A
Discipleship
of
Equals:
Towards
a
Christian
Feminist
Spirituality

A Discipleship of Equals: Towards a Christian Feminist Spirituality

Francis A. Eigo, O.S.A.
Editor

The Villanova University Press

Copyright © 1988 by Francis A. Eigo, O.S.A.
The Villanova University Press
Villanova, Pennsylvania 19085
Library of Congress Cataloging-in-Publication Data
A Discipleship of equals.

Includes index.
1. Women—Religious Life. 2. Spirituality.
I. Eigo, Francis A.
BV4527.D57   1988   248.8′43   87–37257
ISBN 0–87723–051–X

To

Reverend John M. Driscoll, O.S.A.,

who

has supported these endeavors

from

the very beginning,

with

my deepest gratitude

Contents

Contributors

JOHN CARMODY, currently on the faculty of the University of Tulsa, has contributed to scholarly journals and has authored a number of books, including *Contemporary Catholic Theology, Theology for the 1980s, Reexamining Conscience, The Heart of the Christian Matter, Ecology and Religion, Holistic Spirituality, Religion: The Great Questions, Shamans, Prophets, and Sages,* and *Ways to the Center.*

JOANN WOLSKI CONN, presently teaching at Neumann College, has published in *Theology Today, Spiritual Life,* and *Cross Currents,* and is the author of *Women's Spirituality: Resources for Christian Development.*

CONSTANCE FITZGERALD, O.C.D., a member of the Baltimore Carmel, has shared her major life work, the reinterpretation of Teresa of Avila and John of the Cross, in lectures, seminars, and publications in scholarly books and journals.

MARY ANN GETTY, R.S.M., who is on the faculty of the Catholic University of America, is the author of a number of scholarly articles and such books as *Philippians, Philemon* (1980), *Invitation to the New Testament Epistles,* and *Commentary on 1 and 2 Corinthians.*

MARIA HARRIS is visiting Professor at Fordham University and has written more than fifty articles and six books, the most recent of which is *Teaching and Religious Imagination.*

MARY JO WEAVER, on the faculty of Indiana University (Bloomington), is an editor of books, contributor of articles to encyclopedias and journals, and author of a number of books, among which are *Introduction to Christianity* and *New Catholic Women.*

Introduction

Taking as its theme a discipleship of equals, this twentieth volume of the *Proceedings* of the Theology Institute of Villanova University examines the question of a Christian Feminist Spirituality. To do so, it begins with an overview by Joann Wolski Conn, followed by Mary Ann Getty's essay on the biblical roots, Constance FitzGerald's on Teresa of Avila and John of the Cross, John Carmody's on a spirituality for men, Mary Jo Weaver's on a feminist spirituality, and, finally, Maria Harris' on implications for ministry.

As usual, I must express my appreciation to some of the people who have helped me make this volume possible: the President of Villanova University, John M. Driscoll, O.S.A.; the members of the Theology Institute Committee (Walter Conn, Edward Hamel, Bernard Lazor, Thomas Ommen, Suzanne Toton); Patricia Fry, and all the essayists.

Francis A. Eigo, O.S.A.,
Editor

A Discipleship of Equals: Past, Present, Future

Joann Wolski Conn

For ... those who have put on Christ,
There is neither Jew nor Greek;
There is neither slave nor free;
There is no male or female;
For you are all one (Gal: 3:27-28).

This text is best understood as a communal Christian self-definition, an affirmation that within the Christian community no structures of domination can be tolerated.[1] Of all the structures of domination, it has been argued that the patriarchal oppression of women is the deepest and most pervasive.[2] Therefore, to expose its roots and abrogate its claim to legitimacy are not only to liberate women and evangelize men, but also to loosen the bonds of racism, classism, and every other structural obstacle to a Christian discipleship of equals.

How can we promote this discipleship of equals, this new Christianity beyond patriarchy? We can build its foundation: the dialogue of religiously committed women and men, the energy of reciprocal consciousness. Together, we must unpack, examine, and evaluate the baggage of our conflicting religious assumptions. Because religion is the single most important shaper and enforcer of women's role as either equal or subordinate in society, such religious dialogue becomes an instrument not only of religious transformation but also of wider social reform.[3]

Until very recently, Christianity had been interpreted and communicated from an almost exclusively male-centered point of view so that we had a monologue rather than a dialogue. Now, the emerging discipline of women's studies is recovering the forgotten or neglected history of women in every field, including the Christian religion. Consequently, a genuine Christian dialogue becomes possible, one that frees men and women, like Lazarus, from being "bound head and foot" by partriarchy's distortions. "Untie yourselves," Jesus is telling us, "and let yourselves go free" (Jn 11:45).

1

This essay will survey the issues that feminist scholars judge important for discussion in the Christian tradition. Its method is collaborative, in the sense that it selects some of the best feminist scholars as spokespersons for each issue. Therefore, it surveys significant scholars as well as central issues. It will interpret and evaluate the past (Part I) and the present (Part II) in order to imagine the future (Part III) in a way that inspires both action and patience, according to the Spirit's leading. My advisor about the way to approach the future is Teresa of Avila, who notices the pattern of God's interaction with humanity: "Oh, what a good friend You make, my Lord! How you proceed by favoring and enduring. You wait for the other to adapt to Your nature, and in the meanwhile you put up with his!"[4]

I believe that God is now favoring us with the gift of Christian feminist spirituality and enduring our struggles to walk in its light. The term spirituality, here, refers to our deepest self lived in relation to God, the sustainer of all, and so, literally, it touches everything. As feminist, spirituality is that way of relating to God, and to everyone and everything, lived by those who are aware of the history of women's restriction and oppression and now work to ensure women's equality in every sphere. Sensitivity to women's oppression alerts feminists to the wider dimension of human oppression, especially to the relationship of sexism, racism, classism, and élitism in our society. As Christian, feminist spirituality is that mode of relating to God, in Christ Jesus, through the Spirit, which is, like the gospel, inclusive of women and men, universal in its vision and prophetic in its call to be converted from the sins of domination and self-righteousness.[5] Christian feminist spirituality relies on *contemplation* in *action for justice* as its only hope for the future.

I. Interpreting the Past

Christian women's and men's spiritual growth requires knowledge of women's history. It is necessary, first of all, in order to satisfy the basic human need for meaning and identity. Because meaning requires imagination, all of us need an accurate picture of women's own past and role models to support an inclusive vision for the future. Second, knowledge of this history promotes action. When women perceive their condition as deprivation, history demonstrates that they act to change this condition.[6]

Although the field of women's history is young, it has already developed through three phases or approaches. As in human growth, tasks of earlier stages remain significant even when later tasks emerge.[7]

Compensatory history was naturally the first phase. Because so many notable women are missing from traditional history, especially from religious history, this continues to be a long-term undertaking. Here, two questions are basic. To what extent did Judaism and Christianity directly promote misogynism? To what extent were they combating earlier denigration of women and helping women's gradual rise to respect?

Phase two moves from documenting oppression and exploitive interpretations of women's role to investigating the way women operated in a male-defined world on their own terms. Here the task is to recover women's experience expressed in their own words. A significant religious question is: to what extent does women's religious experience indicate that a struggle for self-affirmation, self-definition, and autonomous self-donation is intrinsic to women's conversion and progress in holiness.

A third phase is emerging in which women view themselves, not as another minority but, more accurately, as the majority of humanity. Now the question becomes: what would history itself look like if seen through women's eyes and values?

Even the following modest survey of results in these three phases or tasks provides women with resources for praise, pride, and power to affirm their own religous history in the ongoing dialogue to promote the discipleship of equals.

A. Compensatory History: Documenting Patriarchy and Its Effects

This approach to history documents the relationship of patriarchal religion both to feminine imagery and to the psychological and social self-images of women. It serves as a basis for suggestions of ways in which patriarchal religion must be reshaped to overcome its unjust and debilitating effects on women. The following survey is merely an enticing sample of the results of this approach applied to the Hebrew and Christian scripture, to major periods of Christian history, and to a few individual persons and issues. Some of the positions cited here as having merit could well be debated by other feminist scholars.

Hebrew scripture is a collection of writings by males from a society dominated by males. Phyllis Bird, a Christian scholar of this literature, documents a wide range of images of women in the Old Testament, as she refers to this scripture.[8] In some texts the woman of ancient Israel is portrayed as property. In others she is depicted as possessing considerable freedom, initiative, power and respect.

The woman of the Old Testament, judged by economic criteria or in terms of interest in continuity of the male name, was deemed inferior to the man. In the realm of cult her activity was restricted, and from the law's viewpoint she was a minor and dependent, whose rights were seldom protected. These roles and systems of status are the base line for any discussion of woman's image, but they are not the whole picture.

In many situations, the woman was, in fact or in theory, an equal despite pressures to treat her as an inferior. She was recognized as equal in certain kinds of knowledge and in religious sensibility. In love she might also be an equal, and could exploit as well as suffer exploitation. Man sees her as a partner in pleasure and labor, one whom he needs, and one who can deal him weal or woe. She completes him—but as one with a character of her own.

Genesis' two creation accounts suggest an original and in-tended equality and harmony in creation behind the present state of division and alienation. Some prophets see a renewed creation that would abolish exploitation based on distinctions of age, sex, and social status. That Israel rarely lived up to this vision does not deny its presence in Israel's scripture.

Synthesizing the best New Testament scholarship, Constance Parvey demonstrates that women were educated in the scrip-tures and assumed leadership roles of sufficient magnitude to attract many women in Christian congregations.[9] Their partici-pation was, however, not problem-free. New Testament images of women reflect both theologically and socially a first-century male-centered religious culture. Nevertheless, Paul's theology of equivalence in Christ could support a new religious and social basis for women-men relationshps in the future. The radically new theology of women, however, became obscured in the later epistles. What Paul had understood as a kind of temporary *status quo* ethics—in the context of the imminent end-time—became translated two generations later into moral guidelines for keep-ing things forever the way they are. Consequently, the Church inherited two widely divergent messages: the theology of equiv-alence in Christ; the practice of women's subordination. In attempting to reconcile them it maintained the social *status quo* and affirmed women's equivalence by projecting it as a purely spiritual, otherworldly reality.

Bernadette Brooten concludes that Paul judges the morality of women's sexual relationship to other women entirely on the basis of culturally defined roles and the primacy of undisturbed order.[10] Lesbian relationships are morally wrong, for Paul, because in them women overstep the bounds of the role and status assigned by culture. That is, in them women exchanged the passive, subordinate sexual role that Paul considered "natural" for them for an active, autonomous role that could be natural, and thus moral, only for men. Lesbian women are condemned, in Paul's eyes, because they repeat the pattern of idolatry, that is, of refusal to defer to their head who is man, as man must defer to Christ who defers to his head who is God.

Christians, especially those who promote women's equality, commonly view the Fathers of the Church as ascetics and woman haters. It is true that they usually hated sex and often insulted women, but identifying the two themes obscures the issue. It tends to ignore the high praise of women, in their new role as virgins, in patristic theology. It also fails to explain the rise of that veneration of Mary that characterizes patristic thought in the fourth century C.E. Rosemary Radford Ruether judges that this ambivalence between misogynism and the praise of the virginal woman is not accidental.[11] One view is not more characteristic of the Fathers than the other. Both stand together as two sides of a dualistic psychology that was the basis of the patristic doctrine of humanity viewed as normatively male.

All the patristic traditions of feminine spiritual imagery were gathered together in their emerging theology of Mary. Mary became the epitome of all these images of spiritual womanhood, and the Fathers transferred to her the ancient titles of Queen of Heaven and Mother of God formerly given to the ancient Mediterranean Earth Goddess. They crowned Mary with the moon and stars of Isis, the turret crown of *Magna Mater,* and placed her enthroned with the divine child on her lap in an ancient image derived from the iconography of Isis and Horus. Patristic theology rededicated ancient temples of these Earth goddesses to Mary and finally escorted her to the very throne of God to take her seat beside the Jewish Ancient of Days who, with his son Messiah, ruled the heavens in exclusive patriarchal splendor. The image of Mary's assumption emerged in popular piety in Egypt by the early fifth century C.E. The male ascetic devotees of the virginal woman saw her receiving the prize of heavenly glory. While these men were praising Mary, however, they were despising all real physical women, sex and fecundity, and wholly etherealizing women into spiritual love objects and warning against any physical expression of love with the dangerous daughters of Eve.

Ruether desires not only to decry the patristic tradition's defects. She wishes also to cherish the hard-won fruits of patristic theology: conclusions about transcendence and spiritual personhood won at the terrible price of men's denying their natural affections and fearing, or even hating, women's natural humanity.

While patristic theology developed in Chrisitianity, Jewish tradition synthesized rabbinic legal tradition in the Talmud.

Judith Hauptman presents three general conclusions about the images of women in the Talmud.[12] First, woman's role is well defined along traditional lines of caring for husband, children, and home in which she is always dependent upon a man. Given this framework, the rabbis tried to secure the greatest possible good for women, especially those least fortunate. Second, the rabbis guided their decisions by their ultimate goals. Since they defined Jewish commitment in terms of ongoing concern for the community and a quest for dialogue with God, they had to regulate family life in a way that would lead to optimum achievement of these goals. The easiest way to engage a man's help and his devotion to God was by keeping the woman at home so that her husband could fulfill his duties outside the home. Third, although Talmudic anecdotes taught a woman to accept a supportive role in life, there are numerous stories in which women buck the tradition, assert themselves, and speak their own minds. That Bruria, in many ways the antithesis of self-sacrificing Rachel, is recorded in the Talmud, even at the risk of her potentially subversive influence, is indicative of the fact that womankind was not monolithic nor was rabbinic legislation devoid of changing attitudes toward women.

Biblical, Talmudic, and Patristic scholarship is, of course, more complex than the previous summaries can convey. Ruether, for example, chooses to emphasize the pejorative interpretation of Church fathers, while Hauptman opts to demonstrate that the authors of the Talmud can be read as "moderates." There is more to the two situations than the emphases these authors feature.

Eleanor McLaughlin is amazed at the extent to which medieval assumptions about women remain effective today. Liberation from the misogyny of those assumptions can come only when the implications of that medieval past are made clear.

McLaughlin emphasizes three medieval assumptions.[13] First, for Thomas Aquinas there are in every aspect of the woman's life a tension and confusing ambiguity between her subordination in the order of creation and her equivalence in the order of salvation. This tension can be overcome only when the woman is able to renounce or escape (in heaven) that which has been considered essential to her femaleness, her reproductive function.

Second, these theories confront social reality in two institutions: marriage and monastic or virginal life. Here, the Church attempted to do justice to the equivalance of women and men while assuming and reinforcing their subordination. In marriage, for example, Thomas Aquinas, following Aristotle, speaks of a friendship between husband and wife, but it must be that of inferior to a superior, a hierarchical love comparable to the love of the soul for God.[14] In the virginal life, the religious equivalence of male and female is fundamentally undermined by the Church's development of a rationale for the denial of Holy Orders to the woman. One aspect of this rationale is that ordination confers a superiority of rank that cannot be received by a woman who is by the order of creation in a state of subjection. Thus, the woman, like the slave, may not validly receive Holy Orders. Another example is the refusal of Franciscan and Dominican men to give the female branches of their traditions the status of true membership in their respective orders. The rejection is explicit: both Dominican and Franciscan women wanted and struggled for equal membership with the Friars. Both groups of women wanted to receive pastoral care from the Friars rather than from local secular clergy; but, the men refused, saying that care for these women (in whom their founders had taken such interest!) would interfere with their ability to preach, and other comments implied that association with women would endanger the health of their souls.[15]

Third, medieval theology of Mary has contradictory elements that have serious implications for women. Mary's role in Christ's work of redemption is both essential and characteristic of her sex: secondary, passive, reflecting the male picture of the female as manipulative and seductive. Bernardino of Siena describes Mary's relationship to God this way:

> . . . one Hebrew woman invaded the house of the eternal King. One girl, I do not know by what caresses, pledges or violence, seduced, deceived, and if I may say so, wounded and enraptured the divine heart and ensnared the Wisdom of God. . . .[16]

For this theologian, it seems, the woman to whom God gives such privilege and power could have received it only through seduction and deception.

Calvin's reformation exegesis and pastoral advice continue the patristic and medieval tradition of affirming the spiritual equality of women and men while confirming the submission of women to men, especially in Christian marriage.[17] For example, when advising women who are suffering mental or physical abuse from their husbands, Calvin encourages silent acceptance and submission to what God has sent them and wants to console them with the knowledge that this kind of affliction is nothing compared with the spiritual infidelity of which their husbands are guilty. Mary Potter concludes that although Calvin is not the first to use a double-sided argument for male-female relationships, he is the first to place equal emphasis on both sides of the argument. Calvin proposed a carefully contained spiritual reformation for women in the sixteenth century; nevertheless, it was one that had little effect on social and political structures.

Compensatory history, as we see from these examples, has important implications. First, it demonstrates a pervasive tension between teachings about a new creation of equality between women and men, and assumptions about women's different and inferior nature. Then, it impels us to ask why and how this tension and inequality can continue to shape the Church and society thousands of years later. It is important to recognize that religious teachers in the past were deeply and pervasively sexist; still, scholars agree that it is relatively impossible for anyone of any period, woman or man, to grasp any issue differently from the prevailing culture. It is another matter, entirely, to have twentieth-century men and women resorting to these sexist traditions as refuges from institutional change or personal conversion.

B. History That Recovers Women as Agents

The second phase of women's history asks the question: how did women operate on their own terms in a male-defined world?[18] It recovers women's experience as women interpreted and evaluated it, often in their own words. If often reveals and reverses misconceptions about women, misconceptions rooted in male-centered assumptions.

My own misconceptions about Margery Kempe, a fifteenth-century visionary, pilgrim, and mystic, were reversed by Clarissa W. Atkinson's historical scholarship.[19] I knew Margery Kempe as a middle-class English housewife called to weep and to pray for her fellow Christians and to adopt an unconventional way of life. Separating herself from her husband and many children, she became a pilgrim traveling around England and as far away as Jerusalem. In old age, she dictated to scribes an autobiography that recounts her extraordinary intimacy with Christ as well as her intense, commotion-filled life. To me, she did not seem very "saintly" in character or disposition, and her spiritual experiences had been conveyed to me as extreme or egotistical; indeed, she was usually presented to me as the opposite of her saintly contemporary, Julian of Norwich.

In order to appreciate and interpret properly Margery Kempe's life and spirituality, Atkinson demonstrates that one must go beyond conventional categories of social and religious history. One must examine six perspectives: the character of Margery's autobiography, her mysticism and pilgrim way of life, her social and family environment, her relations with her church and its clergy, the tradition that shaped her piety, and the context of medieval female sanctity.

Margery's *Book* was shaped by the writings of famous holy women and by pressures on memory and motivation that come with age. It is, nevertheless, an authentic autobiography: the story of a life told by its subject.

The vocation that called Margery to mysticism and pilgrimage made her unusual and, therefore, open to suspicion. It required her to leave her husband and children, to dress in white (a color usually reserved for virgins), to go on pilgrimage as a way to participate in Christ's earthly life and death. It graced her with a conspicuous gift: tears she could not control or resist. With the help of repeated assurance from Christ and her advisors, Margery was convinced her mystical gifts and tears were intended to make her a mirror of penitence, compassion, and God's love for sinners.

Margery's domestic and social background gave her the courage to persist in her strange vocation and unpopular way of life in spite of current norms about the behavior of married women. She was not deferential or quiet; she came from a powerful merchant family, so she spoke to her contemporaries (even priests and bishops) with straightforward language. She met scorn from most of her relatives, but found encouragement in Christ, the saints, and some representatives of the Church.

During Margery's lifetime, the Church displayed intense anxiety over the related issues of religious "feelings," discernment of spirits, and female visionaries. Margery consistently sought to have her religious "feelings" and way of life examined and approved. Many trustworthy persons, including Dame Julian of Norwich, advised Margery to accept what God sent her and judged her "feelings" to be "the work of the Holy Ghost."

Atkinson's most original and significant insights are in the area of Margery's spirituality. It is in the tradition of affective piety and of late medieval female sanctity that Margery's religious emotions and expressions can be best understood.

From Anselm of Canterbury in the eleventh century to Prior Nicolas Love in the early fifteenth century, affective writers and preachers aimed to promote intense feelings. Principal among these were compassion, which enabled Christians to participate in the suffering of Jesus and his mother, and contrition, which produced repentance and the emotive aspects of conversion. Margery incorporated these feelings in her own devotional life: identification with the human Christ, conspicuous humility inspired by Saint Francis of Assisi, "boistrous" emotion in sympathy with Mary grieving at the cross. Against this background, the religious life of Margery Kempe seems neither aberrant nor even unusual. Rather, it is her unique response to a tradition established by great saints.

Atkinson notices the way Margery corresponds with the pattern of holiness in many medieval women, such as Catherine of Siena, Birgitta of Sweden, Joan of Arc, and Julian of Norwich. They characteristically saw visions, communicated directly with God, found scribes or biographers who publicized their experiences. An increasing number of them were wives and mothers who struggled, like Margery, with the married state and eventually "transcended" it, becoming in effect "honorary" virgins through their humility and by God's special favor. Traveling widely, speaking publicly, departing from traditional women's roles, these women were a new creation of the late Middle Ages. Atkinson demonstrates the way their lives and works form the only appropriate context in which to recognize and appreciate Margery Kempe's life and *Book*.

Not only does this approach to history correct misconceptions, such as those about Margery Kempe, but it also recovers the lost or neglected story of women's impact on society. A fascinating example of this recovery is the account of Quaker women's influence on American society.

In *Mothers of Feminism,* Margaret Hope Bacon identifies the root of the conflict over women's roles that has plagued our country from the Puritans to the present.[20] What generates conflict is living according to the biblical revelation that every person has God's guiding spirit, so that each individual may and must trust her or his own religious experience. From its origin in the seventeenth century, the Society of Friends consistently acted on the belief that each person has an independent relationship to God, to "the inner Light," whether male or female, slave or free, educated or illiterate. Quakers were unique because they encouraged and expected women to participate equally in worship, to preach, organize, and administer the business of the community.

Other Protestants and Catholics found such Quaker attitudes not only dangerous but also blasphemous because they underminded "God-given" patriarchal authority in households, churches, and governments. In the name of social order, Puritans whipped, imprisoned and hanged brave Quaker women who came into the Bay Colony as "traveling ministers." This fear of sexual equality remains, to this day, the root of conservative religious opposition to a discipleship of equals.

Bacon's description of the role of Quaker women in every major American reform movement, from abolition and universal suffrage to civil rights and disarmament, supports the conclusion that throughout our history there has been a "gender gap." On the one hand, in every era and reform effort there has been an exclusive, male-centered, authoritarian ethic in power; yet, there has also been an inclusive, feminist, uncompetitive minority, incorporating Quaker values.[21]

Quakers were a feminist vanguard influencing other reformers to adopt such practices as shared leadership, consensus decisions, and nonresistant protest. Quaker women were in the forefront. Women like Lucretia Mott, Susan B. Anthony, Alice Paul, M. Carey Thomas, and Grace Abbott led the struggle for prison reform, abolition, temperance, equal rights, coeducation, child welfare, peace and eventually disarmament. Quakers have participated out of all proportion to their numbers (never more than two percent of the population). Quaker women accounted for four out of five of the organizers of the first women's rights convention, in 1848; five of the first eleven women doctors; and an estimated forty percent of the women abolitionists, thirty percent of the pioneer prison reformers, and fifteen percent of the suffragists born before 1830.

Quaker women's heroism not only offers women a "usable past" but also serves as a resource for feminist concepts that are still applicable today in the quest for more humane social systems.

C. Historical Studies as a Copernican Shift in Consciousness

No man has been excluded from the historical record because of his sex, yet most women were. Gerda Lerner, a founding mother of women's studies, reminds us that women have "made history" as actors and agents; however, they have been kept from contributing to "history-making," that is, they have been barred from the task of officially interpreting the past of humankind as a whole.[22] They have not been accepted as writers or teachers of what would be acknowledged as the history of humanity.

This contradiction between women's central and active role in creating society and their marginality in the meaning-giving process of interpretation has been a force, causing women to struggle against their subservient condition. When, in that process of struggle, at certain moments, the contradictions between the centrality of their action and the marginality of their presence in the "official interpretation" of that event are brought into women's consciousness, women's condition is perceived as a deprivation that is shared as a group. This consciousness raising becomes a force moving women into action to change their condition and to enter into a new relationship to the male-dominated society.

The most mature phase of women's history realizes that the "event" which needs reinterpretation now is all of history, because history has never yet been interpreted with women viewed as the majority that they are, rather than as a subordinate minority. Is the goal a reverse discrimination? Exclude men the way they have excluded women? Definitely not. As a temporary measure, civilization needs to be reconceptualized from a women-centered perspective in order to step outside of patriarchal thought and, thus, transform the whole system. The ultimate goal of most feminist historians, however, is a perspective on civilization that pays equal attention to women's and men's experience.

Three metaphors help us capture the desired angle of vision.[23] Feminist historians desire, first, a "doubled vision." Adding the female vision to the male in such a way that both eyes see together allows both a full range of vision and accurate depth perception. In another image, feminist historians picture men and women living on a stage on which they act out their assigned roles, equal in importance. But, the stage set is designed by men who have written the play, assigning themselves the most interesting parts. Realizing their disadvantage, women gradually negotiate for a contract that gives them co-authorship of the play. We do not yet know what the new script will be. A third metaphor imagines us removing the umbrella of male dominance, stepping out under the free sky to observe a new universe in which man is not the measure of all things; rather, women and men are. This vision transforms *consciousness* as decisively as did Copernicus' theory the earth is not the center of the universe. We do not yet know what will emerge as we sail over the horizon of our current preconceptions. Feminist historians have begun and encourage us to follow. The process itself is the way, the goal.

Some scholars have begun to explore this new universe of consciousness and ask: if women were central to an issue in their scholarly field, how would it be defined? Gerda Lerner, for example, explores the question of the origins of class society and finds direct links with women and religion.[24]

Lerner raises and answers two difficult questions: how was class definition different for women from that for men? Why did it take 3500 years for women to realize their subordination; that is, what could explain women's historical "complicity" in upholding the patriarchal system that subordinated them?

Through a series of brilliant and controversial judgments, Lerner concludes, regarding the first question, that men controlled women's sexual and reproductive capacity prior to the formation of private property and class society. Treating women's sexuality as a commodity is at the foundation of private property, rather than the other way around. Lerner's position, therefore, is the opposite of the standard Marxist interpretation of class which regards private property as the foundation, and only then turns to women as one example of men's property.

Women's sexual subordination was institutionalized in the earliest law codes and enforced by the full power of the State. Women's cooperation in this system was secured by various means: force, economic dependency on the male head of the family, class privileges bestowed upon conforming and dependent women of the upper classes, and the artificially created divisions of women into respectable (i.e., attached to one man) and not-respectable (i.e., not attached to one man or free of all men).

Feminist historians recognize that the later symbolic devaluing of women in relation to the divine imaged as male becomes one of the two founding metaphors of Western civilization. The other founding metaphor is supplied by Aristotelian philosophy, which assumes that women are incomplete and damaged human beings of an entirely different order from that of men. It is with the creation of these two metaphors, which are built into the very foundations of the symbol systems of Western civilization, that the subordination of women comes to be seen as "natural," and hence becomes invisible. Therefore, what is now called "women's complicity with patriarchy" was actually assimilation to the only meaning, that is, the only reality available to anyone. As Lerner reminds us, when historical events allow new meaning to emerge, and women perceive their situation as "deprivation," they begin to act to change their condition.

It is this action, based on new meaning, that is the next topic for discussion. "Present issues" are matters for urgent action.

II. Present Issues

In my judgment, growth of the discipleship of equals requires action in four areas. First, every Christian must participate in the ongoing conversion of religious institutions. Second, we need prophetic insistence upon initial conversion of sinful structures. Third, theologians should continue to enlarge the discipline of Christian feminist theology. Fourth, Christians must appropriate a feminist spirituality.

A. Participate in the Ongoing Conversion of Religious Institutions

1. Renewal of Religious Life. I agree with Sandra Schneiders' claim that, as a group, women religious (and those assimilated to them educationally and culturally) are the most creative element

in the Catholic Church today. They are theologically well
informed, have a variety of professional skills, have experience
of ministry in many parts of the United States and the world,
and have been the most enthusiastic about implementing the
renewal of Vatican II in daily life. Therefore, it might be safe to
claim: as women religious go, so goes the Church in the next
decade.[25]

Mary Jo Weaver pinpoints the heart of their conversion as
commitment to a discipleship of equals in the midst of misunderstanding and opposition. Although the Vatican and the
Council originally encouraged the renewal of sisters, the Sacred
Congregation for Religious and Secular Institutes and the
present pope are not supportive of the directions taken by
American "nuns." For Roman authorities, religious life is essen-
tially a matter of dependence, hierarchical authority, and sepa-
ration from the world. For most sisters and many American
Catholics, on the other hand, religion is embodied precisely in
the struggles and opportunities of life in the world, and the
gospel is best expressed in feminist values of collective experience and collegial process. Each group espouses a different
ecclesiology, and those operating out of feminist values believe
that they have the stronger case to claim that a discipleship of
equals is truer to the gospel.[26]

The premier theologian of contemporary religious life,
Sandra Schneiders, specifies the meaning of the vows in terms
related to the discipleship of equals. Religious vows are a
commitment to the transformation of all things and people in
Christ through a life dedicated to mutuality of possessions,
affectivity, and power. Through the vow of poverty, one responds to the world's staggering problems of selfishness and
exploitation by sharing everything, by entering a relationship of
sister to all in Christ. From this perspective, the task is to
renounce artificial dependence on superiors or community for
money, to abandon useless and unreal imitation of the destitute,
and to devote one's energy to alleviating misery and building
structures of solidarity. To vow celibacy is to enter the current
cultural conversion from patriarchy to mutuality of women and
men. Celibate women are in a favored position to challenge male
domination because they have professional competency and
social freedom. They are more likely to demonstrate the possibility of experiencing genuine intimacy in friendship free of
violence and intolerance and marked by mutual acceptance and
love that honors vulnerability. Vowed obedience aims at freedom for union with the will of God mediated, not through
hierarchical authority, but through human events and persons
which call for discernment of the appropriate loving response in

particular circumstances. In this view, reliance on personal religious experience, which is the heart of discernment, is the only ground for confidence that one has found God's will. Here, cooperation is understood to be just as demanding as the older form of obedience.[27]

Religious life in this mode is a revelation of the biblical "eschatological community." By eschatological Schneiders means not so much what lies in the future as what acts as the focus of hope in the present. In the last twenty years, religious life, especially of American sisters, has emerged as an inclusive community bonded by shared love of Christ, dedicated especially to God's reign of peace, justice, nonhierarchical authority, and egalitarian friendship.[28] American sisters understand that the root of the tension between them and the Vatican—evident in the mandated study of United States religious life—does not lie in the presumed dissent and defection of American sisters, but rather in the collision course of following two distinctly different and opposing models of authority based on different ecclesiologies: one is hierarchical, the other is the discipleship of equals.[29]

2. Spiritual Renewal in Women's Organizations. Many Catholic women's organizations now equate spiritual renewal with espousal of feminist values. The contrast between the values promoted by the Grail and those of the National Council of Catholic Women highlights what I mean by the unity of feminism and renewal.[30]

The NCCW has consistently reflected the views of the American bishops. In their pamphlets defending their stand against the Equal Rights Amendment and in their case against the ordination of women they maintain the traditional hierarchical view of women as different from and complementary to men, that is, women are best suited to roles which serve and support men. Here, they echo some medieval assumptions that were explained in the first section of this essay. As a women's organization, the NCCW supports women's issues, but never by way of structural analysis which would uncover the fact that their assumption that women are "different and complementary" works out, in practice, to being separate and unequal. The NCCW testimony at hearings for the forthcoming bishops' pastoral letter on women's issues, for example, assumes that women and men have different "natures" and, thus, are suited to different roles in which women are the primary parent and the support for male leadership.

The Grail, founded to promote the lay apostolate of women, espoused the "traditional womanly role" until the 1960s, when its members began to be more aware of the relations of domination and submission which are embedded in all social structures, including the Church. Small and officially invisible, in contrast to the NCCW, the Grail is much more influential as a forum in which women's concerns are central to the task of a renewed theology and liturgy and search for a noncoercive model of authority.

Other organizations of Catholic women that work from within a feminist perspective do so because they believe that God's Spirit moves within the Church today in the lives of the marginalized. Far from seeing the women's movement as a luxury in a world full of staggering problems, they perceive the real issue as the need to see the direct links between their own oppression and the problems that plague the disenfranchised people of the world. Since most of the world's poor are women and children, and since women have only secondary status in the Catholic Church, these groups see their inclusive Christian feminism as a most valid way to live the gospel in the modern world.[31]

The Womanchurch movement is another example of this fusion of feminism and Christian conversion. Womanchurch, begun in the 1980s, is a coalition of organizations founded in the 1970s around specific causes (e.g., Woman's Ordination Conference, Center of Concern, Black Sisters, Las Hermanas, Women's Alliance for Theology, Ethics, and Ritual). Rather than focus just on the issue for which they were founded, these laywomen and sisters are bonding to form what Elisabeth Schüssler Fiorenza calls "the gathering of the ecclesia of women." It is a forum for exchanging stories of women's experience, sharing spiritualities, celebrating liturgies, identifying issues and resources for future empowerment. In the midst of the hope that this sharing generates is an urgency based on the conviction that women are leaving the Church in growing numbers because it has become irrelevant to their lives.[32]

The significance of Womanchurch is its claim to *be* Church. Participants in the 1983 conference, Womanchurch Speaks, saw themselves, not as exiles from the Church, but as in exodus from patriarchy. As Rosemary Radford Ruether later analyzed it, this community of liberation from patriarchy declares itself to be theologically Church, that is, a community of redemption. Womanchurch makes no claim to "leave the Church" or cut itself off from historical Christianity; rather, it is the beginning of a process of renewal which must include men and historical Christianity, but only when these, too, recognize that exodus from patriarchy is essential to the meaning and mission of the Church.[33]

Since 1984, the original coalition has broadened to include newer and older groups of Catholic women and expects to become ecumenical. It provides political, spiritual, and liturgical possibilities for almost every Catholic feminist still trying to make sense of her tradition. Although the presence of Catholic lesbians and those favoring a pluralistic understanding of Catholic teaching on abortion may frighten conservative women, the inclusion of these groups makes Womanchurch a forum for those with different views to meet one another in dialogue and explore bonding possibilities that go beyond their immediate differences.[34]

B. Prophetically Denounce the Recent Creation of a Second Class "Alternate Christianity" for Women in the Catholic Church

Sandra Schneiders has called attention to a collection of events in the recent past that has had the effect of gradually creating what she calls an "alternate Christianity" for women in the Catholic Church.[35] Preaching is a good example. As women, especially those trained in theology and Scripture, began to emerge as excellent preachers, the Vatican ordered that women were not to preach the homily at the Eucharistic liturgy. While a male deacon without even rudimentary formation in Scripture could give the homily, women with doctorates in Scripture could not. No doubt because the total exclusion of these women was patently absurd, an *alternate* form of preaching was developed for them. While they could not give the homily, they could give "reflections." And, lest anyone conclude that the two were the same, "reflections" were not to be given after the reading of the gospel but at some other time before or after the liturgy.

Assistance at the altar is also a matter that is separate but not equal. Women may assist at the altar, but they may not be installed as acolytes. They may read the scriptures during liturgy, but may not be installed as lectors. Even when women do exactly what men do, their participation is to be understood as an *alternate* form of service rather than an official one.

Due to the increasing lack of ordained ministers in the Church, a situation which could be easily remedied by the ordination of already trained, experienced, and willing women, a number of women have assumed, with ecclesiastical approval, the role of community leadership in parishes without clergy. These women do many things, including presiding at communion services. Yet, their leadership cannot be acknowledged as pastoring, and the services they lead are not the Liturgy of the Eucharist. Again, women are *alternate* pastors, *alternate* leaders of *alternate* worship.

The most serious example, from a theological point of view, of this gradual creation of an alternate Christianity for women was the declaration by the Bishop of Pittsburgh that the Holy Thursday footwashing service which Jesus explicitly commanded his disciples to do in imitation of him was to be carried out only with men because the liturgical instruction speaks of "*duodecim viros.*" In John's gospel, all biblical scholars note, the footwashing plays the role that the institution narrative plays in the synoptic gospels. Therefore, to exclude women from the footwashing is to symbolically declare them ineligible for Eucharist. The outrage of priests, women, and other laity at this sacramental discrimination drew from the Bishop what he considered a conciliatory gesture. He said that women could be included in some *alternate* rite expressing service in the Church. Most recently, this Bishop removed his original ban on women, but continues to favor the creation of alternate rites to include women.[36]

In summary, the increasing difficulty Church officials are experiencing in maintaining women's exclusion from full participation in the Catholic community is gradually leading them to create an alternate and second class form of Christianity for women. While the various restrictions have occurred at different times and places and have differing official weight, women have not failed to notice the pattern of marginalization and exclusion by which the denial of their full Christian identity is made concrete in their daily experience, and they are beginning prophetically to renounce this abuse of pastoral authority.

C. Continue to Enlarge the Discipline of Christian Feminist Theology

Christian feminist theology is participation in and critical reflection upon the religious faith of the Christian community by persons who are aware of the historical and cultural restriction of women in Christian tradition and who intend to re-imagine and articulate Christian faith in such a way that it promotes mutuality and equality.[37] In order to give focus to the complex tasks of Christian feminist theologians, I will limit the discussion to Roman Catholic women and will use some of Mary Jo Weaver's synthesis and evaluation of their contributions.[38]

Christian feminist theologians admit from the outset that their tradition is relentlessly patriarchal in language, custom, practice, symbolism, memory, history, theological articulation, and ritual. They understand the reason some feminists judge that the tradition is so intrinsically sexist that it cannot be revised, or the reason others decide that the patriarchal religious structures are so intrenched that one's energy is better spent on other projects.

Mary Daly is perhaps the most famous feminist to make these decisions about the tradition. Of Roman Catholic background and education, she has parted company with the Church and what she calls "American sado-society" because she finds them both to be unredeemably sexist. Because her first book, *The Church and the Second Sex* (1968), was a groundbreaking event for American Catholic feminists, I agree with Mary Jo Weaver's judgment that Daly must be considered in any discussion of Roman Catholic feminist theology. Weaver notices that, ironically, even now Daly exhibits some peculiarly Roman Catholic dynamics: her later work, especially, is characterized by dogmatic authoritarianism, a flight from and denigration of the world, a strong desire for transcendence, and an élitist understanding of the intellectual life, all hallmarks of preconciliar Catholicism.

Daly's second book, *Beyond God the Father* (1973), was a transitional one: it connected to the past by way of being a theological argument for a process God, dynamic revelation, and a realized eschatology; it mirrored the present because it was a feminist manifesto; it foreshadowed the future by being a book about language.

Most of Daly's subsequent work has aimed at a "transmogrification" of the language: she inverts and invents words, for example, "gyn/ecology," in order to describe a new world of "radical feminist friendship and sisterhood."

If Daly is going to function as a prophet for feminism, Christian readers must weigh critically the alternatives she offers. Daly sees no possibilities within the Christian community. Her choices are clear and dogmatic: one must choose between the logic of radical feminism and the logic of the Christian symbol system. She projects an image of an all-female Utopia, but the identification of this place as "Otherworld" and the absolute exclusion of all men reinstate the divisive dualisms other feminist theologians attempt to overcome.

Elisabeth Schüssler Fiorenza and Rosemary Radford Ruether exemplify the vision of these more inclusive feminists. They have decided to reinterpret the tradition in order to change its direction and open it to the influence of women's religious experience.

Elisabeth Schüssler Fiorenza, a specialist in New Testament studies, has produced an intense vision of feminist theology. German-born and trained, the first woman in her diocese to study theology and needing the bishop's permission to do so, Schüssler Fiorenza devoted herself first to ecclesiological issues. Because of her long-standing commitment to declericalization and structural change within Roman Catholicism, she is wary of

women seeking ordination within the present system without
seeking significant structural change in the way ministry is
practiced and understood.

Schüssler Fiorenza's efforts to articulate a new interpretive
paradigm for New Testament study and to urge a new hermeneutics that can prove that God is on the side of the
oppressed are at the center of her book, *In Memory of Her*.[39]
Here, she argues that an equalitarian interpretive framework is
the only one that can do justice to the dynamics of the Jesus
movement and the only one that has the power to set free the
equalitarian impulses of that movement both in the ancient
traditions and in contemporary practice. Her groundwork for a
new Church has been laid in grass-roots gatherings of women, as
well as in scholarly forums in the academy.

Schüssler Fiorenza works within a creative tension that is both
feminist and Christian: as a feminist, she criticizes Christianity
for being guilty of the structural sin of sexism, while, as a
Christian, she argues that the tradition is not inherently or
necessarily sexist. To sustain this tension she focuses on the
historical struggle of women and other oppressed peoples,
finding here the locus of God's liberating activity. She resists
those outside the Christian tradition who have relinquished
women's biblical heritage, and, at the same time, resists those
within the Church who would judge a feminist reconstruction of
the New Testament period to be eccentric or marginal.

Schüssler Fiorenza establishes theoretically the task of feminist theology, and she connects theory with practice by following
the insight of liberation theology that "only active commitment
to the oppressed and active involvement in their struggle for
liberation enable us to see our society and the world differently
and give us a new perspective."[40]

Rosemary Radford Ruether is the most prolific writer in the
Roman Catholic feminist community. Because her work has
been directed by her own interests and because "social sin" has
been a catalyst for her thinking and writing, Ruether's work is
wide-ranging. She is equally at home in her area of academic
specialization—the classics and early Christian writers—and in
the ecclesiastical and social issues of the times: she has written
articles on a spectrum of issues from birth control, divorce, the
Council and its aftermath, to civil rights, the Jewish-Christian
dialogue, nuclear arms, and base communities. When asked
about the many different causes she has espoused, she says,
"These issues were experienced by me not as a series of
alternating commitments, but as an expanding consciousness of
the present human social dilemma."[41] Refusing to hier-
archicalize oppressions, she sees "sexism, racism, classism and

other kinds of oppression as interconnected in an overall pattern of human alienation and sinfulness."[42]

Ruether (along with Daly) did pioneering work in grasping and communicating the basic issues of feminist theology. Her "Male Chauvinist Theology and the Anger of Women" (1971) and *Religion and Sexism* (1974) were challenging summaries of the issues at a time when very few people understood the dimensions of the problem of women in the Church. Her book, *Women of Spirit: Female Leadership in the Jewish and Christian Traditions* (1979), edited with Eleanor McLaughlin, and the new series she has edited with Rosemary Skinner Keller, *Women and Religion in America* (1982-), make available views of female strength and greatness that have never been glimpsed until now.

Sexism and God-Talk, Ruether's systematic theology, is at once a deconstruction of traditional categories, such as sin and redemption, and a reconstructive vision of theology from a feminist perspective.[43] Like much contemporary theology, she begins with experience rather than with deductive principles taken from scripture or the teachings of the magisterium. What is unusual, however, is the weight she gives to *women's* experience and female cultural paradigms. The critical principle of this theology is: whatever denies or distorts the full humanity of women is appraised as not redemptive. The positive corollary maintains that whatever promotes the full humanity of women is "of the Holy." Feminist theology is not unique in claiming this principle, but women are firm in claiming it for themselves.

Ruether's liberationist theology, like biblical prophecy, is based on a concept of conversion and repentance. For her, prophecy is valid only as a form of self-criticism, not as a means of castigating communities and systems other than one's own. Her criticism of Catholicism and of aspects of American economic and political practice is, she believes, the legitimate task of an American Catholic. Feminism incorporates everything else. "For me," she says, "the commitment to feminism is fundamental to the commitment to justice, to authentic human life itself."[44]

In summary, pioneering feminist theologians have begun to enlarge the discipline of theology by changing its direction from one in which faith was considered primarily from a male centered viewpoint to one which compensates for this imbalance by concentrating on women's experience as its starting point. Expansion of theology's perspective must continue in the direction of attending as faithfully to women's experience of faith as to men's, and articulating the new vision that emerges from the conversation and possible convergence of these commitments of faith. Some of this more inclusive theology comes from men who are feminists. Leonard Swidler, for example, has a distinguished record of attention to feminist issues in interreligious dialogue. With Arlene Swidler, he co-founded the *Journal of Ecumenical Studies* which incorporates feminist convictions.[45] John Carmody brings a feminist perspective to holistic spirituality and to theologies of peace and justice. In partnership with Denise Lardner Carmody, he has pioneered bringing a feminist viewpoint to textbooks on world religions.[46] William M. Thompson brings a feminist viewpoint into his Christology, and Matthew Fox does the same for creation-centered spirituality.[47]

Ongoing conversation will, no doubt, concentrate on such issues as inclusive language in worship and all prayer; prophetic action for conversion to an authority of service and mutuality; shared wealth; declericalization of ministry; renewal of theology to eliminate its use as an ideological support for denigrating women[48] and to enrich its possibilities of conveying revelation by incorporating women's religious insights.

D. *Appropriate Christian Feminist Spirituality*

Everything mentioned so far in this essay has been related to spirituality, for spirituality as life-experience and as a field of study is no longer identified simply with asceticism and mysticism, or with the practice of virtue and methods of prayer. Spirituality encompasses all of life from the perspective of the actualization of the human capacity to be spiritual; that is, to relate to self, others, and God in love, knowledge, and commitment. In relation to God, spirituality is who we really are, the deepest self, not entirely accessible to our comprehensive self-reflection. Spirituality is reflected in all we do; it is consciously cultivated, yet it is deeply informed by class, race, culture, sex, and by our time in history. We each live a personal story about the meaning of our life and the ultimate meaning of all life and death. Making this story explicit means that we have already gained perspective and made the story available for criticism.[49]

To realize that spiritual development is human development is to be aware of the problematic nature of women's spirituality. There are three reasons for this difficulty.[50] First, for women the possibilities for mature humanity, and thus for spirituality, are restricted. Models of human development universally recognize that movement away from conformity and predetermined role expectations and toward greater autonomy or self-direction is necessary for maturity. Yet, women's experience shows that most women are socialized into conformity to a passive role or are arrested at the threshold of autonomy. Second, Christian teaching and practice, instead of promoting women's maturity, have contributed significantly to this restriction. Especially sad is the fact that so many women are estranged from themselves by absorption of the Christian tradition's most common God-images: as male parent, as masculine spirit, as Lord who excludes women from representing him at the altar. Third, women's spirituality is problematic because the desire for spiritual maturity causes some religious women to separate from each other. Some women judge that spiritual maturity can really be accomplished only by rejecting biblical tradition, while others conclude that their spiritual development demands dedication to the challenging, exhausting, long-range task of reconstructing the entire Christian tradition because it is male-centered.

A reconstructed Christian tradition is slowly emerging as women and men become aware of the detrimental effects of patriarchy on everyone, and particularly on women. Women's spirituality can be promoted if all of us make progress in a two-fold process. To begin, we must reexamine presuppositions about human development, discover the history of women's experience and leadership that has not yet become common knowledge, and explicate the women-liberating insights implicit in biblical teaching about God.[51] As soon as these resources become available, we must begin to incorporate them into every aspect of life and ministry: teaching, writing, celebrating, praying, counseling, reconciling, befriending, protesting. As long as this process remains "frontier territory," experienced as the unknown and fraught with risk, women's spirituality will continue to be very problematic.

I am particularly interested in supporting women's spirituality by demonstrating the compatibility of feminist psychology and Christian maturity. Contrary to common expectations, my primary inspiration comes, not from contemporary psychology, but from the classical tradition of Christian spirituality. Teresa of Avila and Catherine of Siena understood the primacy of adequate self-understanding before such psychologists as Carol Gilligan or Jean Baker Miller questioned the assumptions of the dominant psychology. While I regard the latter as valuable teachers, I have been drawn to them because I was already in the school of Teresa and Catherine.

In her *Life,* Teresa advises her readers: "This path of self knowledge must never be abandoned. . . . Along this path of prayer, self knowledge . . . is the bread with which all palates must be fed no matter how delicate they may be. . . ." Catherine, too, images self-knowledge as a basic food for spiritual growth. In *The Dialogue* she pictures God as saying, "So think of the soul as a tree made for love and living only by love. . . . The circle in

which this tree's root, the soul's love, must grow is true knowledge of herself. . . ."[52]

I believe that feminist psychology is a necessary resource for
this self-knowledge. This puzzles people who ask: how can
feminism, which promotes self-fulfillment, be compatible with
Christian spirituality which fosters self-denial?

The answer to this question lies in a critical examination of its
assumptions. First, there is no need to assume conflicting goals.
Both feminist psychology and Christian spiritual development
aim at a common goal: maturity; both emphasize the balance
between relationship and independence. Both spirituality and
feminist psychology value vulnerability as a human quality
capable of generating empathy for others; that is, when vulnerability is accepted as a normal human condition, one can avoid
the harmful defenses against having to admit it, and then one
can be more sensitive to others.

The assumption that Christian spirituality and feminist psychology are incompatible assumes also that the self comes "ready
made" with needs to be either fulfilled or denied. We must,
however, ask deeper questions: how is one's self constructed?
How can one avoid self-deception about what gives fulfillment
and what should be denied?

Closer examination reveals that feminism and Christian spirituality have compatible goals and processes. Feminism teaches
women a method of critical examination through which they
come to recognize the way socialization in a patriarchal culture
affects their self-understanding; it raises their consciousness to
awareness and affirmation of themselves as authors of their own
life-story. Christian spirituality promotes a parallel process:
discernment. Experts on the subject, such as Teresa of Avila,
Ignatius of Loyola, and Catherine of Siena, advocate a process in
which one examines one's feelings and thoughts, one's assumptions and actions in order to distinguish authentic religious
experience from false projections, to separate illusion from
honest self-assessment, to relinquish blind fear and egoism in
favor of courageous adherence to truth and free commitment to
love.

There are also similarities between the goal of Christian
spirituality, which is union with God demonstrated by loving
care for all persons, and the feminist goal of human development, maturity as understood by such psychologists as Carol
Gilligan,[53] Robert Kegan,[54] and Jean Baker Miller.[55] Gilligan
rejects autonomy as the only appropriate goal for human
maturity in moral decisions and presents instead a goal which
equally values relationships. Although she has not yet expanded
the basic insights of her research into a full model of life-span

development, her colleague, Robert Kegan, has done this. Kegan explicitly intends to present a model of maturity which listens as carefully to women's experience as it does to men's. Consequently, his model demonstrates the way the qualities which have come to characterize men and women stereotypically —autonomy or relationship—are the focus of life-span tasks at *every* stage of everyone's development. Whereas Kegan contributes a complete developmental model, and Gilligan evaluates women's moral development, Miller presents characteristics of a whole new psychology of women. She explains that autonomy as the goal of maturity is a carry-over from men's experience and implies that one should be able to give up affiliations in order to become separate and self-directed. Women seek more than autonomy as was defined for men; indeed, they seek a fuller ability to encompass relationships *simultaneously* with the fullest development of themselves. Too often women are misinterpreted or penalized for affirming to men a basic truth: everyone's individual development proceeds only through affiliation as well as differentiation. And, this development involves conflict as an inevitable fact of life which can be helpful if faced honestly and examined with mutuality.

According to feminist psychologists, then, the criterion for human maturity is an integration of both attachment and independence. Do traditional spiritual writers agree that both of these elements are part of the standard of religious maturity? They explicitly agree that the norm of religious maturity is relationship. The ability to sustain a wide range of loving relationships typifies the religiously mature person. I believe they agree also with the need for autonomy or self-direction; yet, only contemporary authors use this language. Agreement in the classical sources is implicit, yet clear, I believe, when one examines their description of religious maturity as the fruit of a strenuous human process. Writers like Teresa, Ignatius, and Catherine speak of maturity as the result of developmental phases which require love even in darkness, loneliness, or misunderstanding. This lack of consolation which throws one back upon one's deepest inner resources is, I believe, the kind of experience which can promote what contemporary language calls autonomy, or what classical language calls perseverance or fidelity to one's inner calling, or discernment of the appropriate response to God's presence in a given situation.[56] Lack of consolation can also promote depression if one has not been helped to have deep inner resources, such as a sense of identity as loved for oneself.

Nevertheless, this recognition of the importance of personal autonomy has seldom been taught to Christian women. Rather, women have been educated to find the meaning of themselves primarily in terms of relationships. At the same time as they have lacked sufficient encouragement in the direction of auton-omy, they have not been helped to see the dangers inherent in a self that finds its meaning only in relationships. Religious models of development that idealize relationships are too often used to reinforce motifs of women's self-sacrifice." This results in conformity to male-approved roles unless the praise for self-sacrifice is coupled with insistence on development of an independent self.

Exhortation to free choice and self-directed action are present, but not obvious, in classical discussion of discernment by such writers as Catherine of Siena and John of the Cross. These themes are implicit, I believe, in their meditation on fidelity in darkness and on perseverance when one feels no consolation. For, it is this struggle to sustain authentic love that forces one to question conventional wisdom and trust one's own religious experience. Discernment enables one to experience both ultimate dependence on God and personal empowerment by God.[57] This is what is important for women today, this conviction that God's Spirit affirms their self-direction as well as their surrender. What is essential for mature spirituality is the conviction that *only* an independent self can achieve authentic religious surrender.

In summary, the gospel call to a discipleship of equals urges us now to act simultaneously on at least four fronts. Participate in the ongoing conversion of institutions, such as religious life and women's organizations. Insist on a reversal of the trend to create an alternative, second class Christianity for Catholic women. Enlarge the discipline of feminist theology, and appropriate a feminist spirituality.

III. Future Issues

Because Christianity believes that the future invites us to greater possibilities of God's reign of friendship, and liberation, we can speak with hope. Because the only way to risen life is through the mystery of the Passover of Jesus, we must set our face toward Jerusalem and prepare for suffering. As I pointed out in the last section of this essay, feminist spirituality values the self-direction and maturity that are the fruit of struggle and suffering. For, this appropriate autonomy makes possible au-thentic religious surrender and the true discipleship of equals.

A theology for the future anticipates the likely experience of the future and discerns the Christian interpretation of that experience that might sustain us. We cannot live without meaning, so we try to anticipate or evaluate, in the light of past experience, what interpretation might sustain hope and reinforce the action we must undertake. Elie Wiesel, in a lecture at Villanova University (March 19, 1987), reminded us that when the unspeakable is spoken, it then becomes possible. Referring to the Holocaust and to nuclear war, Wiesel noted that the ability to speak of these matters as though one were sane when doing so makes these outrages possible and perhaps likely. So too, he reminded us, we must speak words of hope in order to make hope possible. For example, in the Talmudic tradition it is said that the name of the Messiah was spoken even before creation. That is, the ultimate word of hope was spoken before Israel's long experience of struggle in order to sustain Jewish belief that human history is ultimately messianic.

The future holds more possibilities than I could mention or even imagine, but allow me to concentrate on one that I can imagine and then to suggest some theological words of hope that I believe we must develop in the future in order to sustain us in this experience.

A. Action or Experience in the Future

Completing the Exodus from Patriarchy: Adulthood. I agree with those who interpret the signs of the times as indications that the Church, especially the Roman Catholic community of the Church, is moving to complete its exodus from patriarchal institutions.[58] Various segments are moving away from acceptance of the situation in which one male adult has absolute control over others who remain as children in relation to him. Whether this father figure be husband, work supervisor, parish priest, or pope, this person is no longer assumed to be the only one recognized as fully adult. The future will bring stronger claims for adult status, for the discipleship of equal adults, from every segment of the Church. There are clear signs of this future experience, I believe.

For example, Sandra Schneiders notes six signs of demands for adulthood in the Church.[59] First, the movement of women toward full and equal participation in the life and ministry of the Church is a demand for adult status. Second, the laity's insistence on their right to make responsible theological and moral decisions is a claim to adulthood. Third, there is the claim of theologians to the right to dissent from Vatican positions when their research and reflection reach conclusions that differ from those presented by the Vatican. Fourth, various national hierarchies are emerging as genuine leadership groups which formulate teachings and even defend theologians, such as Leonardo

Boff, who are under attack from the Vatican. Fifth, the emergence of spirituality as a central concern of all Catholics is the emergence of the desire to take personal responsibility for one's relationship to God. This attention to spirituality is bearing fruit in greater moral responsibility, ministerial commitment, and concern with justice. Sixth, the emergence of increasing pluralism of thought and practice is an indication of the exodus from patriarchy. Absolutism in doctrine and practice is possible only when the "father" thinks and plans and the "children" meekly follow and obey. Today, all serious Catholics think, plan, and act.

All movement toward adulthood involves an uncomfortable shift from a need for certitude to a search for understanding, and, often, a struggle with parent-figures who exert pressure, try to manipulate, and abuse their authority. We must be prepared to interpret this experience with hope.

B. Words of Hope for Difficult Times to Come

Theological themes that have been used most often in the past to oppress women are now being reimagined in ways that make them capable of giving hope.

1. *Anthropology.* Assuming that women are, by nature, subordinate to men, Church officials have excluded women from ordination and leadership roles, demanded that they remain in abusive marriages, and restricted contemplative women in ways that do not affect contemplative men. Most disagreements between the bishops and representatives of the Women's Ordination Conference are rooted in this issue. Most bishops have a model of "two natures" in which they believe that women and men are different but equal and complementary. In practice, "complementary" means inferior and incapable of representing Christ at the altar. In the national hearings for the forthcoming pastoral letter on women's concerns in the Church, the same "two nature" anthropology was used by conservative women's groups to bolster requests that only traditional roles be affirmed in the future.[60]

Now, feminist theologians are reimagining this "two nature" anthropology according to a transformational model. They connect the transformation of gender stereotypes with the transformation of the social and cultural structures which promote and reinforce them. Any adequate understanding of the natures of women and men must have the power of social critique.[61]

2. *Self-denial and the Cross.* Influenced by Constance FitzGerald's writing on impasse and the dark night,[62] Carolyn Osiek has

begun to reformulate the theology of the cross.[63] This is one of the most difficult symbols to use in a feminist context. Under this sign, powerful men have identified their own cause with that of God and slaughtered "unbelievers," tortured "heretics" and "witches," and silenced dissidents. It has been used according to a double standard. Both women and men have embraced rejection and suffering in order to "die with Christ." Yet, women's self-sacrifice was evaluated according to criteria set by men, and not vice versa; indeed, men set some standards which assumed that women should subordinate themselves to men. Women should "carry their cross," for example, by enduring an abusive husband or by accepting the rejection of their request for full participation in ministry. "The cross" has been manipulated by people who would submit others to it, but not themselves.

This double standard is most evident in its application to women of the notion of "bearing one's cross" in passive acceptance. Though seen as weaker by nature, women have been seen as capable of bearing greater suffering. For example, St. Bonaventure says, "It is for man to act, for woman to suffer";[64] that is, woman is naturally suited to endure, to be passive.

Osiek's theology of the cross aims to integrate feminist convictions about self-direction and free decision with traditional notions of the cross. To this end, she emphasizes the relationship of suffering, choice, vision, and redemption.

First, Christians must look to Jesus. He chose to devote his life to a vision and to the attempt to bring it about: the vision of the reign of God begun in this life. Jesus believed it was possible and was willing to give all for it. The suffering he experienced was not imposed but came as a consequence of his choosing "with a passion" to remain faithful to his vision.

So it is with the disciples of Jesus who envision the reign of God as the discipleship of equals. We must prepare to live under the cross of Jesus as a sign of contradiction. We choose to live coherently with a perception of gospel life as that of the discipleship of equals; this much is chosen. The contradiction results from the unexpected, irrational, and sometimes violent opposition which such a choice attracts. Or, even for those who expect suffering, the contradiction arises from the fact that an opposing vision of the gospel generates a powerful determination to enflesh that dream in society. The ideal might be, for example, God's reign as the "order" of obedient unanimity in which women "know their place"; or, it might be as the harmony that results when women accept their complementary roles as "handmaid," and "Martha." In her novel, *A Handmaid's Tale* (which was on the *New York Times* "bestseller" list for months in

1986-87), Margaret Atwood presents the harrowing story of a
woman's life in the American society that would result from a
political takeover by Christian fundamentalists who have just
such a vision of truth.[65] In any case, the contradiction which is
the cross results from the violent reaction of opposition that is
aroused by a choice for the discipleship of equals.

The cross tears at us heart and soul, Osiek reminds us,
because we wish to have the vision without the cost. Women's
affinity for harmony and peace-making is violated; the feminine
original sin of passivity lurks at the door as a tantalizing escape.
There is no point in trying philosophically to see the conflict as
"paradox," as only "seeming contradiction." It is true contradiction; it is opposites which cannot be reconciled, but which must
be lived with in their intolerable conflict and ambiguity as long
as the vision is judged worth living for. There is always the
temptation to abandon the vision of a discipleship of equals in
order to have at least the peace of being left alone. But, this
choice too, Osiek advises us, would take its toll in bitterness and
disillusionment, and thus is not really a viable option.[66]

The focus here is not on who is to blame or the reason we must
suffer, but on what happens to us in the process of suffering: we
enter into the suffering of God.[67] Contemporary theology
describes this "pain of God" as the result of the conflict between
anger and love: God's anger at human sinfulness is counteracted
by the depth of love that is also an integral aspect of the divine
relationship with us. The result is forgiveness. Jeremiah, voicing
the feelings of God imaged as a mother, cries: "Is Ephraim not
my favored son, the child in whom I delight? Often as I threaten
him I still remember him with favor. My womb stirs for him. I
must show him my mercy" (Jer 31:20). The only way in which we
can enter into that divine conflict, that suffering love of God, is
to experience it within our own lives. The conflict is between
anger at injustice in the Church and an abiding love of the
Church that refuses to be killed by anger; the conflict is between
a vision of the discipleship of equals and the price to be paid in
individual lives—our lives, my life—to bring it about. This is the
way we enter into the mystery of the cross of Christ, into the
suffering of God. This redemptive love is the only hope for the
future of a discipleship of equals.

NOTES

[1] Elisabeth Schüssler Fiorenza, *In Memory of Her* (New York: Crossroad, 1983), p. 213.

[2] See, for example, Gerda Lerner, *The Creation of Patriarchy* (New
York: Oxford University Press, 1986); Mary Briody Mahowald, ed.,
Philosophy of Woman (Indianapolis: Hackett, 1978); Alice S. Rossi, ed.,

The Feminist Papers (New York: Columbia University Press, 1973).

3 Rosemary Radford Ruether, ed., *Religion and Sexism* (New York: Simon & Schuster, 1974), pp. 9-10.

4 St. Teresa of Avila. "The Book of Her Life," in *The Collected Works*, 1, trans. Kieran Kavanaugh, O.C.D., and Otilio Rodriguez, O.C.D. (Washington, DC: Institute of Carmelite Studies, 1976): 68-69.

5 Anne Carr, "On Feminist Spirituality," in *Women's Spirituality: Resources for Christian Development*, ed. Joann Wolski Conn (New York: Paulist Press, 1986), pp. 53-55.

6 Lerner, *Creation of Patriarchy*, p. 2.

7 Gerda Lerner, *The Majority Finds Its Past* (New York: Oxford University Press, 1979), pp. 145-59.

8 Phyllis Bird, "Images of Women in the Old Testament," in *Religion and Sexism*, ed. Ruether, pp. 41-88. See, also, Phyllis Trible, *God and the Rhetoric of Sexuality* (Philadelphia: Fortress Press, 1978).

9 Constance Parvey, "Theology and Leadership of Women in the New Testament," in *Religion and Sexism*, ed. Ruether, pp. 117-49. See, also, Letty M. Russell, ed., *Feminist Interpretation of the Bible* (Philadelphia: Westminster Press, 1985).

10 Bernadette J. Brooten, "Paul's Views on the Nature of Women and Female Homoeroticism," in *Immaculate and Powerful*, ed. Clarissa W. Atkinson, Constance H. Buchanan, and Margaret R. Miles (Boston: Beacon Press, 1985), pp. 61-87.

11 Rosemary Radford Ruether, "Misogynism and Virginal Feminism in the Fathers of the Church," in *Religion and Sexism*, ed. Ruether, pp. 150-83.

12 Judith Hauptman, "Images of Women in the Talmud," in *Religion and Sexism*, ed. Ruether, pp. 184-212.

13 Eleanor Commo McLaughlin, "Equality of Souls, Inequality of Sexes: Woman in Medieval Theology," in *Religion and Sexism*, ed. Ruether, pp. 213-66.

14 Thomas Aquinas, *Summa Theologica*, ed. English Dominican Province, 3 vols. (New York, 1947), II-II, 10, 1, ad 3, as referred to in McLaughlin, "Equality of Souls," p. 229.

15 Micheline de Fontette, *Les religieuses à l'âge classique du droit canon: Recherches sur les structures juridiques des branches féminines des ordres* (Paris, 1967), p. 116, as referred to in McLaughlin, "Equality of Souls," p. 242.

16 Hilda Graef, *Mary, A History of Doctrine and Devotion* (London, 1963), p. 317, as quoted in McLaughlin, "Equality of Souls," p. 249.

17 Mary Potter, "Gender Equality and Gender Hierarchy in Calvin's Theology," *Signs* 11 (Summer 1986): 725-39.

18 Outstanding examples include: Carolyn Walker Bynum, *Jesus as Mother: Studies in the Spirituality of the High Middle Ages* (Berkeley: University of California Press, 1982); Rosemary Ruether and Eleanor McLaughlin, eds., *Women of Spirit* (New York: Simon & Schuster, 1979); William L. Andrews, ed., *Sisters of the Spirit: Three Black Women's Autobiographies of the Nineteenth Century* (Bloomington: Indiana University Press, 1986).

19 Clarissa W. Atkinson, *Mystic and Pilgrim: The "Book" and the World of Margery Kempe* (Ithaca, NY: Cornell University Press, 1983).

[20] Margaret Hope Bacon, *Mothers of Feminism* (San Francisco: Harper & Row, 1986).

[21] Elizabeth Griffith, "Friends Indeed," review of *Mothers of Feminism*, by Margaret Hope Bacon, in *New York Times*, 1 February 1986, p. 28.

[22] Lerner, *Creation of Patriarchy*, p. 5.

[23] *Ibid.*, pp. 11-14. See, also, Joan Kelly, *Women, History, and Theory* (Chicago: University of Chicago Press, 1984).

[24] *Creation of Patriarchy*, pp. 123-230.

[25] Sandra M. Schneiders, I.H.M., *New Wineskins* (New York: Paulist Press, 1986), p. 11.

[26] Mary Jo Weaver, *New Catholic Women* (San Francisco: Harper & Row, 1986), pp. 105-06.

[27] Schneiders, *New Wineskins*, pp. 95-113.

[28] *Ibid.*, p. 263.

[29] Weaver, *New Catholic Women*, p. 107.

[30] *Ibid.*, pp. 118-27.

[31] *Ibid.*, pp. 127-36.

[32] Kevin Klose, *Washington Post*, 13 November 1983, as quoted in Weaver, *New Catholic Women*, p. 133.

[33] Rosemary Radford Ruether, "Womanchurch Calls Men to Exodus from Patriarchy," *National Catholic Reporter*, 23 March 1984, p. 16, as quoted in Weaver, *New Catholic Women*, p. 133.

[34] Weaver, *New Catholic Women*, p. 134.

[35] What follows is a paraphrase of Sandra M. Schneiders, I.H.M., "New Skins: A Legacy for the Third Millennium," *Delta Epsilon Sigma Journal* 31 (October 1986): 51-52.

[36] This paragraph benefits from clarifications suggested by Gerard S. Sloyan, as do other sections of this essay.

[37] This definition adapts John Macquarrie, *Principles of Christian Theology* (New York: Charles Scribner's Sons, 1966), p. 1, to a feminist perspective.

[38] This next section of the essay is a digest of material from Weaver, *New Catholic Women*, pp. 156-77.

[39] See note #1.

[40] Elisabeth Schüssler Fiorenza, "Toward a Feminist Biblical Hermeneutics: Biblical Interpretation and Liberation Theology," in *The Challenge of Liberation Theology*, ed. Brian Mahan (Maryknoll, NY: Orbis Books, 1981), p. 100, as referred to in Weaver, *New Catholic Women*, p. 164.

[41] Rosemary Radford Ruether, "Feminist Theology and Religion," unpublished paper presented at Lily Endowment Seminar, March, 1983, p. 23, as quoted in Weaver, p. 164.

[42] Rosemary Radford Ruether, "Of One Humanity," *Sojourners* 13 (January 1984): 17, as quoted in Weaver, p. 165.

[43] Rosemary Radford Ruether, *Sexism and God-Talk* (Boston: Beacon Press, 1983).

[44] Ruether, "Of One Humanity," p. 19, as quoted in Weaver, p. 170.

[45] See, for example, Leonard Swidler, *Biblical Affirmations of Woman* (Philadelphia: Westminster Press, 1979).

[46] See, for example, John Carmody, *Holistic Spirituality* (New York:

Paulist Press, 1983), and *The Progressive Pilgrim* (Notre Dame, IN: Fides/Claretian, 1980); see, also, Denise L. Carmody and John T. Carmody, *Ways to the Center* (Belmont, CA: Wadsworth, 1981).

47 See, for example, William M. Thompson, *The Jesus Debate* (New York: Paulist Press, 1985); and Matthew Fox, *Original Blessing: A Primer in Creation-Centered Spirituality* (Santa Fe, NM: Bear & Co., 1983).

48 See, for example, the use of St. Monica to reinforce stereotypical roles for women, as explained by Clarissa W. Atkinson, " 'Your Servant, My Mother': the Figure of Saint Monica in the Ideology of Christian Motherhood," in *Immaculate and Powerful*, ed. Atkinson et al., pp. 139-200.

49 See Joann Wolski Conn, "Women's Spirituality: Restriction and Reconstruction," in *Women's Spirituality*, ed. Conn, p. 9; Carr, "On Feminist Spirituality," pp. 49-50.

50 See essays in my *Women's Spirituality*, pp. 3-5, 9-57.

51 See, for example, Susan Cady, Marian Ronan, and Hal Taussig, *Sophia: The Future of Feminist Spirituality* (San Francisco: Harper & Row, 1986). The authors demonstrate the way the image of God as *Sophia* (wisdom) is less likely to be coopted by the white race or the upper class.

52 Pertinent texts from Teresa and Catherine are reprinted in my *Women's Spirituality*, pp. 177-200.

53 Carol Gilligan, *In a Different Voice* (Cambridge: Harvard University Press, 1982). See, also, the critique of Gilligan by a panel of feminist scholars and Gilligan's reply in *Signs* 11 (Winter 1986): 304-33.

54 Robert Kegan, *The Evolving Self: Problem and Process in Human Development* (Cambridge: Harvard University Press, 1982).

55 Jean Baker Miller, *Toward A New Psychology of Women* (Boston: Beacon Press, 1976).

56 Saint Thérèse of Lisieux, for example, developed an independent, original vision of holiness by struggling with spiritual darkness and reevaluating the tradition common in her nineteenth century French Carmel. See my "Thérèse of Lisieux from a Feminist Perspective," *Spiritual Life* 28 (Winter 1982): 233-39.

57 This theme is developed in Constance FitzGerald, O.C.D., "Impasse and Dark Night," in *Women's Spirituality*, ed. Conn, pp. 287-311.

58 See, for example, Richard A. McCormick, S.J., "Dissent in Moral Theology and Its Implications," *Theological Studies* 48 (March 1987): 87-105, esp. 104; Madonna Kolbenschlag, *Authority, Community and Conflict* (Kansas City, MO: Sheed & Ward, 1986).

59 Schneiders, "New Skins," pp. 50-60.

60 *Origins* 14 (21 March 1985): 652-66; 15 (3 October 1985): 242-56. See, also, Sidney Callahan, Sally Cunneen, Monika Hellwig, Margaret Brennan, and Doris Smith, "The Pastoral on Women: What Should the Bishops Say?," *America*, May 18, 1985, pp. 404-13.

61 See, for example, Anne Carr, "Theological Anthropology and the Experience of Women," *Chicago Studies* 19 (Summer 1980): 113-28; report of Mary Ann Donovan's presentation on this theme in *Proceedings of the Catholic Theological Society of America* 41 (1986): 151-52; Mary J. Buckley, "The Rising of the Woman is the Rising of the Race," *Proceedings of the Catholic Theological Society of America* 34 (1979): 48-63;

Mary Ann Hinsdale, "Women's Experience and Christian Anthropology," as reported in *Proceedings of the Catholic Theological Society of America* 42 (1987).

[62] See note #57.

[63] Carolyn Osiek, R.S.C.J., *Beyond Anger: On Being a Feminist in the Church* (New York: Paulist Press, 1986).

[64] *III Sententiae,* d. 12, a. 3, q. 1, as noted in Osiek, *Beyond Anger,* p. 91, footnote #2.

[65] Margaret Atwood, *A Handmaid's Tale* (Boston: Houghton Mifflin, 1986).

[66] Osiek, *Beyond Anger,* pp. 73-74.

[67] *Ibid.,* pp. 75-76.

A Discipleship of Equals: Biblical Roots

Mary Ann Getty, R.S.M.

Introduction

The title of this volume suggests a loaded agenda. That is good. The phrase, "discipleship of equals," calls to mind the important ground-breaking work of Elisabeth Schüssler Fiorenza, especially in her monumental work, *In Memory of Her*.[1] The subtitle, "Towards a Christian feminist spirituality," suggests numerous possibilities: that we are on a journey progressing toward a goal, that it is possible to be both Christian and feminist, and that these help define the common goal. There is a deepening hunger for spirituality in our world, and we are involved in helping to address that need in this volume.

My own assignment is to explore the biblical roots of this project. I would initially like to unpack some of my own agenda which both adds to the already loaded one and proposes some clarifications which I hope will ease the way of these reflections. First, some thoughts about the terms of the title and a hint of a rudimentary outline to set the direction these reflections will take. My plan is to proceed along these lines:

1) clarify some terms,

2) propose methodological considerations and describe basic principles of feminist hermeneutics,

3) explore some biblical texts that mention women and alternate ways of interpreting them,

4) provide examples of the application of feminist hermeneutics to selected biblical texts and suggest some ramifications for a developing Christian feminist spirituality.

Clarification of Terms

Feminism is a values transformation.[2] It values cooperation rather than competition, reciprocity rather than hierarchy, and

integration rather than dualism. Feminism seeks to value and
respect all people in all areas of life so that freedom and
mutuality characterize our relationships, both personal and
societal. Feminism opposes all forms of discrimination based on
sex—that is, distinctions or prohibitions that apply to a whole
class of people simply because they are male or female. It
opposes the pattern of domination and subordination that such
distinctions and inequality imply.

A feminist consciousness rejects the win-lose pattern. It works,
not by exclusion, but by incorporation. A feminist perspective is
wholistic—not monolithic or tyrannical, but organic and differ-
entiating. It allows for differences in ideology, lifestyle, religious
expression, work patterns—and seeks to learn from these differences. Feminism is life-supporting. It values a sense of
stewardship toward all life and makes choices to preserve life
now and for the future. If feminist values are able to flourish,
they will lead to a transformation in the patterns of relationship
between persons, within communities and among nations.

Having considered some of the implications of feminism, I
would like to say a word about other aspects of this title that call
for some clarification, specifically what is meant by "equals" and
the relationship between theology and spirituality.

The concept of "equals" could be misleading. The Constitu-
tion of the United States says that we hold as basic that all "men
are created equal," that included in their rights are "life, liberty
and the pursuit of happiness." Yet, besides this being restricted
to "men," it takes no genius of history to remember that this
equality and these rights were neither inalienable nor inviolable.
And, maybe the basic concept of equality needs some explanation. Does this notion not set up false expectations? Is it not
possible that not only were we created unequal, but that equality
is not even a desirable goal? Are not our lives more interlocked
than as if we live side-by-side, each individually having equal
opportunity and therefore competing on equal terms? More
practically, I find that the notion of equality too often translates
into a confrontative power struggle. In relation to the equality of
men and women, too often it is set up as a win-lose situation with
what men have and are becoming what women are perceived to
be aspiring to. I find it hard to grant that men have arrived and
that women are now catching up or that equality is an absolute
value worth striving for.

Yet, there surely is something to the notion of equality as
opposed to and contrasted with a dominance-subordination
model that is present in the gospels' description of discipleship.
I personally prefer the phrase, "egalitarian discipleship," to
describe the community of faithful, but I will use the phrase,

"discipleship of equals," as described by Elisabeth Fiorenza and as I understand its meaning.[3]

A final note is concerned with spirituality. In our time, spirituality, once subordinated to and controlled by theology, has come into its own.[4] Spirituality as an essential expression of human experience has helped develop a new respect for the workings of the Spirit, for the role of prophecy and, of particular importance for us, for the voice of the feminine and feminism. In the words of Sandra Schneiders:

> . . . we can simplify the discussion by agreeing that the referent of the term "spirituality" is *Christian religious experience* as such. What that means is that spirituality for Christians is *Christian* and therefore theological considerations are relevant at every point; it is also *religious*, which means that it is affective as well as cognitive, social as well as personal, God-centered and other-directed all at the same time; and it is *experience*, which means that whatever enters into the actual living of this on-going integrating self-transcendence is relevant, whether it be mystical, theological, ethical, psychological, political or physical.[5]

Regarding its biblical roots, I believe that a Christian feminist spirituality is both critical and constructive.[6] It will include at least the following three elements:

a) a critique of patriarchal values and a call to conversion of grace which demands a transformation to an alternative order of reality,

b) a challenge to prophetic imagination which would create new, more liberating structures and ways of relating to one another,

c) an emphasis on truth as incarnated in human events and story (as interpretation and communication of those events), including the experience of women.

Other Methodological Considerations

In addition to exploring texts about women, a feminist hermeneutic understands the importance of reading the texts' silences, of examining the social setting that produced the text, and of interpreting texts from the perspective of furthering the Kingdom of God already inaugurated in Jesus.

1. Interpreting the Silences

A number of additional presuppositions have to be made explicit. First, not all the texts that omit mention of women are therefore exclusive of women. Women are mentioned in the scriptures either because they are exceptional or because there arose a problem concerning them.[7] Often when women are not mentioned, their presence can be taken for granted. So, for example, the infrequent mention of women (comparatively speaking) in the gospel of Mark does not indicate that they were not present, especially since the whole of the gospel is conceived as a journey from Galilee to Jerusalem. Women's sudden appearance at the end of the gospel, at the cross and at the empty tomb on the morning of the resurrection testifies eloquently to their faithful presence with Jesus throughout the journey. This accompaniment is made explicit by Luke (cf. 8:1-3) who develops his source, Mark, especially regarding the symbolic meaning of the journey for its implications for discipleship. Disciples are those who were "with Jesus," persevering with him in trials (Lk. 22:28), hearing the word of God and bringing forth its fruit in patience (8:15). The women were there, even if the men did not count them. The addition, "those who ate were about five thousand, not counting women and children" in Matthew (14:21), is a corrective of this oversight and an emphasis on the potency of the multiplication of bread—since women and children do get hungry just like the others, and since *all* were satisfied. Matthew stresses the abundance of Jesus' miraculous feeding and corrects the exclusive male count of his Jewish source, Mark.[8] Thus, women represent the messianic aspect of the banquet where all, without prejudice, are fed and satisfied.

2. *Examining the Social Context*

Secondly, feminist interpretation poses such imaginative and liberating questions as: What was it like to be a Christian woman in the first century? Are there any limits to Christian ministry and/or are there any just qualifications that would limit who can minister? Such questions force us to go beyond only those texts that directly mention women. We are challenged to consider the whole context, to ask what is Christian ministry, to examine the qualification of those who serve to promote the Kingdom of God. We are led to ask old questions in new forms, such as, "Should men be ordained?" We become suspicious of those ways of relating to one another that are merely expressions of cultural biases to which we have been born (e.g., should Americans hate the Russians?).

Contemporary biblical criticism has become intrigued with such sociological issues as the development of house churches, the freedom of individuals of whatever status to become Christians and, once baptized, to create a new community, not modelled after this world, but on the justice of the kingdom. The impact of the questions of what it was like to be a Gentile Christian woman in Corinth or a Jewish Christian woman in

Galatia which eluded interpreters for so many years has been explored by feminist interpreters like Elisabeth Fiorenza.[9]

Principles of a Feminist Christian Spirituality

Thus, we need to consider not only those texts and contexts that deal with women, but that point us in a direction of fleshing out the Kingdom of God in our midst. Other texts that have to do with 1) inclusion of all, especially the outcasts and disenfranchised, 2) the call to egalitarian discipleship as following the example of Jesus and in imitation of God, and 3) the challenge to participate in the liberation of all people from all oppressive structures. These are texts that demand feminist revisioning and the development of a feminist interpretative tradition. The feminist perspective is necessarily liberationist, egalitarian and inclusive. I would briefly describe what I mean by each of these three points.

1) All theology and spirituality worthy of the name Christian must be a form of *liberation;* it must be on the side of the disenfranchised, the marginalized, the poor and the outcast.[10] Theology has been used to justify an established order of Church and society, to defend the powerful, to reinforce the rights of the few while sacrificing or reducing the rights of others. Theology has been used to make exceptions even to the most basic commandments—for example, in the case of the development of the Just War theory, it has been recognized that under a certain set of circumstances the fundamental injunction against killing can be mitigated. From the time of Josue until the Second World War, elements justifying killing helped construe some wars as just and even holy so that land and revenge and similar ends were seen as legitimate reason for killing many. In a world progressively oriented toward the Kingdom of God, the notion of any war ever being holy is challenged at last. When such elemental principles as discrimination and proportionality are no longer viable, as in our own times, the hope of justifying war as holy must be abandoned. Christian theology necessarily liberates humankind from its propensity to inhumanity, for whatever reasons. The question of timing is significant in view of our collective and progressive movement toward realizing the Kingdom of God. The liberation movements, liberation theology, peace and women's studies, are opening up new possibilities for becoming more and more conformable to the gospel mandate to establish the Kingdom of God on earth.

2) A second essential value of feminist theology is that it is *egalitarian.* There are many indications that such was Jesus' instruction to his disciples. In contrast to the Gentile leaders who

lord it over them while being addressed as "benefactors," the disciples of Jesus are reminded that "It shall not be so with you" (Lk. 22:25-26). The question of rank was a subject of debate in various Jewish circles of Jesus' day. For example, it was an issue in the Qumran community. The fact that it also plagued the early Christian Church helps explain the reason the gospels portray the disciples' preoccupation with it, even in the most sensitive of times. Jesus' response to this question, according to Mark, is to take a small child whom he puts in their midst (Mk. 9:36). Then, Jesus identifies personally with this child, a representative of those who have no rights at all in the society of Jesus' day. Jesus instructs his followers: "Whoever receives one child such as this in my name, receives me; and whoever receives me, receives not me but the one who sent me" (9:37). Further, Jesus warns, "Whoever does not accept the Kingdom of God like a child, will not enter it" (10:15). But, the most powerful of Jesus' responses is in his own example: "The Son of Man did not come to be served but to serve and to give his life as a ransom for many" (10:45). John portrays a similar message when he pictures Jesus washing the feet of his disciples, telling them: "You call me Lord and Master and well I am; but I have treated you as friends. I have given you an example; so you ought to do for one another."

3) A spirituality that is feminist and Christian must be *inclusive*. It seeks the removal of boundaries and limitations of all kinds. Sin divides people. Grace unites. Jews and Gentiles, slaves and free, women and men are included in the gospel and its mission. "The gospel was preached unhindered" (Acts 28:30), as the disciples discovered the meaning of becoming Jesus' witnesses to the "ends of the earth" (Acts 1:8). The miracles are stories of Jesus' boundary-breaking, recorded in the gospels to remind the Church of its own mandate to reach out to the handicapped, the lost, the imprisoned, the hungry. The parables, too, are Jesus' usual manner of teaching the surprises of a universal God who challenged the expected, the limited, the binding.

The three principles of liberation, egalitarian discipleship and inclusion ought to be identifiable in a Christian feminist spirituality. Let us consider, first, the way they might operate as a critique to patriarchy regarding interpretation of texts that deal with women and then as essentials to reconstructing an alternative hermeneutic for sample texts within a wider perspective.

Biblical Texts on Women

An initial possibility for developing the biblical basis for a feminist spirituality is to examine all the texts that speak about women. From the outset there has been caution about this project, concern that its perspective is anachronistic. By implication, then, there has been the acknowledgment that the scriptures have an androcentric bias and have not been concerned with women. The scriptures were written by the "historical victors," portraying what was of concern to those in control of and maintaining the "real world" of history, religion and politics where women were seldom seen and even less heard. The cautions were often well intentioned and well taken.

For example, it was with a certain amount of trepidation, therefore, that the women who responded to Elizabeth Cady Stanton's invitation to uncover and revise (i.e., re-view) the scripture texts referring to women proceeded. They experienced the sobering awareness that, for different reasons, both suffragettes and experts in higher criticism viewed their task with disdain. Cady Stanton herself was keenly aware of the political implications of her task, and it was precisely because of these that she persevered.

Thus, these amateurs went forward despite the criticism. In 1898, they published *The Women's Bible,* a review of texts and chapters referring to women, which they found to constitute one tenth of the scripture, and a commentary on these texts.[11] They had been forewarned, too, that their efforts were merely self-serving, "engaged" as they were subjective.[12] It appears that women were naturally disqualified from seriously studying scripture since their feminine eyes would prejudice them against a more serious and objective reading such as had always been done. This was suggested as if all rational, male, theological probing had been value free and as if that is therefore the more truthful. It was Cady Stanton's realization of the political implications of the task that fortified her. She was engaged in a critique and a reconstruction. Perhaps it was fear of her success that challenged her opponents.

Some extremely interesting and fruitful insights were gleaned from these alleged amateurs. For instance, the study of Genesis 1-3 is enlightening. Some excerpts serve as tantalizing samples of the work of these interpreters. According to these commentators, Gen. 1:26, 27, 28, presents

> the sacred historian's first account of the advent of woman; a simultaneous creation of both sexes in the image of God. It is evident from the language that there was consultation in the Godhead and that the masculine and feminine elements are equally represented.[13]

As for the second creation account, in Gen. 2:21-25, Elizabeth Cady Stanton says:

Accepting the view that man was prior in creation, some scriptural writers say that as the woman was of the man, therefore, her position should be one of subjects. Grant it, then, as the historical fact is reversed in our day, and the man is now of the woman, shall his place be one of subjection? . . .[14]

Lillie Devereux Blake of the Revising Committee writes:

It is evident that some wily writer, seeing the perfect equality of man and woman in the first chapter, felt it important for the dignity and dominion of man to effect woman's subordination in some way. To do this a spirit of evil must be introduced, which at once proved itself stronger than the spirit of good, and man's supremacy was based on the downfall of all that had been pronounced very good. The spirit of evil evidently existed before the supposed fall of man, hence woman was not the origin of sin as so often asserted.[15]

The commentators further note that in Gen. 2:23 Adam proclaims the eternal oneness of the happy pair, "This is bone of my bone and flesh of my flesh"; no hint of her subordination. How could men, admitting these words to be divine revelation, ever have preached the subjection of woman? And, they point out that if there is any superiority in this story, it is of the woman over the man: they claim that the

assertion of the supremacy of the woman in the marriage relation is contained in v. 24: "Therefore shall a man leave his father and his mother and cleave unto his wife." Nothing is said of the headship of man, but he is commanded to make her the head of the household, the home, a rule followed for centuries under the Matriarchate.[16]

But, perhaps the most challenging of all is *The Women's Bible* reading of Genesis 3:

Note the significant fact that we always hear of the "fall of man," not the fall of woman, showing that the consensus of human thought has been more unerring than masculine interpretation. Reading this narrative carefully, it is amazing that any set of men ever claimed that the dogma of the inferiority of woman is here set forth. The conduct of Eve from the beginning to the end is so superior to that of Adam. The command not to eat of the tree of Knowledge was given to the man alone before woman was formed (Gen 2:17). Therefore the injunction was not brought to Eve with the impressive solemnity of a Divine Voice, but whispered to her by her husband and equal. It was a serpent supernaturally endowed, a seraphim . . . who talked with Eve and whose words might reasonably seem superior to the second hand story of her companion—nor does the woman yield at once. She quotes the command not to eat of the fruit to which the serpent replies, "Dying ye shall not die" (v. 4). In other words telling her that if the mortal body does perish, the immortal part shall live forever and offering as the reward of her act the attainment of knowledge.

Then the woman fearless of death if she can gain wisdom takes of this fruit; and all this time Adam standing beside her interposes no word of objection. "Her husband with her" are the words of V. 6. Had he been the representative of the divinely appointed head in married life, he assuredly would have taken upon himself the burden of the discussion with the serpent, but no, he is silent in the crisis of their fate. Having had the command from God himself he interposes no word of warning or remonstrance, but takes the fruit from the hand of his wife without a protest. It takes six verses to describe the "fall" of woman, the fall of man is contemptuously dismissed in a line and a half. . . . Again we are amazed that upon such a story men have built up a theory of their superiority.[17]

Yet, an androcentric reading of these passages has produced a theory of male superiority allegedly based on an objective and therefore true reading of these passages. Not only the texts but their androcentric interpretation have been canonized. The supremacy of males and the subjection of females have been said to have a scriptural basis, especially in the stories of creation. Thereby customs of domination down through history have been sanctified. The New Testament writers revert to this "amazing" interpretation whenever the question of "women's place" becomes enough of an issue to challenge "right order" in the Church or men's place. For example, 1 Tim. 2:11-15, says:

A woman must receive instruction silently, and under complete control. I do not permit a woman to teach or to have authority over a man. She must be quiet. For Adam was formed first, then Eve. Further, Adam was not deceived, but the woman was deceived and transgressed. But she will be saved through motherhood, provided women persevere in faith and love and holiness, with self-control.[18]

And, 1 Pet. 3:7 will advise husbands:

Likewise you husbands should live with your wives in understanding, showing honor to the weaker female sex, since we are joint heirs of the gift of life, so that your prayers may not be hindered.

And lest we think we can expunge all traces of chauvinism from Paul, we are struck by a similar thought in 2 Cor. 11:3, a passage that almost no one argues is not from Paul, "But I am afraid that, as the serpent deceived Eve by his cunning, your thought may be corrupted from a sincere (and pure) commitment to Christ." For Paul, Eve is the traditional image of sin, and she is easily seduced. So says Genesis 3, it is claimed, and so interpret centuries of Jewish and Christian tradition based on

Genesis 3, as if no other implications are possible or admissible. But, the same Paul, in another passage where the heat of his differences and problems with the Corinthians does not intrude, contrasts the second Adam, Christ, with the first who caused sin to enter the world (Rom. 5:12-21; also 1 Cor. 15). The last Adam is not at all like the first, but is life-giving spirit, and his resurrection is a promise of the resurrection of all (including women of whom nowhere else, besides 1 Tim 2:15, is it ever said that she will be saved in a manner different from men).

But, even these traditional interpretations of the fall of Eve may be on to something—it is important to include Eve in the fall since the Genesis 3 account has to implicate all humanity. If it were only a matter of the "fall of man," the entire human family would not have been involved. "The Mother of all the Living" (i.e., Eve) represents all humankind in a way that Adam does not. Eve's creation and her Fall are in some respects more important than Adam's since they signify all.

Further, the traditional interpretation and even the story of Genesis 3 contain their own corrective, a significant observation about revelation itself. The subordination of woman is an expression of sin, manifesting what is wrong with humanity. The promise of a redemption through the woman is given even before the "curse" on humanity (3:15). The woman, through her seed, shall crush the head of the serpent and will ultimately be victorious over evil. The "curse" involves the domination of man over woman. In other words and curiously enough, the writers of the scriptures (who were almost certainly all male) recognized this domination of man over woman for what it is— a consequence and a continuing sign of sin.

Thus, the recognition that male writers and interpreters of scripture gave it an androcentric bias does not preclude the also present realization that a remedy is necessary. There is a built-in critique of male dominance over woman. A similar appreciation of other stories of the Old Testament is expressed even in the long tradition of scripture writing and interpretation. So, for example, the organization of women across cultural, national, class lines is responsible for the preservation of Israel at the beginning of the Exodus with the rescue and care of Moses, with the entrance into the Holy Land with the cooperation of Rahab, with the preservation of God's people despite many threats with the heroism of Tamar, Deborah, Judith and Jael, Vashti and Esther, Bathsheba, Huldah, the Mother of the Maccabees.

In the story of the Exodus, patriarchy represents a negative force that perceives a threatening aspect of Israel's growing population and the competition Israel represented to Egypt. The Pharaoh planned the extermination of this competition, ordering first the Hebrew midwives and then all of his own subjects to kill the male Israelite babies (Ex. 2:15-22). The Pharaoh perceives that the way to oppose a threat is by killing; he even tries to enlist the help of women whose work it is to cooperate in producing life. The women conspire to thwart all the powers of such an evil empire—the Pharaoh's daughter, the midwives, the mothers and sisters join not only to insure the preservation not only of one man's life, Moses, but to insure their own rights of self-determination and the future of the people. This is salvation. Moses owes his life to Miriam. She is also the first liturgist, celebrating the people's victory with instruments and song. But, Moses' adaptation of his sisters' words are the ones remembered. And it is the "sons of Aaron" who are the priests entrusted with the liturgical celebrations in the customs of the people.

Melchizedech was to be forever remembered because he served Abram bread and wine once (Gen. 14:18-20); his act of hospitality was so unusual that it is reckoned as a model not only for Christian priesthood but of the High Priesthood of Christ himself. But, Abraham and his visitors ate bread regularly kneaded and baked by Sarah. There was nothing exceptional about the fact that she and millions of other women offered such hospitality and more every day of their lives. For Peter's confession of Jesus he is said by Matthew to have received the keys to heaven (16:18-19); when Martha made the same profession of faith, she does not receive a comparable award (Jn. 11:27). No androcentric interpretation ever based any Church doctrine on Martha's confession, to my knowledge.

Even in the face of the androcentric bias of the scriptures, the perspectives, the texts selected for canonization and the interpretations given them, there is also a critical tradition built in recovering and insisting on the faithful role of women not only as objects of reflection but as participants, as agents of history, as representatives of a critique of the dominant male culture and of an alternative which is often perceived as preferable in the plan of God. The task of explaining the androcentric bias of the scriptures and their interpretations is easy. But, this bias and these interpretations are also suspect since they are culturally conditioned. Wherever these same scriptures also include good news for women, sometimes subtle, sometimes less so, this can be a key for understanding the cultural critique of the scripture and ways in which "God's ways are not man's ways" (cf. Is. 55:8).

Thus, the elements of scripture that can easily be explained in the light of cultural biases are the least likely to contain revelation of the God of Israel and of Christians who is "Other," "One," transcendent while personal, but unable and unwilling to be made an idol. On the other hand, those values which are consistent with such a view of God, with the covenant and the promises, which challenge the *status quo* and which could not have proceeded from cultural bias, are the more trustworthy for the challenges they represent.

The Mission to the Outcasts (Women and Slaves)

The Jesus movement was inclusive—the boundaries that had held religions and religious people were broken. The criticisms against Jesus were basically addressing this boundary-breaking quality of his ministry. He ate with sinners; he heals on the Sabbath; he is unwilling to call down fire from heaven on the inhospitable Samaritan nor even to answer his accusers; he speaks with women and touches them. The biblical promise that "wherever the gospel is told, what the woman who anointed Jesus has done will be told in memory of her" (Mk. 14:9) testifies that the gospel is not just a story about Jesus but is about the characters who interact with Jesus, who create the revelatory gospel moments, who receive the gospel with open and generous hearts and proclaim it with perseverance.

Baptism held open to women the possibility of an improved status, an alternative identity apart from the patriarchal family and state. It never was an issue whether women could be baptized. Although this was an issue concerning Gentile men, from earliest times women were included in the basic inclusive symbol of salvation. Also, very early on other underprivileged (from the androcentric viewpoint) categories of persons were also included—slaves and children, for example. The New Testament references to Jesus' permitting the children to come to him and his blessing of them could signify that infant baptism and even the whole project of marriage for Christians were seriously questioned. Perhaps this is due to a certain bias for celibacy, at least in predominantly Gentile-Christian communities. In any case, the saying of Jesus regarding the eschatological state of Christians, where there is "Neither giving nor taking in marriage" (Mk. 12:25; note the androcentric perspective), and even Jesus' views on the indissolubility of marriage caused some disciples to conclude, "Then it is better not to marry" (Mt. 19:10). The option to become Christian and consequently to lead a celibate lifestyle held up by some as ideal became an early crisis for the Church. It is not difficult to perceive how Baptism could be extremely threatening to patriarchal society.

The matter of the freedom of Baptism involved more than just the status of women and the possibility of celibacy. Another special case was slaves. A common practice was that whole households were converted at once (cf. Acts 10:2, 24, 44). That seems to be the case when early problems crop up in Corinth, and Paul receives questions regarding the options available to married women and slaves with reference to their new status in Christ.

The advice Paul gives in 1 Corinthians 7 seems simplistic and short-sighted; he says four times in this one chapter that no one should change her state in life (1 Cor. 7:8, 17, 24, 29-30). "Stay the way you were when you were first called" is Paul's general advice. He will promise in 1 Cor. 11:34 to answer other questions or to resolve some of the more complex aspects of his advice when he gets there. Paul does appreciate some of the complexity of the situation, apparently. For example, in the case of women who become believers without their husbands (cf. 7:12-16), he allows that a serious dilemma could exist. On the basis of Baptism, Paul believes that Christians are "one" in Christ (cf. Gal. 3:28). Therefore, in the case of a "mixed marriage" between a non-believing husband and a believing wife, "if the unbeliever separates, let him separate. The brother or sister is not bound in such cases" (7:15). This despite the blanket injunction of the Lord against divorce. The woman is not bound to society's patriarchal values as a Christian. Paul realizes the social problem of the authority of a husband over his wife. But, Paul is more fundamentally convinced of the woman's new status and identity in the Lord. And, despite its potentially threatening and even revolutionary implications, Paul allows that the believing woman may divorce her non-believing husband, "because God is a God of peace." The Baptism of the believer is a more basic commitment than marriage and grants a freedom greater than the limits of marriage.

Philemon: A Case Study

In 1 Cor. 7, however, Paul does not go further than his "stay as you are" advice with regard to slaves (7:20-24). Development will have to wait until a problem arises, as in the case of Philemon and Onesimus, Christians of Colossae. The short letter of Philemon provides a good example of the way feminist spirituality reaches beyond the borders of those texts that deal with women.

In summary, the story behind the text is simply this: Onesimus was a slave of Philemon. For some reason we cannot know for sure, Onesimus did not become a Christian when Philemon did. Perhaps Onesimus has already stolen money or valuables from Philemon and run away at the time of Philemon's conversion. That detail we cannot know. Paul calls himself

Philemon's father and brother, as he also is Onesimus,' which
suggests that they both became converts under influence of
Paul's preaching. Nevertheless, remember that Paul says in 1
Cor. 1:14-17 that he rarely baptizes; that he "was not sent to
baptize but to preach the gospel" (1:17). It also appears that
many others of Philemon's household, Apphia and Archipus,
for example, were converted and probably by Paul since they are
also known to him. Philemon is the head of a house-church; his
leadership is recognized not only by those who meet in his
house, but by Paul himself.

In prison, Paul encountered Onesimus who becomes a Christian and thereby develops with Paul a relationship comparable
to the one Philemon has with Paul. Paul recognizes Onesimus'
great gifts and clearly feels genuine affection for him. Indeed, as
is frequently the case with Paul, the Apostle is dependent on his
converts, including Onesimus. Paul claims that the relationship
is one of mutuality, that he relies on Onesimus and is reluctant
to part with him. Baptism has overcome all other social distinction. Onesimus is "brother" to both Paul and to Philemon. Yet,
Paul also recognizes that Philemon has another claim to
Onesimus since not only was Philemon Onesimus' master, but
Onesimus has wronged Philemon and owes him something.
And, Paul owes Philemon the opportunity to decide what to do
now that he has been found.

The lack of reconciliation between Onesimus and Philemon
bothers Paul. He, therefore, equips Onesimus with a letter and
sends him back to Philemon with a request that remains oblique.
It is far from clear that Paul is asking Philemon to manumit
Onesimus. What is clear is that Paul identifies with both
Philemon and Onesimus, not identifying himself as an apostle
who would underscore his authority, and refusing to invoke his
authority, although he not so subtly reminds Philemon that he
does possess both the authority and the courage to command.
Paul identifies himself as father, brother, old man and guest; he
enlists members of Philemon's household and the entire Church
that gathers in Philemon's house. He implies that the liturgy
ought to be the context for a public reading and scrutiny of the
letter and discernment about what action to take.

Paul identifies with Onesimus so completely that he promises
that he himself will make retribution for any wrongs Onesimus
may have committed. At the same time, Paul reminds Philemon
of his debt to Paul himself. Elsewhere Paul describes charity as
both the remission of debt and the only legitimate debt a
Christian incurs and recognizes. In Rom. 13:8-10, Paul says,
"Owe nothing to anyone except to love one another." In 15:29,
he speaks of the Gentiles' debt to the Jews: having shared their

spiritual blessings, they owe the Jews their material support. Perhaps in the same way, Paul thinks of a new approach to Onesimus as the "debt" incurred by their sharing of the same faith (cf. Rom. 1:8-11).

While the exact nature of Paul's request to Philemon cannot be definitively decided, what is clear is that Paul enjoins, in modern terms, a process of communal discernment that calls for new levels of their relationship. Things cannot go on as if they had not been baptized. The letter is addressed not only to Philemon whose rights as Master are recognized and would seem in a social context to be the only issue. The whole church is involved. The letter discusses not only Onesimus and his sins but the mutual indebtedness of Paul and Philemon and Onesimus.

Much has been written about the dilemma with which this letter faces Philemon,[19] given that slavery was part of the social and economic fabric of society and that a suggestion to free a runaway errant slave was tantamount to revolution. Outside of his Christian concerns, Philemon had no choice but to prosecute Onesimus to the fullest extent of the law, which could have included death. For his part, Paul realized that continued service as a slave was not the worst thing that could happen to Onesimus. In a Christian home slaves would have fared better than they would have even if let free without support or preparation (cf. Paul's admonishment to slaveowners in Colossae to treat their slaves justly and fairly: Col. 4:1). Nowhere does Paul advocate revolution, with its wholesale rejection of societal mores. Nor even did Jesus call for the abolition of slavery.

By normal standards, Onesimus should have been an object lesson, made an example for not only robbing his master but for running away, which threatened slaveowners everywhere. The least Onesimus could hope for was that his chastisement be kept private, and perhaps he could be personally forgiven by Philemon and sent away in disgrace. But, by writing not only to Philemon but to the whole church, Paul asks for something more that challenges both Philemon and Onesimus. After all, Onesimus must have trusted both Paul and Philemon a great deal. For, if Philemon's fortune were threatened, this was a matter of life and death for Onesimus. The letter to Philemon indicates not only a growing personal social awareness in Paul but also a growing Christian consciousness of the implications of a discipleship of equals. The community needs to resolve this multi-faceted problem from the perspective of the social ramifications for baptismal promises.

What is clear is that Philemon is interdicted from taking

retaliatory measures; he cannot exact an "eye for an eye or tooth for a tooth." There is no question about whether he can demand retribution from the offender: Philemon cannot invoke his authority merely as slaveowner or as head of household or as leader of church. Paul himself does not even invoke his own apostolic authority. Everyone involved is required to go the extra mile, to be reconciled before offering a gift at the altar. Philemon and Onesimus and Paul require the help of the church in discerning what is the "good and perfect thing to do" (cf. Rom. 12:1-2) in this case. The issue of slavery, previously so clear, has become more complex and weightier in the light of a new understanding of Baptism.

Christology and the Mission of Jesus

The God of Israel, of Paul and of Jesus is a God of surprises. Israel was always reluctant to present images of God, concerned as she was about idolatory. Necessarily, the symbols and parables and images used in the scriptures are more than one since any single image would be a form of idolatory. Although Jesus himself gives us many images of God: Father, Wisdom, searcher of the lost, Jesus also tries to teach that God is "Other," not reasoning as humans do, manifesting a notion of justice that surpasses merely human projection. One gospel image in particular vividly portrays Jesus' God of mercy.

In his chapter 15, Luke has Jesus telling three parables descriptive of the Kingdom of God. These represent Jesus' response to the criticism of his enemies that he eats with sinners (Lk. 15:1-2). The Kingdom of God, Jesus says, is like a man who had two sons. So far so good—he seems extremely blessed until this point. But, this man had some problems—apparently with his younger son in particular. Bored, perhaps restless and certainly ungrateful, this boy suggests a revolutionary plan. He wants to take his due and run. He is disowning his father; he implies that he deserves something—probably a great deal. Even today, we can understand that as younger son he is really overstepping himself. Especially in the patriarchal world of Jesus' day, the boy's arrogance was appalling. Certainly while his father is living and even when he dies, the younger son is not due much at all. So Jesus' audience should be shocked already and cheering for the lad's comeuppance.

But then we have the Father, whose behavior and attitudes are equally shocking, although they might explain the spoiled son. The father not only gives in—but even after the son's departure with the money, the misled father acts like a fool. Jesus' audience would not have appreciated his reducing to such depths the most cherished and, in fact, one of the last bastions of respected institutions of the times, fatherhood. This would be all the more shocking in an already troubled and irreverent world. Worse, when the wayward son returns, the foolish father further degrades himself, running to greet the son, substituting the folly of a celebration for the punishment the kid deserves!

It is rather natural to identify with the third character, the elder son. He is the only reasonable reaction of the story. It is not right. The younger first gets some of the elder's portion; he gets it in advance; he wastes it, and yet the father acts as if he is a hero. The elder's complaint is just, and many of us have learned that the logic of this elder's position is justice. Other sayings of the gospels, like "the last shall be first and the first last," are mysterious but abstract enough to accept. But here, as, for example, also in the story where those who labor only one hour are given the same as those who have borne the heat of the day, God's sense of justice is threatening to our own and perhaps too hard to hear.

At least one of the "morals" of this story is that God is *not* like a Father as defined by the society of Jesus' day. Fatherhood at that time was a very much constrained concept. The Kingdom of God is like when a Father breaks out of these constraints and does not act like any ordinary human father; when not the elder son, the safer one, inherits all the wealth upon the death of a watchful father; but when the younger son, even after much sin and waste, is restored and reconciled and celebrated because he is a witness to new life. The justice of the kingdom of God is mercy, freeing all who are locked up in the inhumanity of a "to each his due" attitude, a correcting, healing challenge to the measured sense of right that actually does violence to everyone. In this view, the elder son becomes the most pathetic of all characters. Yet, sometimes our systems called justice cannot, any more than this man could, look beyond petty horizons of rewards and punishments which have nothing whatever to do with what is good in the Kingdom of God.

Jesus, Word and Wisdom of God

Jesus presents many images of God, none of which are detached figures. How would we know God whom we have never seen and whose image we are forbidden to create lest we fall into idolatry? The gospel's answer is that God is known through the image, the Word, Jesus. The gospels' portraits of Jesus are testimony that God's best efforts at becoming intelligible are through Jesus. Thus, in trying to discover the meaning of Jesus, Christians searched the scriptures for usable symbols and traditions. One of the oldest traditions they found suitable and which was quickly and widely used was that of Sophia (= Wisdom). Recently, some feminist studies have recovered this ancient symbol and stirred new interest in and potential for exploring further the fascinating history and meaning of this tradition.[20]

Christology, theoretically one of the most potentially liberating of all aspects of Christian theology, has been used as a way of emphasizing the incarnation of Christ as male and, therefore, excluding and even oppressing women. Clearly, this avenue of interpretation, however long and authoritative its tradition, is not consistent with a liberationist, inclusive and egalitarian model, such as we find in the gospels' own representation of Jesus. It is not a new idea to explore the Wisdom tradition for its impact on Christology, but the feminist voices of Elizabeth Johnson and Elisabeth Schüssler Fiorenza have suggested some exciting possibilities of Sophia-Wisdom as a biblical basis for non-androcentric Christology.

One of the oldest and most commonly used scriptural figures to understand Christ was the Jewish image of personified Wisdom, whose words, functions and attributes were quickly transferred to Jesus (e.g., 1 Cor. 1:24; Jn. 1:1-18). Implicated in this use of this female image of the goddess incarnated in Jesus are consequences for understanding such traditional biblical categories as pre-existence and divinity, the inclusive nature of Jesus' ministry and mission. This image has also been evoked by the Church to attribute cosmic significance to Jesus' death-resurrection and to relate his saving message to the creation and governance of the world.

The figure of personified Wisdom appears not only in the Bible but in intertestamental apocalyptic, in the Dead Sea Scrolls, the works of Hellenistic Jewish philosophers, Gnostic sects and rabbinic Judaism. In the Old Testament, Wisdom is introduced subtly in the Book of Job (chap 28), and more noisily in Proverbs (1:20-33; 4:13; 8:15-35; 9:1-6). According to Proverbs, she gives life, she teaches righteousness and justice while opposing evil. She also helps in the creation of the universe (3:19), existing before the world (8:22-31), and delighting in human company whom she invites to eat her bread and drink her wine (9:5). Wisdom is a searcher of people, especially the lost and forgotten; she entrusts her secrets to them.

According to the biblical wisdom literature, wisdom is allied with the Torah (Sir. 24:23). She invites people to herself, calling, "Come to me all you who desire me, and eat your fill . . ." (v. 19). For the author of the Book of Wisdom, her gifts are manifold;

she is "mother of all good things" (7:12), and all are saved by wisdom (9:18).

The influence of even these few selected texts on New Testament Christology is clear to see. Nevertheless, a few examples serve to illustrate how widespread this impact was across the New Testament. For Paul, Christ is the Wisdom of God (1 Cor. 1:24). It is through the Lord Jesus Christ that all things are and through him we exist (1 Cor. 8:6). The Christological hymn of Col. 1:15-20 celebrates Christ as "the firstborn of all creation, in whom all things were created."

Everyone is aware of John's portrait of Jesus as the word of God, preexisting creation, revealing the glory of God and saving all. The synoptic writers also depend on the Wisdom tradition to develop their Christologies. Jesus befriends the outcast and thus proves wisdom right (Lk. 7:35). Jesus is a prophet sent by Sophia and rejected as one in a long line of murdered envoys (cf. Lk. 11:49).[21] But, Matthew is even more explicit; he puts Sophia's words into Jesus' mouth, portraying Jesus as Sophia speaking (Mt. 23:34). "When John heard in prison about the deeds of the Christ," he sent his disciples to Jesus, questioning Jesus' identity. Part of Jesus' answer, according to Matthew, is "Wisdom is judged by her deeds" (11:19). The deeds of Christ and the deeds of Sophia are the same. Matthew had narrated the mighty deeds in Galilee in chapters 8 and 9; immediately after this testimony to John's followers, Jesus is described as "upbraiding the cities where most of his mighty deeds were done, because they did not repent" (11:20).

These are but a few of the many references we could cite, noting Jesus' intimate relation with wisdom. It is startling that implications of this association had to await development by feminist exegesis in our own times. It is not hard to understand the maintenance necessities of the androcentric bias of traditional Christology. What is challenging about the reevaluation of the wisdom imagery as related to Christology concerns the fluidity of the gender symbolism inherent in the tradition and essential for a truly inclusive Christology.

Thus, the biblical roots of Christology afford us a feminist way of interpreting not only who Jesus as image of God is but what the Christian mission of faithful discipleship involves. The feminist principles of inclusion, egalitarian discipleship and imitation of God characterize a biblical Christology, with its implications for carrying out the mandate to "Go and teach all nations what I have taught you" (Cf. Mt. 28:20).

Discipleship as Imitation of God

The scripture frequently enjoins imitation of God. From the keeping of the Sabbath through the command to Abraham to the mandate of Jesus, the model for the faithful is no less than God. The Law prescribes the observance of the Sabbath, the Sabbatical Year, and the Jubilee Year as ways in which the people of Israel are to reflect their faith in God through the quality of their relationships with one another (see Leviticus 25). The Sabbath requires leisure (abstinence from work) for the sake of meditating on the God who accomplishes all things. Thus, "to keep holy the Lord's day" is an imitation of God; Israel becomes like God when she studies God's way. The Sabbatical Year is likewise a time given over to the study of God's instruction. The Jubilee Year allows for the numerous ways in which dedication to God might affect human/social relationships. In accordance with God's instruction, then, the Jubilee Year is an opportunity to act like God by freeing the captives, restoring land to the disenfranchised, granting forgiveness and grace freely.[22]

The passage Jesus read from Is. 61:1-2 as part of his inaugural address in the Nazareth synagogue, according to Luke (4:16-20), was a commentary on Leviticus 25. There Jesus proclams that his mission is to give sight to the blind, to restore hearing to the deaf, to preach the gospel to the poor, to proclaim the Jubilee Year. His commentary, including his statement that this is being fulfilled "today," excites his listeners to reject him and conspire to kill him. In accepting his mission to the poor and outcasts, Jesus is accepting the terms of his baptism by which he became the child of God.

Jesus' temptation is recorded by Luke (4:1-13) between the description of his Baptism, with the heavenly voice that said, "This is my Son" (3:21-23), and Jesus' inaugural address in his hometown synagogue (4:16-30). Jesus is depicted as being tempted on the very grounds of his identity as the son of God. Jesus' acceptance of his mission to the outcasts is his rejection of the temptation. Jesus' mission to proclaim the Lord's Year of Favor is the expression of his identity as God's son.

The disciples of Jesus request a prayer, as John taught his disciples (Lk. 11:1-4). Jesus' response is the "Our Father," a prayer that gives not only the words to say but the context in which to pray. Jesus' disciples pray for the coming of God's kingdom. They pray out of an experience of God they know. Prayer is drawing strength to imitate God.

Jesus' instruction to his disciples included the command to imitate God (cf. Mt. 5:45; Lk. 6:36). According to Matthew, Jesus says, "Be perfect as your heavenly father is perfect."

Fortunately Matthew includes a further illustration of the way we are to imitate God:

> You have heard that it was said, "You shall love your neighbor and hate your enemy." But I say to you, love your enemies, and pray for those who persecute you, that you may be children of your heavenly Father for he makes his sun rise on the bad and the good and causes rain to fall on the just and the unjust. For if you love those who love you, what recompense will you have? Do not the tax collectors do the same? And if you greet your brothers only, what is unusual about that? Do not the pagans do the same? So be perfect as your heavenly father is perfect.

It has been said that this command of enemy love is the distinctive mark of Christianity, a kind of summary of the New Testament message. Such a statement requires further examination.

The command to enemy love appears as the sixth and last of a series of antitheses in Matthew 5, part of the Sermon on the Mount. These antitheses are all introduced with the phrase, "You have heard it said . . . but I say . . ." The radical quality of Jesus' demand in relation to the teachings of the law is demonstration of the spirit of Jesus' insistence: "Your righteousness must surpass the righteousness of the scribes and Pharisees" (5:20). Yet, nowhere in the Old Testament does it say, "You shall hate your enemy." Rather, it seems that love of neighbor was sometimes construed as a limit to the requirement to love. Human experience tells us it is necessary, if not easy, to love those who love us and to take care of our own, to provide for our neighbors, to render good to others in order to live well. Yet, there arises the question of limits: What are the boundaries of love? Enemy love is an intrusive mandate, challenging all boundaries and going far beyond the apparent reasonableness of neighborly love.

Yet, enemy love is not unique to the gospels. A number of pagan sources of the first century speak about enemy love and consequently remind us that this seems to have been a widely debated issue around the time of Jesus. Thus Seneca, the tutor of Nero and Roman philosopher of the first century, writes:

> If you are imitating the gods, you say, "Then bestow benefits also upon the ungrateful; for the sun rises also upon the wicked, and the sea lies open to pirates." This point raises the question whether a good man would bestow a benefit on an ungrateful person if he knew that he was ungrateful. Understand that according to Stoicism there are two classes of ingrate: one type is ungrateful because he is a fool; another—the common meaning of the term—because he has a natural tendency to do this vice. The good man will benefit the first type of ingrate, but he will no

more benefit the second type than he would lend money to a spendthrift or to a person whom many have already found to be false.[23]

Jewish sources also describe a kind of enemy love, at least in so far as they prescribe renunciation of vengeance. Thus, for example, the apocalyptic group of the Essenes taught that one should not repay evil for evil, but leave that to God (cf. I QS x, 17-20). The speaker adds that he will not, however, forget: "I will not be content until he begins the day of judgment." The Hellenistic-Jewish author of the *Letter to Aristeas* considers a similar question about the right attitude toward one's enemies:

> The King asked . . . "To whom should one show liberality?" He replied, "All agree that we ought to show liberality toward those who are well disposed toward us, but I think that we ought to show the same spirit of generosity toward those who are opposed to us so that in this way we may win them over to what is right and to what is advantageous to us. But we must pray to God that this be accomplished, for He rules the mind of all." (#227)

Thus, the question of the treatment of one's adversaries is not a purely Christian one. Further, neither the idea of imitation of God nor the idea of renunciation of retribution is in themselves Christian. The powerlessness of Christians in the early centuries of the Church could be interpreted as making a virtue of necessity. The command to enemy love and "doing good to those who hate you" for Christians in a hostile state, who faced dire consequences should they be imprudent enough to either resist authorities or retaliate against powers much stronger than themselves, simply makes good sense to a Church in a survival mode. But this context of powerlessness is hardly adequate as an explanation of the crux of the Christian ethical teaching.

The ideology of power as described by Seneca and Aristeas has as its purpose the preservation of dominance over others. The basic Christian message, on the other hand, cannot be cynical about power, even the power of the humane ruler. Both these pagan and Jewish references refer to the behavior of the "King" or the "wise man," symbolizing those who are dominant and depicting their treatment of those under their authority. They also have to do with the behavior of individuals ultimately to serve their own purposes.

As Luise Schottroff points out, essential to discerning the uniqueness of the Christian teaching about charity is some attention to social distinctions together with a clear emphasis on equality as an expression of authentic Christian love.[24] In short, it is not virtue to merely avoid either crushing an underling or courting sure punishment from a superior. With those of different levels in society, patient endurance is basically a matter of prudence.

Schottroff goes on to say, "An attitude of submission subject to the contempt of the aristocrat or the sympathy of a superior" is not merely elevated in the gospels to an ideal "without taking into account the relation of dependence."[25] Schottroff further cautions: "If we simply ignore social differences and assume that texts like Matt. 5:38ff inculcate a universal ethic intended for everyone in all circumstances," we would miss the specifically Christian impact of this command and reduce it to a justification of structures of domination.[26]

Neither "love of enemy as an exercise of one's own power nor love of enemy as the resignation to one's own powerlessness captures the sense of Matt 5:38ff and of the spirit of the Christian gospel."[27] Socrates figures in many ancient legends as a symbol of one badly treated in a society gone mad. And, for Plutarch, the absence of anger "is the victory of the strong."[28] The individual philosopher is head and shoulders above the crowd. The legends regarding Socrates revolve around the principle that the individual is confronted by a crowd of madmen, beasts, or misguided children. He accepts their blows without resisting in order to proclaim, not only in words, but also in his body the rottenness of society. If we compare those legends with Mt. 5:38ff, the difference is clear. It is important for the understanding of the ethical teaching of the synoptics to remember that addressed is not an isolated individual but members of the Christian community.

The call to nonviolence, to renunciation, and love of enemy has come down to us in several versions. The common tradition used by Matthew and Luke (=Q), Paul and Peter all attest to some part of this command. Among the common elements of this tradition is the mandate to pray for one's persecutors, to do them good, to bless and not to curse them (cf, Rom. 12:14; Lk. 6:22 par.; 1 Thess. 5:18; 1 Cor. 4:12-13; 1 Pet. 2:12, 23; 3:9, 16; 4:4, 14). The Christian is challenged to include his persecutor in his community. The enemy are those who reject and refuse this invitation and, on their part, wish to detach themselves. Consequently, the command to love the enemy is thoroughly aggressive, although not in a destructive sense. The command to enemy love is an appeal to take up a missionary attitude toward one's persecutors. Even the enemies of the community are given a place in its common life and in the kingly rule of God. This challenge may not have pleased the enemies at all. Hence, it is only partly true to say that love of enemy is the central content of the Christian proclamation. It is certainly also a means for mission and conversion.

The community teaches by its own example. The expected salvation is for all. This makes a difference to the practice of Christian life. "Overcome evil with good," Paul says in Romans (12:21). The aim of enemy love is to conquer evil and not to "surrender oneself to the hands of evil."[29] As Luise Schottroff indicates:

> Since there is no claim to domination here the ambiguity of loving the enemy can only be cleared up by taking social distinctions into account. The desire of the powerless for the salvation of their enemies is the precise opposite of the desire of the ruling classes to integrate their enemies or rebellious subjects into their dominion after they have defeated them.[30]

Within the Christian community, none of the social barriers that separate persons is recognized. In Christ, there is neither Jew nor Gentile, slave nor free, male nor female. This is a very early Baptismal formula Paul quotes in Gal. 3:28. It is not an adequate description of the early Church to say it attracted only the uneducated, the underclasses, women and slaves and the poor. Rather, characteristic of the early Church was the formation of a new society, a class inconsistency.[31] An outcome of the gospel was the Church which became a "new creation," where distinctions recognized in society were no longer valid. Women, for example, were disenfranchised and subject to men in the patriarchal household and state. But, women were often the heads of housechurches, influential members of the Church.

The impact of this new creation, which is to model a discipleship of equals, can be applied to various social distinctions that caused problems within the Christian communities. These problems were particularly acute in the case of the disenfranchised who lived in close contact with their "enemies"—slaves, children, wives, Christian citizens in a hostile state. The critical nature of this "status inconsistency" vis-à-vis the patriarchal climate of the first century helps contextualize and better understand the so-called *haustelfn* of the epistles (e.g., Eph. 5:21-6:9; Col. 3:18-4:1; 1 Pet. 2:11-3:7; also in 1 Cor. 7). The basic Christian position is the one Paul articulates in Gal. 3:28: in Christ, all are one. The household rules draw out some implications for living in society. (Note that Eph. 5:1 begins the paraenetical instructions with, "Be imitators of God."). Christians need neither flee society nor merely accept the patriarchal order as God-given. In a word, the authors of Ephesians, Colossians and 1 Peter agree: Christians can subvert the enemy society from within. The enemy must be won over, persuaded to a different kind of life. Love is the way of winning over, the only debt legitimately recognized by a Christian (Rom. 13:8-10), the only thing that will not hurt another.

Thus, such phrases as "Wives be subject to your husbands" must be interpreted within the context of Peter's continuing advice and explanation: ". . . converting them with the beauty of your lives" (1 Pet. 3:1-2). Marriage is a viable option for a Christian woman (just as celibacy is), according to both Paul and Peter. But, as Christians, women do not have to either divorce or embrace the religion of their husbands. From within the marriage they can influence and convert their husbands. In this way, Christians exercised subversive power in society, refusing to recognize patriarchal and hierarchal structures and offering an alternative in their relationships with one another. In effect, Christians recognize a "double standard": love towards outsiders looks to their conversion and integration into the community. The community practices the love that effects a discipleship of equals.

We may ask why, if the Jesus movement so consistently stressed a discipleship of equals as an alternative to a dominance-subordination model of relating in the world and to each other, the emphasis was so soon lost. Why is there evidence that Christianity readopted so quickly the partriarchal order? What went wrong with the Christian movement that it lost its apocalyptic edge? The model of the patriarchal household was too readily adapted by the Church, and too early. The household churches became the household of God. Order was seen as ordained by a God who acted like a patriarch, who spoke through men. The command to wives to be obedient and submissive to husbands was quickly decontextualized and applied universally and absolutely to relationships between women and men. Celibacy, originally an alternative option and sign of women's new freedom in the Church, became one more oppressive structure and symbol, regulated by a patriarchal institution struggling to survive. The Church lost its prophetic edge and the courageous imagination that goes with it. It retreated quickly to the security of the patriarchal order which defined a place for everyone, and manifested the comfort of the domination-subordination pattern rather than the constant call to conversion of relationships of mutuality and equality.

Conclusion

We can trace progress in the development of a Christian feminist spirituality characterized by a discipleship of equals. But, the road ahead is long indeed. Sometimes it seems as if we are only beginning. Even the appropriate vocabulary for our project is still wanting. Probably "feminism" and "equals" can be best understood in contrast with such perspectives as patriarchy, hierarchy, domination and subordination. This is not said by way of apology but by way of challenge. Some of the biblical roots of the growing Christian feminist spirituality are liberation, egalitarian discipleship, and inclusion. Fleshing these out in response to the mission to engender and foster them, to teach them to the ends of the earth has a long way to go.

NOTES

[1] E. Schüssler Fiorenza, *In Memory of Her: A Feminist Reconstruction of Christian Origins* (New York: Crossroad, 1983).

[2] Adapted from a description by Carol Coston, *Network Newsletter,* July, 1979.

[3] Cf. especially Schüssler Fiorenza, *In Memory of Her;* also *Bread Not Stone: The Challenge of Feminist Biblical Interpretation* (Boston: Beacon Press, 1984); "The Sophia-God of Jesus and the Discipleship of Women," in *Women's Spirituality: Resources for Christian Development,* ed. Joann Wolski Conn (New York/Mahwah: Paulist, 1986).

[4] Cf. Sandra Schneiders, "Theology and Spirituality: Strangers, Rivals, or Partners?," *Horizons* 13 (1986): 253-74.

[5] *Ibid.,* p. 267.

[6] Some feminists have abandoned hope of "redeeming" the Bible, permeated with a patriarchal viewpoint, for feminism; e.g., Mary Daly, esp. in *Gyn/Ecology: The Metaethics of Radical Feminism* (Boston: Beacon, 1979).

[7] Fiorenza, *In Memory,* pp. 41-67.

[8] Mk. 6:44 says, "Those who ate were five thousand men."

[9] For example, in Schüssler Fiorenza, *In Memory.*

[10] Cf. Schüssler Fiorenza, *In Memory,* p. 6.

[11] Cf. Elizabeth Cady Stanton and the Revising Committee, *The Women's Bible* (New York: European Publishing Co., 1898). (Printed by The Coalition Task Force on Women and Religion, Seattle, 1974.)

[12] Cf. Schüssler Fiorenza, *In Memory,* pp. 7-14.

[13] Elizabeth Cady Stanton, *The Women's Bible,* p. 14.

[14] Her rhetorical question seems to be motivated by the absurdity of the idea. How is it that the absurdity of the notion of man's dominance by creation has not been so recognized, but on the contrary canonized even in the scriptures themselves and since their writing? See 1 Tim. 2:11-15; and 2 Cor. 11:3, and 1 Cor. 11:2-16, etc.

[15] Lillie Devereux Blake, *The Women's Bible,* p. 21.

[16] *Ibid.,* pp. 21-22.

[17] *Ibid.,* p. 27.

[18] This translation and most of the others used in this essay, unless otherwise specified, are from the *New American Bible,* New Translation.

[19] E.g., J. Burtchaell, *Philemon's Problem: The Daily Dilemma of the Christian* (Chicago: ACTA Foundation, 1973).

[20] Elizabeth Johnson, "The Wisdom of God: A Biblical Basis for Non-Androcentric Christology," *Ephermerides Theologicae Louvanienses*

LXI (Dec., 1985): 261-94; also Elisabeth Schüssler Fiorenza, "The Sophia God of Jesus," in *Women's Spirituality,* pp. 261-73.

[21] E. Johnson, *art. cit.,* pp. 280-83.

[22] Cf. John Howard Yodder, *The Politics of Jesus* (Grand Rapids: Eerdmans, 1972), for a description of the Jubilee Year and for Jesus' ministry as a fulfillment of this description.

[23] Seneca, *De Ira,* 3, XXIV, quoted in Luise Schottroff, "Non-Violence and the Love of One's Enemies," in *Essays on the Love Command,* ed. Reginald Fuller (Philadelphia: Fortress Press, 1978), p.19.

[24] *Ibid.,* pp. 9-39.

[25] *Ibid.,* p. 18.

[26] "The Jesus tradition requires love of enemy—but the attitude of kindness shown by a stronger party to the dependent weaker person does not do justice to the social conditions of early Christianity." Nor do texts like Matt. 5:38ff merely "deal with grace toward the conquered enemy because such grace of the stronger party has as its purpose the preservation of its dominance over others. . . ." *Ibid.,* p. 20.

[27] *Ibid.,* pp. 20-21.

[28] Plutarch, *De Cohibenda Ira* 9 (Loeb trans.); quoted in Schottroff, *op. cit.,* p. 35.

[29] *Ibid.,* p. 23.

[30] *Ibid.,* p. 24.

[31] Cf. Wayne Meeks, *The First Urban Christians: The Social World of the Apostle Paul* (New Haven/London: Yale, 1983).

A Discipleship of Equals: Voices from Tradition—Teresa of Avila and John of the Cross

Constance FitzGerald, O.C.D.

INTRODUCTION

In the epilogue of *In Memory of Her*, Elisabeth Schüssler Fiorenza suggests that in the past, women's relationship to God has been defined by their sexual relationship to men and through the patriarchal structures of family and Church. Now, a Christian feminist spirituality wants to probe and define women's relationship to God in their concrete experience of being called today beyond patriarchal structures into "a discipleship of equals."[1] What the great mystics like Teresa of Avila and John of the Cross teach us is that it is in the very development of their relationship with God that both women *and men* will first of all discover and then finally embrace their equality in life and discipleship. In the dark fire and the bright living flame of God's Spirit, equality is inescapably appropriated, even when this is not consciously recognized because of the pressures of culture and education. This means that the **experience** of equality and solidarity in a common humanity is conditioned by the depth of one's interiority or religious consciousness or relationship with God.

In the sixteenth century reform of the ancient Carmelite Order, the Spanish mystics, Teresa of Avila and John of the Cross, stand together through time and mirror in their lives and writings this experience of equality. Teresa, older by twenty-seven years, is the charismatic leader who envisioned, initiated and directed the reform of Carmel, first for the women and later for the men. John looked to her as the mother of the

Teresian Carmel, not only for her gifts of vision and leadership
—she taught him practically the way to live in the new reform—
but also because she embodied in her life and writings the
deepest experiences of God the human person can know. In his
own incomparable mystical works, he refers to her writings to
enlarge on or complete his own.[2]

John, on the other hand, is the father. He went with Teresa to
open the first house for men in the reform. His poems, the
primary expression of his experience of God, are thought by
many in our day to be the greatest poetry in the Spanish
language. They have been the fire in the Teresian Carmel for
four hundred years. John was the father of Teresa's soul, her
confessor and confidant in prayer from at least 1572-1575,
during which time she experienced the most profound depths
of communion with God in the "spiritual marriage." In a letter
to Mother Ann of Jesus, Teresa sings John's praises and urges
Ann and her sisters in Beas to "talk to him with the utmost
frankness, for I assure you," she says, "that you can talk to him
as you would to me, and you . . . will find great satisfaction, for
he is very spiritual and of great experience and learning. Those
who were brought up on his teaching miss him greatly."[3]

An often told story illustrates the character and extent of the
collaboration, communion, and equality of this great woman
and man. On the feast of the Blessed Trinity, John was talking
to Teresa about the profound mystery of the feast "when
suddenly both of them were seized by the ardor of the Spirit and
raised aloft" in ecstasy.[4] In this context of a common experience
of God's Spirit, it is significant that while Teresa's writings were
published before John's and she was also canonized before he
was, he, a man, was declared a Doctor of the Church almost fifty
years before the structures of the patriarchal Church could
bestow that same highest approval of her writings upon Teresa,
a woman.

Now, in our time, we ask whether the writings and the lives of
these two saints and doctors can contribute to a Christian
feminist vision of a "discipleship of equals." Can they function
for both the liberation and development of women and for the
ultimate equality of women and men? What do these two giants
of contemplation, these two friends and companions, tell us
about the process of becoming equal?

To examine this question I want to do two things. First of all,
I will try to trace the evolution of Teresa's image of Christ by
analyzing the complex symbolism of her visions of Jesus. Secondly, I will look at Teresa's development in the light of specific
teaching of John of the Cross. In this way, we will see Teresa's
lifelong movement from confusion of heart, inferiority and fear

of abandonment to connectedness, mutuality and equality. If Christology has, indeed, been used to subordinate and exclude women, as Elizabeth Johnson suggests, I want to study Teresa's visions to see whether her experience of Jesus Christ validates that subordination and exclusion.[5] It is my hope that the deepest meanings of her life, revealed in the imagery through which her psyche expressed its experience of God, will intersect with our questions and struggles and even redescribe our reality. The functioning of the image of Christ in Teresa's life really transformed her self-image, and an investigation of the development of her God-image may transform our self-understanding as well.

SYMBOLISM OF DESIRE AND THE IMAGE OF CHRIST IN JOHN OF THE CROSS

We can begin to study the process of becoming equal by concentrating on the symbolism of desire and friendship, or relationship, which is central in any interpretation of Teresa's and John's works. Teresa and John are always talking about desire—the desire of the human person first of all, but also the desire of God. God, says John, has only one desire for a person, and that is to exalt her and make her equal:

> If anything pleases him, it is the exaltation of the soul. Since there is no way by which he can exalt her more than by making her equal to himself, he is pleased only with her love. For the property of love is to make the lover equal to the object loved. Since the soul in this state possesses perfect love, she is called the bride of the Son of God, **which signifies equality with him.** In this equality of friendship the possessions of both are held in common, as the Bridegroom himself said to his disciples: I have now called you my friends, because all that I have heard from my Father I have made known to you . . . As a result they are truly gods by participation, equals and companions of God.[6]

The person, on her part, can never be satisfied, will never have what she desires, says John, until she has attained this equality of love, until God has "put her somehow in himself and made her his equal."[7] The desire of God and the desire of the human heart coincide, therefore, although we often feel they are at odds with each other. It took Teresa many years to understand and to accept this reality and the equality it implied.

The itinerary of meaning we find in Teresa's experiences will be understood better if we look briefly at John of the Cross' teaching on the image of Christ. John counsels his readers to immerse themselves in the Jesus of the Gospels so that Christ will gradually become the focus of meaning in their lives. He wants them, in this way, to build up more and more conscious references to Jesus Christ in order to redirect their deepest desire toward him. In this prayer process, an image of Jesus, unique for each person, slowly forms within and is the basis for any relationship with Jesus Christ. Furthermore, it is the basis for the experience of equality. All our life experience becomes a part of and is in dialogue with this image in some way or another. In the poem, *The Spiritual Canticle*, John sings:

> O spring like crystal!
> If only, on your silvered over face,
> You would suddenly form
> The eyes I have desired,
> Which I bear sketched deep within my heart.

Commenting on this stanza, John says: the person "experiences within herself a certain sketch of love . . . and she desires the completion of the sketch of this image, the image of her Bridegroom, the Word, the Son of God, who . . . is the splendor of his glory and the image of His substance." When John, therefore, decries the destructive counsel of inexperienced spiritual directors, it is because they cause their directees to "lose the sublime image God was painting within [them]." [8] In Teresa's visions of Christ we see a very explicit illustration of John's doctrine.

TERESA'S DEVELOPMENT A DIALOGUE: SELF IMAGE AND THE IMAGE OF CHRIST

Basic to any study of Teresa's visions is an understanding of the way of prayer she learned, during the solitude of a prolonged illness, from Francisco Osuna's *Third Spiritual Alphabet*, which was given to her by her uncle when she was a young, sick nun. "I tried as hard as I could," she writes, "to keep Jesus Christ, our God and our Lord, present within me, and that was my way of prayer. If I reflected upon some phase of the Passion, I represented him to myself interiorly." Even though this was difficult for her and she often resorted to good reading to collect her thoughts and quiet herself into God's presence, still she says beginners "must strive to consider the life of Christ" and use their own creativity and ingenuity to do this:

> The soul can place itself in the presence of Christ and grow accustomed to being inflamed with love for his sacred humanity. It can keep him ever present and speak with him, asking for its needs and complaining of its labors, being glad with him in its enjoyments and not forgetting him because of them, trying to speak to him not through written prayers but with words that conform to its desires and needs . . . I consider the soul advanced

who strives to remain in this precious company and to profit very much from it, and who truly comes to love this Lord to whom we owe so much.[9]

According to Teresa's self-report, however, her life was a story of vacillating desire. At one time, the focus of her desire was a human love; at another time, the focus of her longing was Jesus Christ. She is quick to tell us when someone is her friend. She always mentions when someone loves her. Her life energy came from friendship. Yet, for many years she was certain that God and others—"the world"—were in competition for her affection.[10] She found out very slowly, and not without mistakes, just **how** Jesus Christ was the fulfillment of her deepest desire.

Teresa felt that the almost reckless desire for God and eternity that characterized her youth was in adolescence dimmed and overshadowed by the desire for pleasure, vanity, romance, approval, and honor. In the company of her young friends and cousins, her desire for God grew cold.[11] Later, during her prolonged illness, after the fervor of her first years in religious life, Teresa's heart wavered again and rested in an intimate friendship with her confessor who was involved in a "sinful" relationship with a local woman.

We should note just how much Teresa appropriated without reflection the prevalent patriarchal attitudes toward woman as the temptress, the one who leads man into sin:

> . . . Men [should] be on their guard with women who desire to carry on in this way. Men should believe that since these women have lost their shame before God **(FOR WOMEN ARE OBLIGED TO MODESTY MORE THAN MEN)**, they can be trusted in nothing, for they will stop at nothing in order to hold on to this friendship and passion the devil has placed in them. (emphasis mine)

While the woman, herself, **may** have been the seducer, neither equality of responsibility nor the reality of men who seduce and then desert was part of Teresa's awareness when she wrote her *Life*. Furthermore, Teresa paints herself as one who also "seduces" the priest!

This confessor loved Teresa for her goodness, and she "loved him deeply." She used his affection for her to win him away from the woman, and though her intention was good and the priest was converted and "died a very good death," Teresa always felt guilty about the relationship. It was somehow competitive and diverted her desire from God, she thought. It placed her in danger of almost dying in mortal sin. "Damned be such loyalty [friendship] that goes against the law of God," she writes.[12] It should be noted that when Teresa saw herself as one whose salvation was in jeopardy, she blamed it on the poor guidance of confessors who did not understand the significance and seriousness of misdirected desire.

Because of her divided heart, Teresa marveled she could endure suffering so patiently and associated it with the deep prayer experiences she was having. "All my conversations were with him [Jesus Christ] . . . the Lord [who] raised me from the dead," she writes.[13] In the frightening experience of almost dying, Teresa felt her desire swing again toward Jesus Christ. But, THIS time of focused attention on God was not to last either.[14]

Here, Teresa brings two important symbols—*abandonment* and the *hand* of Jesus—into relationship with the image of Christ as one who not only relates in interpersonal *dialogue* but even *raises up* and makes whole. Because Teresa seemed to fear abandonment all through her life, she was very sensitive to the vacillation and treachery of her own heart. **She** abandoned the conversations of intimate prayer for human conversation and superficial pastimes, and, though Christ held out his hand to her, she did not want it. She felt unfit to face Christ because of her human friendships and was therefore "ashamed to return to the search for God by means of a friendship as special as is that found in the intimate exchange of prayer . . ." She writes:

> It seemed impossible, my Lord, to abandon you so completely. And since I did forsake you so many times I cannot but fear. For when you withdrew a little from me, I fell to the ground. Although I abandoned you, you did not abandon me so completely as not to turn to raise me up by always holding out your hand to me.[15]

In response, as it were, to her self-understanding and world view, came Teresa's first **vision** of Jesus Christ.[16] While she was actually with a friend, she "saw" a very severe looking Christ before her, making her understand his disapproval of such friendships. It is hardly mere coincidence that this vision reflected and validated Teresa's own fragile self-image. Nor is it inconsequential that at this time she described and found meaning in the appearance of a large ugly toad (a well-known symbol of evil) in the middle of the day, moving more quickly than usual toward her and her friend.[17] There seems to be a profound relationship both here and in her other visions between Teresa's image of herself and her image of God. Each calls forth and responds to the other in some mysterious way, giving a much deeper meaning than we might suspect to the *dialogic* character of Teresian prayer, which Teresa, herself, describes

> . . . as nothing else than an intimate sharing between friends; it means taking time frequently to be alone with Him who we know loves us.[18]

Teresa, however, continued her "worldly" conversations. She *needed* friendship, and she did not want to face the warnings she received. Her desire was focused elsewhere! It was only in the terrible wrenching caused by the sickness and death of her beloved and holy father, "who was everything to [her]," that she slowly and with good guidance began to pray regularly again. And, even though she never again abandoned prayer, neither did she forgo her frivolous pastimes for "almost twenty years." Thus, she was torn in two and found happiness in neither God nor her worldly enjoyments. *TERESA'S* God wanted everything! Her experience of Christ's severe judgment of her seemed only to validate this perception and widen the gulf between friendship with God and friendship with the world.[19]

What is the full import of these initial images of Christ? First of all, **hand** functions as an important symbol from the beginning of Teresa's prayer life all the way through to its fulfillment in the "spiritual marriage." Putting out one's hand is the first simple gesture of friendship, a movement of concern and reassurance. The hand can be a promise of tenderness and delicate care, even intimate union. But, there is a long way between the **touch** of a hand and that kind of communion. Moreover, the hand can be withdrawn along the way. A hand can be stretched out to touch in acceptance and encouragement or pulled back in rejection and condemnation, as the image of the severe, judging Christ indicates. From the other side, a stretched out hand can be refused because of the guilty confusion within one's own heart or out of the fear of being abandoned in the end.

When Christ holds out a hand not only to touch but also to *raise up* Teresa, the hand also signifies strength, power, authority, and even superiority. There is a certain inequality implied in the support, just as there is inequality implied in the severe judgment of Christ. This inequality is carried further in the symbol of being raised up *from death* which, while it does speak of potentiality and new life, seems to emphasize the disintegration, powerlessness, and brokenness of the one who is lifted up. In this powerlessness, we circle back to the symbol of abandonment which recurs throughout Teresa's life and is parallel to the symbol of death and resurrection. To feel abandoned or to fear abandonment is, according to J. E. Cirlot, "to feel forsaken by the 'god within us'; [it is] to lose sight of the eternal light in the human spirit." It points to Teresa's sense of estrangement from her own deepest self, her own Center, and God as she imagines God to be. Abandonment as a recurring symbol indicates the need for deeper interiority.[20] Furthermore, it underlines Teresa's experience of a deadly evil within herself. "I wanted to live," she writes, "for I well understood that I was not living but was struggling with a shadow of death, but I had no one to give me life, and I was unable to catch hold of it. He who had the *power* to give it to me was right in not helping me, for so often had he brought me back to himself; and so often had I abandoned him." [21]

It was an image of the "wounded Christ," a statue, that finally stirred up resonances in Teresa's weary, broken, tired soul and called her, through the words of Augustine's *Confessions*, to "conversion." Only a human God, broken by human life, could have spoken into the life of this woman, wounded by years of conflicting priorities and vacillating desires. She identified with Jesus Christ and tried to picture him within her in the gospel scenes where he was more alone. It seemed to her that being alone and afflicted and in need, he had to accept her as she tried to companion him in the darkness of her own faith life.[22] We see here the first faint seed of equality which will bear fruit in the difficult experience of the Dark Night.

For now, Teresa began to experience the **feeling** of God's presence, tenderness, and love, entering and pervading her life as she dwelt with increasing attention and care on the humanity of Jesus, particularly the poor, suffering Jesus. The pendulum of her desire swung once again, and she reached for satisfaction toward a God who was tender, who comforted, who gladdened, who satisfied, who gifted her. Now *she* placed herself in the *"hands of God"* and, while she desired to speak of nothing but Jesus Christ who was showing her such love, she was overcome with her ignorance and lack of education as a woman, her weakness and unworthiness as a person, and her general inability to measure up to the favors of *her* God. These very favors made her inferior not only to a strong and powerful God but even to men. In the context of trying to give an account of her gifts to her male advisors and confessors, she says: " . . . Just being a woman is enough to have my wings fall off—how much more being both a woman and wretched as well." [23]

Her self-doubt, complicated, or perhaps *caused* by the marginal position of women in her society, battled with the inner affirmation she received. Even the experience of a God comforting as a mother, tender as a lover, could not reassure her in the face of the negative masculine evaluations of her life and prayer. Still, she persevered in prayer and really began to love "the most sacred humanity." In fact, she thought she was ready

to forfeit everything for Christ *until* her confessor was transferred to another place! Then, her "soul was left as though in a
desert, very disconsolate and fearful." In the face of this
abandonment, the old fear reasserted itself and in it one of
Teresa's deepest life questions: Is abandonment the finality? Is
there anyone for me who is ultimately trustworthy? The need
for reassurance and friendship was overpowering. She was too
fragile to give up her friendships, and, therefore, her new
confessor advised her to commend the whole matter to God.[24]

In response, the dialogue extended itself to **inner words**—
effective words heard and understood—that changed the heart
and could not ever be forgotten. Teresa, in her first rapture,
heard deep within her being words *verifying her own suspicions*
that her human friendships conflicted with her relationship with
Jesus Christ: "No longer do I want you to converse with men but
with angels." [25] Concerned chiefly with her conflict over the
incompatibility of her relationships, Teresa did not understand
at first the extent of the liberation offered her: No longer was
she to be victim to human words of wisdom, controlled by
human words of love and assurance, but she was to own her own
life and be guided by her own inner voice. The challenge of the
word was to find the focus of motivation, of wisdom, within her
own heart, but Teresa made this transfer only with difficulty.
However, in the light of this inner assurance, Teresa's motivation did shift again, and she made a decisive choice of the heart
for Christ—Wisdom who speaks, changes, refreshes, quiets,
makes strong. Out of this experience, Teresa articulated certain
basic beliefs about human friendship, and later she developed
these extensively in *The Way of Perfection*. Although she never
seemed *consciously* to grasp the full import of the word, she
expresses her freedom: ". . . I have never again been able to tie
myself to any friendship or to find consolation or bear particular
love for any other persons than those I understand love Him
and strive to serve Him." [26]

While the inner autonomy, freedom, and strength that Teresa
experienced in herself grew, she discovered her appropriation
of them was only partial when she was faced with the negative
evaluations of her numerous locutions by learned and wise
MEN. When they decided that her experience was clearly from
the devil(!), Teresa was terrified, and "her fear made her forget
her self-worth." As a WOMAN in sixteenth century Spain, she
needed their reassurance and approval. In challenging the truth
of Teresa's inner word and attempting to lead her away from her
own interior wisdom, these "wise" MEN drove this WOMAN
into deeper inferiority. It was they who quite unconsciously
spoke the word of the "devil" whose "aim . . . is [always]

regression or stagnation in what is . . . inferior. . ," according to
Cirlot.[27] In the dichotomized world of patriarchal Spain,
Teresa's inner experience was either from God or the devil (or
her own deluded self). The devil here stands as such a strong
archetypal symbol of societal domination, control and power-
over. It surfaces in every age and exerts its demonic influence
whenever a person, a group, or a nation appropriates power and
structure to keep a race, a sex, a people, in an inferior,
powerless, oppressed position.

Teresa's agitated feeling of being deluded, alone, and without
any human support was answered by another word in the
dialogue which effected peace, strength, courage, and security:
"Do not fear, daughter, for I am, and I will not abandon you; do
not fear." Teresa's whole person was touched by reassurance as
the pathway back to her own Center opened up. She *began* to
experience a sporadic, though often fearless, mastery over not
only human condemnation but even her own inner contradictions:

> O, my Lord, how you are my true friend . . . Oh, who will cry out
> for you, to tell everyone how faithful you are to Your friends! All
> things fail; you, Lord of all, never fail. O my God, who has the
> understanding, the learning and the **new words** with which to
> extol your works as my soul understands them? All fails me. . , *but
> if you will not abandon me, I will not fail you.* Let all learned men rise
> up against me, let all created things persecute me, let the devils
> torment me [but] do not you fail me, Lord.[28]

One can feel her remembering the intimidation she suffered
when she writes a few years later to her nuns in *The Way of
Perfection* that "since the world's judges are sons of Adam and
all of them men, there is no virtue in women they do not
suspect." [29]

But, the Lord did not fail Teresa. When, in 1559, the
Inquisitor General published an Index of Forbidden Books
which prohibited the reading in the vernacular of many books
on prayer she enjoyed, Teresa was very upset. The Lord said to
her: "Don't be sad for I shall give you a living book." In
retrospect, she understood this as a promise of the visions to
come in which Jesus, eternal Wisdom, became the "true book" in
which she saw all the truth she needed impressed upon her
forever.[30]

This whole period was a turning point for Teresa. In the
experience of numerous words of Wisdom, Teresa, the woman,
was being given to herself and empowered to claim her own
inner wisdom. She was being lifted out of her inferiority and
fear. She saw she was "another person" and "would have

disputed with the entire world that these words came from God." Later, she was even to pray in *The Way of Perfection* to possess "all human eloquence and wisdom together" in order to know the way to explain clearly the path to the knowledge of God.[31]

The fact remains that Teresa was so affirmed as a woman by this "Master of wisdom . . . Wisdom itself, without beginning, without end, without any limit to [her] works" that her view of herself changed, and she began to see women from the perspective of God. Her later writings stand as a clear and forceful defense of women's wisdom; so forceful, in fact, that the censors of her writings sometimes intervened, and Teresa was forced to revise her work.

Some years later, in an era still suspicious of interior prayer and wary of false mysticism, especially in women, Teresa wrote to her nuns with bold conviction in*The Way of Perfection*:

> You will hear some persons frequently making objections: "there are dangers"; "so and so went astray by such means"; "this one was deceived"; "another who prayed a great deal fell away"; "it's harmful to virtue"; "it's not for women, for they will be susceptible to illusion"; "it's better to stick to their sewing"; "they don't need these delicacies"; "the Our Father and Hail Mary are enough." This last statement, Sisters, I agree with. And indeed they are sufficient.[32]

Teresa, the woman, was no longer to be intimidated by the oppressive words and decisions of fearful men into dichotomizing deep, interior prayer and vocal prayers—the Our Father and the Hail Mary. Now, she trusted her own inner wisdom and did not hesitate to point accusingly at the senselessness of what was being urged upon women:

> Well, what is this, Christians, that you say mental (interior) prayer isn't necessary? Do you understand yourselves? Indeed, I don't think you do, and so you desire that we all be misled. You don't know what mental prayer is, or how vocal prayer should be recited, or what contemplation is, for if you did you wouldn't on the one hand condemn what on the other hand you praise.[33]

Realizing that the only real danger lay in the neglect of the interiority in which the God of wisdom would call them to own their own lives, Teresa urged her sisters not to pay any attention to the fears men raised or to the picture of the dangers they painted. She exclaimed with determination, with inner authority, and even a hint of sarcasm: "Hold fast, daughters, for they cannot take from you the Our Father and the Hail Mary." Kavanaugh explains:

> Here the censor, quick to catch the point, intervened and, going a step further than his usual method of simply crossing out the passage, wrote in the margin; "It seems she is reprimanding the Inquisitors for prohibiting books on prayer." [34]

Teresa's visions apparently began in earnest after the locution mentioned above. Although she was counselled to pray to be led along a different path, her own inner experience prevented her from sincerely wanting this "deliverance." Nevertheless, she was torn by the controversy and her own efforts to be obedient:

> There were enough things to drive me insane . . . [and] I didn't know what to do other than raise my eyes to the Lord. For the opposition of good men to a little woman, wretched, weak, and fearful like myself, seems to be nothing when described in so few words . . . if the Lord hadn't favored me so much, I don't know what would have happened to me. [35]

But, the lifelong dialogue did continue, and the Lord urged Teresa deeper into the inner Mystery in ways that defied her expectations. She felt Jesus Christ *beside her* even though she did not see him with her eyes nor even, she thought, with her imagination. Yet, she "saw" it was he who was "speaking" to her—a human person who shared life with her (accompanied her and witnessed her life) in a deep mutuality of understanding, friendship, and love. They were like two people who love each other very much and who, even without signs, with only a glance, understand each other perfectly. She writes:

> The Lord puts what he wants the soul to know very deeply within it, and there he makes it known without image or explicit words . . . And this manner in which God gives the soul understanding of his desires, and great truths and mysteries is worthy of close attention. [36]

What are the specifics of what Teresa here calls "vision"? Along with the "impressions of the Divinity" that Teresa felt earlier, in the prayer of quiet, it was now Jesus in his *humanity* who was present, who "spoke," who was, above all, known with an intuition "clearer than sunlight." This knowledge was engraved upon her mind, her understanding, with a clarity and permanence that could not be erased or doubted, that could not have been even *consciously* desired. It was, she explains, as if someone who had never even tried to learn to read suddenly possessed all knowledge. This woman who was so convinced of her own inadequacy and ignorance could say, "The soul sees in an instant that it is wise."

It is intriguing that in the intersubjective union that was slowly taking over Teresa's consciousness, it was the *human* Jesus, son of Mary, whom she "knew" and enjoyed. But, her experience was subtle and profound. In her determination to forgo dependence on human approval and honor in identification with this man who suffered such contempt and rejection for her sake, she realized that the clearsighted wisdom she discovered in herself was closely related to this Jesus who was not only man but also divine Wisdom. She says, "How rich will [she] find that [she] is, [she] who has left all riches for Christ . . . How wise will [she] be, [she] who rejoiced to be considered mad because that is what they called *Wisdom Himself!*"[37]

When one looks at Teresa's experience of inner wisdom and self-affirmation, the growing ability we see in her writings to trust that experience and inner truth, and the strong conviction of feminine worth she later passes on to her sisters, we are reminded of the investigations of feminist theologians today regarding "Sophia." If the New Testament does indeed identify Jesus with Sophia and if we can speak, therefore, as Elizabeth Johnson suggests, of the union of female divine Wisdom (Sophia) and male humanity in Jesus, we can understand better the dynamics of Teresa's appropriation of her own feminine truth.[38] Divine Wisdom, who is Jesus, was, as it were, a mirror in which Teresa saw the reflection of herself as a wise WOMAN. Teresa, in a sense, became what she saw, for in Jesus, eternal Wisdom, the feminine was lifted up and cherished. In a society where "weak, ignorant" women lived on the margins of knowledge in subordination to the men who controlled them, Teresa's sexual identity was affirmed by God. Therefore, even though Church men continued to warn her of the danger of deception, she was reassured from within and conscious of being brought to new "frontiers."[39] Had the culture and theology of the sixteenth century fitted Teresa to articulate this, she might have echoed the words from *for colored girls who have considered suicide/when the rainbow is enuf*:

> I found God in myself
> And I loved Her
> I loved Her fiercely.[40]

While Teresa experiences and writes of Jesus as Wisdom, John is the one who clearly validates the identity and place of Wisdom in mystical union, particularly in *The Living Flame* and the latter part of *The Spiritual Canticle*. For him, Jesus Christ is uncreated Wisdom, and union with God is seen as transformation in Divine Wisdom. He says, ". . . [the] soul . . . will then be transformed into . . . Wisdom, the Son of God." And, at the end of the second book of the Dark Night, John explains that when the person is ready, "Divine Wisdom unites herself with the soul in a new bond of the possession of love."[41]

It is critical to note, however, that even though Teresa
experienced growing inner certitude, the symbols which appear
in her descriptions of her visions continue to point also toward
connectedness, relationship and tenderness, suggesting that
autonomy and intimacy are not mutually exclusive but, rather,
integrally connected. She writes:

> . . . The Lord desired to show me only *his hands* which were so
> very beautiful . . . After a few days I saw also that *divine face* which
> it seems left me completely absorbed. Since afterward he granted
> me the favor of seeing him entirely, I couldn't understand why
> the Lord showed himself to me . . . little by little until later I
> understood that his Majesty was leading me in accordance with
> my natural weakness.[42]

Let us look at *hands*, masculine hands, held out to support and
strengthen, perhaps even to convey power and authority. But,
these are beautiful hands. They are somehow *for* Teresa. They
promise deeper self-donation and, though they initially frighten
because of their other-worldly "splendor," they invite trust.
Teresa frequently mentions her surrender to or withdrawal
from "the hands of God." Jesus' hands have a power over Teresa
all the way through to the "spiritual marriage."

The image of "so beautiful a face" complements the hand
image, but it is a different metaphor. It is one thing to hold a
hand, to be held in another's hands, even to be caressed by
hands. It is another experience to look into a beautiful, light
filled face. I cannot recall without tears the words my mother
wrote to me on my fiftieth birthday: "I will remember," she said,
"the first time I looked into your beautiful little face," and I
reflect on the meaning of a mother's face in a baby's life and
development. Whether a child sees herself as beloved or blamed,
worthwhile or inferior, is dependent on what she has seen in the
face of her mother. Face has a primary association with mother.

In her work on Julian of Norwich, Elizabeth Koenig draws on
an essay by D. W. Winnicott who argues that "the mother's face
is the precursor of the mirror in its contribution to the sense of
personal identity."[43] This essay intrigues me because, in one of
the last visions Teresa describes in the *Life*, Jesus is a mirror
filling her soul. Koenig tells us that when an infant looks at her
mother, what the baby sees is not the mother but the baby
herself. The mother is looking at the baby, but what she looks
like [to the baby] is related to what she, herself, sees. If she is so
pre-occupied with herself that she reflects only her own mood
or, worse still, the rigidity of her own defenses, the baby may
spend a lifetime trying to find someone who can give her to
herself. If the mother's face is not a mirror in which the baby

may learn about herself, she will move through life attempting to be seen in a way that will make her feel she exists and is worthwhile.

When we reflect on Teresa's early descriptions of her own self-image, we sense she needed to receive something of herself from the face of another. This can throw new light on the significance for Teresa of the face of Jesus Christ which she says "gives the most intense delight to the sight" in its splendor and soft whiteness and beauty. It suggests that the Face functions as a maternal, feminine symbol, even when the face belongs to a friend, a lover, or a god. To look into a face that is **for us**, in whose beauty and total regard we see our own unsuspected beauty and potential, is expressive of a whole new level of self-understanding.

Here we see, as John of the Cross suggests, that God moves through human ways of knowing according to the mode of the soul, according to the way the human person is made. God does not violate our deepest needs, but fulfills slowly in our life situations our most profound desires for reassurance, unconditional love, tenderness, and special regard.[44] We see also that God, like a mother, is on the side, not of lifelong subordination and inferiority, but of development characterized by mutuality.

This was Teresa's learning as the experience of Jesus risen imprinted itself on her heart as a vibrant living image. Then she discovered that although she had sinned and was weak, she really was an image of God. When she compares the light of this vision to the sun and assures us the brightness of the sun appears very much tarnished beside the glorified Jesus, she could be describing the movement of her own self-understanding. "It's like the difference between a sparkling, clear water that flows over crystal and on which the sun is reflecting and a very cloudy, muddy water flowing along the ground." Teresa saw very clearly, as did those who knew her, that these experiences had radically changed her. Even her health improved![45]

What must be stressed here again is the all pervasive presence of the dialogue, or the dynamic of reciprocity, between Jesus and Teresa. Each responded to the other in a day by day companionship that stretched over the years and "changed" both Teresa and God. Jesus Christ accommodated his presence to Teresa's moods and the circumstances of her life. She tells us that, although it was the risen Jesus who accompanied her, when she was suffering and when she was wounded by misunderstanding and persecution, he appeared on the cross or in the garden, wounded or crowned with thorns. In fact, he took her part and guided her through the misunderstandings, suspicions and poor counsel of her confessors who continued to believe she was deceived by the devil and should resist her visions.

When men continued to press her to repudiate her own inner experience, a challenge was thrown to Teresa (and perhaps to Jesus!). Would she repudiate the love experience, would she choose self-hatred over self-acceptance, would she accept the self being shown and given to her—a self connected, related, possessed—rather than the isolated self being forced upon her? We sense the struggle and more than a hint of humor when she tells us that Jesus seemed annoyed when she was forbidden to practice prayer. "He told me to tell them that now what they were doing was tyranny and He gave me signs for knowing that the vision was not from the devil." Furthermore, when she tried to obey the command to reject and resist her experiences, "there was a much greater increase in them." Jesus taught her what she should say and gave her so many adequate reasons that she felt "completely secure." [46]

We get the full import of Teresa's internal conflict in Jesus' next move. He took in his own hands the cross Teresa was holding to drive him away. When he returned it to her, it was made of precious stones. After that, she always saw the cross this way, but no one saw it except her!! This is powerful symbolism to express not only the continual challenge to Teresa to accept her own inner truth, her whole humanity, but also the integration of many seemingly contradictory elements in her life: outer obedience with inner freedom and certitude; conflict and opposition with genuine maturation; personal autonomy and strength with fidelity and surrender in relationship; inner light with inner darkness. All this was the fruit of the experience of being in love with God. And, she was in love with God precisely because she, herself, was loved without restriction.

Teresa's life and desire, therefore, stood open to God's next move in the dialogue! She had reached another intersection. She tells us:

> I saw close to me . . . an angel in bodily form . . . very beautiful, and his face was so aflame that he seemed to be one of those very sublime angels that appear to be all afire. I saw in his hands a large golden dart and at the end of the iron tip there appeared to be a little fire. It seemed to me this angel plunged the dart several times into my heart and that it reached deep within me. When he drew it out, I thought he was carrying off the deepest part of me; and he left me all on fire with great love of God.[47]

In the beautiful fiery angel we see the antithesis of the devil who was, according to many, the cause of Teresa's visions of Christ. As a symbol of the world of God, the angel is, first of all, another confirmation of Teresa's very self and a promise of eventual victory over the power of evil. The experience of an angel complements the visions of devils and hell, which we see in Teresa's *Life* at this time, and brings to consciousness Teresa's ongoing struggle to understand her own humanity even more deeply and to integrate into a wholesome self-image both the light and the darkness in her own heart. But, there is much more in this rich symbolism.[48]

Standing as it did just before the beginning of her reform of the Carmelite Order, at a time of intense persecution and suffering, this vision signaled a *painful* breakthrough to a whole new level of life, motivation, and energy for Teresa. The awesome configuration of symbols—the fire, the arrow, the pierced heart, the wound—tell of a shattering intrusion and of a demand for total self-donation and availability. The heart, with all its great, conflicting desires, was torn open, pierced to its very depths, possessed by a compelling power capable of either destroying what it touched, or changing it into itself. Teresa, in a sense, became the fire; she did not surrender to destruction. Instead, her insatiable desire and passion absorbed the fire and were transformed into boundless spiritual energy. But, we must not miss the implication that this creativity was bought at a price: disintegration—change—for the sake of God.

Heart is one of the basic, primordial images of the self. To see it thrust itself into Teresa's consciousness with such intensity and power clearly manifests that a process of unusual spiritual maturation and fulfillment is going on in the depths of her soul. The psyche is moving toward its full expansion in a decisive moment of illumination. This means that while the *heart*, pierced and wounded with the *flaming arrow*, certainly indicates, in Teresa, an explicit awareness of an intersubjective union of love with God, the emotional identification with that God that we see here is possible only because of the unity and wholeness of the self that have slowly developed in the life long relationship with Jesus Christ.[49] Because her self-image had been purified, to some extent, of its sinful tendencies toward inferiority and excessive self-depreciation, Teresa could surrender to being loved and claimed by God. Stripped of concern for human respect, she could receive the creative energy of love that would issue in an alternative vision, new life and service in the sixteenth century Church.

John of the Cross clearly understood the relationship of this experience to Teresa's role as foundress and/or reformer. He writes explicitly about her in the *Living Flame of Love*:

The soul feels its ardor strengthen and increase and its love become so refined in this ardor that seemingly there are seas of loving fire within it, reaching to the heights and depths of the earthly and heavenly spheres embuing all with love. It seems to it that the entire universe is a sea of love in which it is engulfed, for, conscious of the living point or center of love within itself, it is unable to catch sight of the boundaries of this love . . . The soul is converted into the immense fire of love . . . Few persons have reached these heights. Some have, however; especially those whose virtue and spirit was to be diffused among their children. For God accords to founders, with respect to the first fruits of the spirit, wealth and value commensurate with the greater or lesser following they will have in their doctrine and spirituality.[50]

If Teresa's text is read well, we see that the God of Teresa did not want a fearful, subservient woman. The expectations of the friendship were far too demanding for that. Only a strong woman, capable of capitalizing on her own inner experience to create imaginative life alternatives, could bear to hear the Lord's next "compelling" words in the dialogue which commanded her to strive to found a new monastery—no matter how others would judge the venture. We have to read chapters 32-34 of Teresa's *Life*, where she describes the reactions of her own community, her confessors, superiors, and even the people of Avila, to understand the dramatic and sometimes comical dialogue between Jesus and Teresa. Beneath it, we touch Teresa's profound life struggle between self-doubt and fear on the one hand and a whole new vision of reality on the other. Teresa was being urged to take the image of Christ that had slowly been etched into her inner being and to create in her own social milieu, far beyond the boundaries of her own soul, a likeness of that love-image.[51] Because she was being pushed toward an autonomy stronger than her society allowed or would approve, she cried out:

> My Lord, how is it that you command things that seem impossible? For if I were at least free, even though I am a woman! But bound on so many sides, without money or the means to raise it or to obtain the brief or anything, what can I do, Lord?[52]

During this time, Teresa's obsession with self-doubt, with fear of deception, with a consciousness of her own sinfulness, was balanced by repeated moments of inner affirmation and assurance. While so many around her condemned her, belittled her and attempted to stop the new foundation, she vacillated between extreme anxiety and an amazing ability not to take the reprimands to heart. That she was growing steadily in self-esteem and trust in her own inner wisdom is evidenced by a plethora of images in her numerous visions and locutions. For instance, she experienced herself clothed in a robe of shining brightness by our Lady and St. Joseph who promised to watch over her and who placed around her neck, as a sign, a beautiful golden necklace. Our Lady took Teresa *by the hands* and encouraged her to make the foundation of St. Joseph's. Moreover, she says, "I was given to understand that I was now cleansed from my sins." Later, she saw Christ who seemed to be receiving her with great love and who placed a crown on her head and thanked her for what she did for his Mother.

Teresa's God was forcing her to believe in herself in spite of a patriarchal culture which put little store in the wisdom, judgment or abilities of women. The Lord told her to proceed and not to listen to the various opinions because few would counsel her prudently! Furthermore, she was not to be distressed about making the foundation under the protection of the Bishop of Avila and, therefore, not giving obedience to the Order, for "the Lord had told me," she said, "it wasn't suitable to give it to my superiors! He gave me the reasons why it would in no way be fitting that I do so. But he told me I should petition Rome in a certain way . . . and that he would take care that we get our request. And so it came about . . ."[53]

Teresa's ability to envision and then pursue creative life alternatives was not based on an isolated, autonomous, go-it-alone ego. Rather, it was rooted in a deep connectedness and identification with "Another" to whom she was related in unconditional love. Hence, she could say with a hint of exasperation when everything seemed to be failing: "Lord this house is not mine; it was founded for you; now that there is no one to take care of its affairs, you . . . must do so." And earlier, when she was worried that the house and grounds she had were much too small for a monastery, she heard an irritated Lord say to her: "Oh covetousness of the human race, that you think you will be lacking even ground! How many times did I sleep in the open because I had no place else."[54]

The easy familiarity and affirmation of this constant companionship signaled a growing feeling of equality with others, even with the nobility. Teresa tells us that she conversed with them with the freedom she would have felt had she been their equal in social position. Even more significant, though, is the subtle experience of equality with Jesus Christ. She admits:

> I began to talk to the Lord in a foolish way, which I often do without knowing what I am saying. It is love that is then speaking, and . . . the soul is so transported that *I don't know the difference there is between it and God.*[55]

In the context of this identification and equality, we finally see the resolution of Teresa's life-long conflict over human friend-

ship. When, after many years, she met again the Dominican
Garcia de Toledo, they were drawn irresistibly to share their life
experiences with each other. Since Teresa liked him so much,
she longed for him to give himself totally to God and God's
service, and so she prayed: "Lord, you must not deny me this
favor. See how this individual is fit to be *OUR* friend." Then she
adds, "O the goodness and great humanity of God!" But, then
Teresa was overcome with great affliction and guilt lest she had
seriously offended God. She was not yet consciously at peace
with her human loves. The Lord, however, gave her a message
for the priest through which he turned completely to God.
Later, when Teresa was rejoicing over the graces given to the
man and thanking God for *fulfilling her desires*, and making "a
little old woman wiser . . . [than] a very learned man," she was
overcome by rapture, and she tells us:

> I saw Christ with awesome majesty and glory showing great
> happiness over what was taking place. Thus he told me and
> wanted me to see clearly that he is always present in conversations
> like these and how much he is pleased when persons so delight in
> speaking of him.[56]

Here we see a reversal in Teresa's God. Before, she was to talk
with angels, not human persons. Now, her God not only rejoiced
in her human conversations and loves, but understood her love
and concern and compassion for others as an extension of the
love that was flooding her life. In fact, her God rushed to answer
her prayers for others and to verify her relationships, even with
those who had died.[57] Teresa's awareness had changed, and she
no longer saw her human friendships as conflictual. It was as if
they were given back to her. In her deep emotional identification with the humanity of God, she herself experienced a new
solidarity with everything human in herself and others.[58]
    In one of her "most sublime visions," she "saw" with deep
inner knowledge the humanity of Jesus, and *humanity in Jesus*,
being taken into the bosom of the Divinity in whose presence she
experienced herself to be. What did it mean for humanity to be
taken into God? Certainly, she could never be the same. In fact,
this vision was symbolic of a radically altered world view. She
tells us she understood with contemplative intuition what Truth
is and what it is for a human person "to walk in truth before
Truth itself." She "knew," finally, that just as every truth
imaginable depended upon this Truth, so all her human loves
were a part of this love, and every grandeur she could know was
a reflection of this Grandeur.[59]
    In the symbolism of one of the last experiences she describes
in the book of her *Life*, we glimpse the extent to which she

passed over into the perspective of God regarding both her own self-understanding and her whole vision of reality. She writes:

> [My soul] seemed to me to be like a brightly polished mirror, without any part on the back or sides or top or bottom that wasn't totally clear. In its center Christ our Lord was shown to me . . . It seemed to me I saw him clearly in every part of my soul, as though in a mirror. And this mirror also . . . was completely engraved upon the Lord himself by means of a loving communication I wouldn't know how to describe.[60]

There is no vision in the whole of Teresa's writings that thrills me like this imagery. Teresa looked into herself, a mirror, and she saw Christ. There was nothing but this completed imprint of Christ, etched within her, totally filling the mirror. She looked at Christ and, yet, she saw herself—engraved upon the Lord. Christ, the self-knowledge of humanity, gave her to herself. We marvel at such mutual indwelling, such mutual imprinting, that speaks not only of radical self-donation but just as strongly of self-possession. Teresa's heart had found its dwelling place. Yet, she herself was a dwelling place. She was at home in her own house, her Self! "Each is transfigured in the other," says John. The truth of the self and the truth of the other were revealed, and the desire of the human heart was fulfilled without restriction. Teresa really experienced herself and her acts united to the self and acts of Christ. John of the Cross writes in *The Spiritual Canticle* that Christ "will really transform her into the beauty of both his created and uncreated Wisdom, and also into the beauty of the Word with his humanity."[61] Could there be any deeper answer for Teresa to the question of ultimate reliability or the fear of abandonment? The mirror is a striking symbol of mystical consciousness all through spiritual literature. It shows us Teresa, the woman mystic, effectively connected in reciprocal mutuality with God and with the entire universe.

For, not only is her soul a mirror, not only is Christ a mirror, but for Teresa, Divinity is, as it were, a mirror or a very clear diamond, "much greater than all the world," in which she clearly sees everything in the universe joined together, everything part of the whole. All things are held in God—good and evil and all loves. And God is, after all, the embrace of human love, of friendship. The experience of Teresa deals a death blow not only to going it alone, but even going it alone with God.[62]

DARK NIGHT

One might think that now Teresa's development was complete, but she tells of a time of deep pain and insatiable desire when she was overcome by a sense of total estrangement and

extreme desolation. Her human powers were paralyzed from
the pain:

> The soul begins to grow so weary that it ascends far above itself
> and all creatures. God places it in a desert so distant from all
> things, that however much it labors, it doesn't find a creature on
> earth that might accompany it . . . it desires only to die in that
> solitude.[63]

The desert symbolizes Teresa's experience of human powerlessness before the incomprehensible mystery of salvation. It was
Teresa's final temptation to disavow her self-worth and to
succumb in despair to inferiority, subordination, and "wretched-
ness." She stood on the brink without a final answer to the
question of ultimate reliability and value. She was challenged to
see in the mirror without any defenses, filters, or support
whatsoever, not only the stark reality of her own darkness,
which was hard enough, but even the evil of humanity, and still
believe in unconditional love.[64] This is the blackest time of night,
John of the Cross tells us, when the last delicate shading of the
image of Jesus, crucified and abandoned, is being sketched
within the human heart in total darkness and absolute silence.
He says, "The soul cannot see herself in the beauty of God unless
she is transformed in the Wisdom of God" (divine Wisdom) . . .
and made to resemble her . . . "who is the Word, the Son of
God." But, the gate entering into the fullness of these riches of
Wisdom is the cross of Jesus. It seems that a final phase of the
transfiguration of Teresa and Jesus in each other could occur
only in the dispossession of the Cross and the desperate scream
of the heart, "My God, why have you abandoned me?" The
image was, as it were, being finished when Teresa no longer had
any consciousness of it, when she no longer saw it, or when all
the images she had known had lost their cogency.[65] When we
realize the power and the fullness of the image or vision of
Christ in Teresa's experience over a lifetime, we can grasp the
significance and extent of this deprivation.

In the Dark Night we are, in fact, always purified and
transformed through what we cherish and through what gives
us security and support. In other words, for Teresa, the relationship itself became the cause of pain. Its intense reciprocity
actually highlighted human limitation, and even the limitations
of God. This was Teresa's most profound experience of abandonment, and it preceded what both she and John call the
"spiritual marriage." For Teresa and John, God seemed to walk
away, seemed to break the connectedness: "Where have you
hidden, Beloved, and left me to my moaning. You fled like the

stag after wounding me; I went out calling you and you were gone." [66]

John throws a very clear light on this experience of Teresa. I want to move, therefore, to him for an understanding of this Dark Night which, he says, shows us the whole person deprived in her entire life situation. John, a man and a theologian, writes from the side of the powerless, the inferior, the poor and the abandoned. He tells of the darkness enwrapping their minds, their empty terror and hopelessness in the face of the overpowering burden of their memories, the anguished longing for a lost hope, a lost dream, a lost love. John's God of the Dark Night has such power over him, such power to disturb and control. He says:

> God divests the faculties, affections and senses, both spiritual and sensory, interior and exterior. He leaves the intellect in darkness, the will in aridity, the memory in emptiness, and the affections in supreme affliction, bitterness and anguish, by depriving the soul of the feeling and satisfaction it previously obtained from spiritual blessings. [67]

If we attempt to interpret John's teaching, we discover that here there is no reassurance nor affirmation that one can discern. All supports drop from one's consciousness and only the experience of emptiness, vulnerability and abandonment remains. In earlier times, the desert had woven its way in and out of life, bringing dryness, boredom and the absence of pleasure, but now the dark desert night eclipses the very support systems that have given life meaning and value and through which reassurance has been forthcoming. When John says the intellect is empty and in darkness, he seems to suggest that everything the person has understood and has accumulated by way of knowledge, everything that has given it "faith" and "God"—its concepts, theology, systems of thought, symbolic structures, relationships, institutions, et cetera—becomes meaningless. Nothing makes any sense, so that the mind, while full on one level of everything the person "knows," is in total darkness on another level—the level of meaning. The knowledge, the understanding, that has provided support for a lifetime, becomes a vast, painful, dark emptiness. In other words, nothing Teresa understood from her past experience gave her satisfaction or security. She explains: "The fact is that it seems everything the soul understands then adds to its pain, and that the Lord doesn't want it to profit in its entire being from anything else." [68]

When John describes the emptiness of the memory, our minds stumble because we know human memory is *full* of experience. But, in the afflicted, anguished memory, memories once so life-giving, significant and affirming now rise like piled ash in a bottomless void. The imagination can no longer connect life's memories to produce meaning and hope. One can speak of emptiness in the memory, not because one remembers nothing, but because all that the memory holds, which once provided motivation and security, which engendered trust, hope and promise for the future, now mocks the abandoned heart. Memories do not mean now what one thought or imagined they did. The memory is indeed empty, holding only the scattered remains of cherished experiences—experiences one thought revealed God and were the ground in which trust in the "Other" germinated and grew. Someone has written that the day will come when one must go on *in spite of* memories.[69]

Yes, one must will to go on even when the will is touched by sorrows, deadness, affliction, and painful longing. We have to understand that abandonment and the seeming betrayal of trust and love are the heart of this dark experience. What one wants and needs and clings to more than anything in life, that which one cherishes above all else, is withdrawn, taken away, denied. Moreover, the loved one, the very focus of one's love and desire, becomes the cause of one's agony and distress. There is nothing so destructive of affirmation and, therefore, of motivation and meaning as the seeming rejection and abandonment by one who has loved you, who has touched your naked vulnerability, and on whom you have counted with complete assurance.

The destruction of mutuality, with its deep frustration of desire, is a humiliation, a dispossession, and a death which leave the person (the WILL) unable to grasp anything affectively. A transcendence is forced upon a person in which she is not at home, against which she rebels. Depression invades the whole structure of personality with the certainty that one's life is over and that there is nothing to live for because one's good is gone forever. Life becomes absurd when one feels that there is no one anywhere who is "for me." With no home within or without, the thought of a deeper union than one formerly knew is beyond comprehension. One looks, therefore, with the eyes of absolute doubt toward a hell of eternal nothingness. Certainly, an eternal life where affectivity and desire are fulfilled is a mockery. Bitterness, anger and hate well up like an uncontrollable flood, from the very heart of one's frustrated desire and betrayed love, to threaten destruction and collapse. Rejection and abandonment surface so much human "shadow" and all the unintegrated contents of the human soul.[70]

Let us look at the dynamic in Teresa. The intensity of mutuality between her and Jesus Christ put in strong relief human limitation and even the "limitations" of God. In the mirror everything was seen; there was too much self-knowledge, and the feeling of extreme unworthiness resulted. Her love was not great enough, she thought, and she was too "wretched" to be loved. Therefore, she was being abandoned once and for all. The temptation to inferiority was overpowering, and in her depression she was angry not only with herself but with those others who could not measure up to her expectations of human life. She describes her experience:

> Nor does its will appear to be alive, but it seems to be in so great a solitude and so forsaken by all that this abandonment cannot be described in writing. For the whole world and its affairs give it pain, and no created thing provides it with company, nor does it want any company but only the Creator . . . it . . . dies with the longing to die.
> . . . The devil gives a spirit of anger so displeasing that it seems as if I want to eat everyone up, without being able to help it . . .[71]

The only way to get a new perspective on this impasse, John tells us, is to accept the alternative vision of faith, hope and love and so pass over into the perspective of God:

> We must lead the faculties of the soul to these three virtues and inform each faculty with one of them (faith in the intellect, hope in the memory, and love in the will) by stripping and darkening it of everything which is not conformable to these virtues.[72]

We know the theological virtues are gifts of God, but we act and speak as if we can muster them up in crisis. So we hear, "She had such strong faith. Her faith got her through." This is, of course, true to some extent. However, in *this* darkness and hopelessness, when we no longer feel any faith or any hope, when we hang over the abyss of atheism, absolute doubt and total loss of trust, we truly learn *they are gifts* "made possible and effective by the divine self-bestowal itself," as Karl Rahner explains in his "Theology of Hope."[73] They become the only way, the only "response," to an *unsought*, inescapable darkness and emptiness. They are gifts that bring us blindness and agony, gifts we all but reject in our despair. They must overcome an anger, fear and rebellion that want to refuse grace rather than be left with "nothing." These gifts are known *only in retrospect* by their power to catch and bind the falling, desperate person to God. Perhaps we learn the critical importance of the theological virtues only at this stage of development! What is harder to understand is WHY we, perhaps, believe and hope in God truly, theologically, only when nothing else any longer sustains us. John must have struggled deeply to find the answer to human suffering to write as he does.

Thus, John explains, faith causes darkness in our very power to understand. Now it is at cross purposes with our ability to make *logical* sense out of life, death, and eternity, out of loss, rejection, and abandonment. Faith moves us into Mystery which is incomprehensible, unimaginable and uncontrollable. Only in some kind of searing loss, it seems, do we begin to know experientially that God is indeed *the DARKNESS* beyond all our concepts, images, experiences, feelings, and perceptions, and that, as John writes, no knowledge or feeling bears any resemblance to God.[74]

The horizon of the mind is boundless. The one we call God dwells in this nameless and pathless expanse of our consciousness. When Jesus Christ seems to recede from our consciousness, when nothing human satisfies because of losses without and bitterness within and we, therefore, come to the very limits of human understanding, is this a signal that God waits over the brink? When we look back and nothing is left, when ahead we see only meaninglessness, when the images and representations of life are empty, is God then the unimaginable darkness over the brink?[75] John writes:

> This [night] guided me
> More surely than the noon
> To where he waited for me
> —Him I knew so well—
> In a place where no one else appeared.[76]

The hopelessness and emptiness of the Dark Night are precisely the condition that makes hope in the strictly theological sense possible. Hope can come into play only when we really are radically at the end, absolutely unable to find any further resources within ourselves to connect the memories, feelings, images, and experiences of life into a meaningful pattern or a promising future. Yet, it is hard to surrender to hope, hard to believe there is a possession worth possessing beyond everything we have known. Hope, as John of the Cross and Rahner see it, is free and trustful commitment to the impossible, to that which cannot be built out of what one possesses. In hope we allow ourselves finally to be grasped and drawn out of ourselves by the absolutely uncontrollable, who is God. Hope, therefore, perfects the memory [and imagination], John says, and prepares it for union with God.[77]

Estrangement and abandonment administer the final test of love—genuine love of the self that continues to believe in its own worth, and a love of the other that will not surrender in the end to hate or violence. It is a love which overcomes the will to die, to give up, to commit suicide literally or figuratively, and instead truly lives with the pain of its woundedness and longing. We can identify this experience in a woman, or a man, who is abandoned after many years of marriage or after total, self-giving love and who does not surrender finally to cynicism and hate. We see it when a spouse or child is taken away, tortured and murdered and a person continues to labor for the well-being and freedom of those left behind.

Any feeling of superiority or exclusivity is destroyed in this experience. In this sense, Dark Night is, indeed, a leveller. Love, care, compassion for "us," a common humanity, flower here. When we stand in this kind of nakedness with all our masks ripped away, we see our common bonding, and we *know* that we are "equal."[78] Then, faith affirms "for us" a Wisdom and light beyond our own reason. It affirms life and meaning beyond any carefully reasoned plans for meaningless destruction. Then, hope is exercised "for all" against domination, abandonment, and final annihilation. Then, love affirms "for us" the bondedness, communion and equality of all women and all men beyond rejection, violence and inequality.

TRANSFORMATION AFTER DARKNESS

Teresa's sense of herself survived the onslaught of the fire of self-knowledge. Fidelity in this dark faith, hope and love completed her transformation, and she was transfigured by the love, wisdom, and power of God.[79] The fear that had repeatedly made her a victim of male domination gave way to the experience of inner Power. Her feelings of inferiority and ignorance were put to rest in the certainty of the Wisdom she possessed. Her questions about ultimate exclusion, rejection, and abandonment were finally answered in the experience of a mutuality of love and gifts that could not be doubted. John explains Teresa's experience of wholeness in *The Spiritual Canticle*:

> This is the transformation in the three persons in power, wisdom and love and thus the soul is like God through this transformation. God created her in his image and likeness that she might attain such resemblance.[80]

Teresa speaks of this "imprinting" of the Blessed Trinity in the center of her being as an experience of indescribable understanding and communion. In her use of the word imprinting, we realize that the image of Christ that had been in process over a lifetime was completed. She truly was a likeness of God. John says: "The Spouse will really transform her into the beauty of both created and uncreated Wisdom, and also into the beauty of the union of the Word with his humanity."[81]

The totality and depth of Teresa's relationship to God were symbolized in a beautiful vision of the risen Jesus when she was fifty-seven years old. He gave her his right HAND, as one gives his hand in marriage to his bride, and told her that now it was time that she consider as her own what belonged to him and that he would take care of what was hers. The hand which Teresa experienced in so many ways throughout her life was finally the symbol of the fulfillment of her desire, for Jesus said to her:

> Behold this nail; it is a sign you will be my bride from today on. Until now you have not merited this; from now on not only will you look after my honor as being the honor of your Creator, King and God, but you will look after it as my true bride. My honor is yours and yours mine.[82]

In the nail we understand that all the painful past was brought into this union. The nail sealed forever Teresa's identification with the dying, abandoned Jesus. Because they had shared a common pain, all their possessions were now held in common. John tells us the soul is called the bride of the Son of God to signify her equality with him. God, he says, "makes her love him with the very strength with which he loves her. Transforming her into his love . . . he gives her his own strength by which she can love him . . . She always desired this equality . . . for a lover cannot be satisfied if [she] fails to feel that [she] loves as much as [she] is loved."[83] For God and for Teresa, the heart of equality is love. Only love creates equality. Love gives equality. Love receives equality.

It is interesting to see honor appear as a symbol of the "spiritual marriage." It is another symbol of equality. In sixteenth century Spain, honor was prized more than life itself. It was *the* value that determined personal worth and social acceptance. In her writings and her reform, Teresa was, like the people of her time, "obsessed with honor which stands out everywhere and in the most unexpected passages."[84] Here we see Teresa's concern for honor (the material of ordinary human life and culture) transformed into a symbol of equality and love and made the heart of the mutuality. The nail of Jesus' cross, the honor of Teresa's Spain: real life symbols to show the total sharing of life in God's world.

Now, John tells us, the person "always walks in festivity," and so John of the Cross sings for Teresa at this point:

> Let us rejoice, Beloved,
> Let us go forth to behold ourselves in your beauty,
> To the mountain and to the hill,
> To where the pure water flows,
> And further, deep into the thicket.[85]

This means, he says, "Transform me into the beauty of divine Wisdom and make me resemble [her] which is the Word, the Son of God." And then "she asks that he inform her with the beauty of this other lesser wisdom, contained in his creatures. . . . The soul cannot see herself in the beauty of God unless she is transformed in the Wisdom of God, in which she sees herself in possession of earthly and heavenly things . . . God permits it in this state to discern its beauty and he entrusts to it the gifts and virtues he has bestowed."[86]

Beyond anything she could have dreamed of, Teresa, *the woman*, was affirmed in a definitive way. In the face of eternal Wisdom she saw the giftedness of her own self, precisely as woman, and the power and possibilities of the insight she now possessed. With God's view of things—her mind united to the mind of God, her will to the will of God, her memory attuned "so as to have in its mind the eternal years"—she saw a new way of life rooted in the reality of what she experienced: love, connectedness, relationship, communion, and equality.[87]

She envisioned, in fact, a new social order where all were to be equal.[88] In her small communities of contemplative women, Teresa set in motion a reversal of the social and religious order by a spiritual one that would eradicate the highest principles of the established order and undermine the current images of social status. Her fearless struggle to destroy concern for honor and wealth, and therefore uphold the value of person over money and ancestry, her unswerving struggle for the recognition of women's rights to deep interior prayer and therefore to significant service in the Church at a time of great ecclesial danger and turmoil: these constituted the framework on which she built her renewal of the Carmelite Order in the sixteenth century Church, as well as her teaching on prayer, wholeness, and union with God.[89]

While John was also a major figure in the Reform of Carmel, and contributed deeply to its spiritual formation, his creativity lives majestically and above all else in his poetry which has survived for four hundred years. It witnesses, as nothing else can, to the grandeurs of an equality of love with God. John was so affirmed by God in his life that nothing could destroy his self confidence. Though he was persecuted, blamed and pushed aside after Teresa's death, he could die singing of the treasures of God and the beauty of the human person living in communion and equality with God. It is not without significance that one of the reasons he was removed from a leadership position and deprived of influence in the Carmelite Order was his defense of the rights of the Carmelite Nuns, the daughters of that great woman Teresa who was, he knew, his companion and equal not only in the depth and intensity of her experience of God but even in her ability to write about the ways of God.

CONCLUSION

John of the Cross obviously writes from his own experience. However, he also describes Teresa's experience, and he describes the experience of many women, past and present. His doctrine on the Dark Night raises the painful, paradoxical question: Is it necessary for women today to "accept" the place in which they find themselves and stand without the comfortable connections and belongingness and loves they have known; to stay in the place where previous understandings and memories are not consolations but only burdens, and where **faith and hope** in the face of the unacceptable, the totally unfathomable, are the absolutely only doorway to insight, healing, vision, creative new life, the intimate touch of communion and equality? Must we be able to stand without the God we once "saw" and even, to some degree, the understanding and support of men and institutions, as Teresa did? In *The Living Flame*, John answers through the author of the book of wisdom: "If the spirit of the One who has power descends upon you, do not abandon your place (the place and the site of your probation), for the cure will make great sins cease."[90]

Our dark night comes to us because of our particular time and place in history. The consciousness of our age shapes it just as the particular awareness of Teresa's time shaped hers. When we can respond with enduring faith, hope and love to the dark presence of an incomprehensible God who calls us to something new, we will perhaps, like Teresa, be led finally to the fulfillment of our deep human desires in a relationship of love and equality. Then we might know the way to create and express a vision of connectedness and equality in our own groups and communities and thereby move our world and our Church beyond the unequal power relations that are tearing them apart. The only question is this: Can we, women and men, do it without becoming mystics? In Teresa, we see that becoming a mystic, a contemplative, is possible for fragile human people like us. Moreover, in her transformation we understand just how true it is that the degree of our religious consciousness, the depth of our communion with God, does indeed condition the *DEPTH* of our experience of equality and solidarity.

In tracing the image of Christ through Teresa's writings, and following the movement of her self-understanding from inferiority, confusion of heart and fear of abandonment to connectedness, mutuality and equality of love, we grasp the centrality of

Jesus Christ in the Christian mystical experience. Moreover, an analysis of her complex experience/visions reveals a Christology that certainly does not validate either the subordination or the exclusion of women. On the contrary, the "world" of these texts reveals quite a different vision of reality, a vision that confronts and challenges our personal and societal lives. Here I can only say that as I have appropriated these texts in this study, the inequalities we maintain, one toward another, in so many of our relationships and structures, appear absurd to me—the work of the evil one who prefers inferiority, exclusion, and submission to equality of love.

Teresa makes an interesting comment about women at the end of the book of her *Life*. I want to close with this:

> There are many more women than men to whom the Lord grants these favors. This I heard from the saintly Friar Peter of Alcantara—and I, too, have observed it—who said that women make much more progress along this road than men do. He gave excellent reasons for this, all in favor of women; but there's no need to mention them here.[91]

Perhaps John agreed because he wrote both the commentary of *The Spiritual Canticle* and *The Living Flame* for women.

NOTES

[1] See Elisabeth Schüssler Fiorenza, *In Memory of Her* (New York: Crossroad, 1983), p. 349.

[2] See John of the Cross, *The Collected Works of St. John of the Cross* (*CW*), trans. Kieran Kavanaugh and Otilio Rodriguez (Washington, D.C.: Institute of Carmelite Studies, 1973), *The Spiritual Canticle*, st. 13, no. 7; *The Living Flame*, st. 2, nos. 9-12.

[3] John, *CW*, "Introduction," p. 23; see Teresa of Avila, *The Collected Works of St. Teresa of Avila* (*CW*), trans. Kieran Kavanaugh and Otilio Rodriguez, 3 vols. (Washington, D.C.: Institute of Carmelite Studies, 1976-1985), vol. 1: *Spiritual Testimonies*, no. 31; vol. 2.: *The Interior Castle*, VI, chap. 9, no. 17, with note no. 14. (This article's extensive end notes are provided as an aid for in-depth study of Teresa's and John's texts. I have, however, in some cases grouped a number of references for a single section into one note.)

[4] John, *CW*, "Introduction," p. 30.

[5] See Elizabeth Johnson, "Jesus, the Wisdom of God: A Biblical Basis for Non-Androcentric Christology," *Ephemerides Theologicae Lovanienses* (Dec. 1985): 263.

[6] John, *CW*, *The Spiritual Canticle*, st. 28, no. 1; st. 39, no. 6; see also st. 30, no. 6, and *The Ascent of Mount Carmel*, chap. 5, no. 1.

[7] John, *CW*, *The Spiritual Canticle*, st. 32, no. 6; st. 38, nos. 3-4.

[8] John, *CW*, *The Spiritual Canticle*, st. 12; st. 11, no. 12; *The Living Flame*, st. 3, no. 45; see also *The Ascent*, Book I, chap. 13, no. 3; chap. 14, no. 2; *The Spiritual Canticle*, chap. 37.

[9] Teresa, *CW*, vol. 1: *Life*, chap. 4, no. 7; chap. 11, no. 9; chap. 12,

nos. 2-3; see also chap. 13, no. 11; chap. 12, no. 22; vol. 2: *The Way of Perfection*, chaps. 26, 27, and 28, nos. 3-4.

[10] According to Colin P. Thompson, *The Poet and The Mystic* (Oxford: Oxford University Press, 1977), p. 10: "One of the most insistent calls echoing through the whole [western] tradition is the renunciation of the self and every thing created for God. Its roots lie in pre-Christian antiquity and it occurs in other faiths." (See note on Zaehner's *Mysticism Sacred and Profane* in Thompson.)

[11] Teresa, *CW, Life*, chap. 2, nos. 1-8.

[12] *Ibid.*, chap. 5, nos. 5 and 4. See nos. 4-10.

[13] *Ibid.*, chap. 5, nos. 8, 11.

[14] As Teresa here describes her fervent life and her carefulness of conscience, one is reminded of the description she wrote years later of the good, reasonable, careful person in the third dwelling places. See *Life*, chap. 6, and *The Interior Castle*, III.

[15] Teresa, *CW, Life*, chap. 7, no. 1; chap. 6, no. 9.

[16] In *The Seeing Eye, Hermeneutical Phenomenology in the Study of Religion* (University Park and London: The Pennsylvania State University, 1982), pp. 78-79, Walter L. Brenneman et al. write: "Seeing is a metaphor for a broad spectrum of cognitive experiences, including visions that come from beyond the boundaries to which senses and reason extend and revelations that have radically changed people's views of the world and of the meaning of life. . .Sight involves a realization of what was previously undisclosed. . .and it implies a prior blindness to that which was always there to be seen if only one had had the eyes to see it."

[17] See Teresa, *CW, Life*, chap. 7, nos. 6-9; see also J.E. Cirlot, *A Dictionary of Symbols* (New York: Philosophical Library, 1971), for the entry on toad to understand the fascinating and even lethal effect of a toad's gaze. See also *Life*, chap. 22, no. 13, where Teresa compares the person at this stage of development to a toad who tried to fly on its own.

[18] Teresa, *CW, Life*, chap. 8, no. 5.

[19] *Ibid.*, chap. 8, no. 2; chap. 7, no. 6; chap. 8, no. 3.

[20] See Cirlot, *Dictionary*, p. 1, "abandonment." Although we cannot pursue this here, we become aware at this point of significant relationships between some of the major symbols in Teresa's writings: garden, castle, way, and even water which is given little by little, and abandonment and death/resurrection.

[21] Teresa, *CW, Life*, chap. 8, no. 12.

[22] See Teresa, *CW, Life*,chap 9, nos. 1-7.

[23] *Ibid.*, chap. 10, no. 8. See also all of chap. 10; chap. 22, no. 12; chap. 23. This is the prayer of quiet.

[24] *Ibid.*, chap. 24, nos. 4-5.

[25] *Ibid.*, chap. 24, no. 5; see also chap. 25, no. 1, and John, *CW, The Ascent*, Book II, chap. 31.

[26] Teresa, *CW, Life*, chap. 24, no. 6; see *The Way of Perfection*, chaps. 4, 6, 7.

[27] Cirlot, p. 80; see Teresa, *CW, Life*, chap. 25, nos. 14-15.

[28] Teresa, *CW, Life*, chap. 25, nos. 17, 18, 19.

[29] Teresa, *CW, The Way of Perfection*, chap. 3, no. 7.

30 Teresa, *CW, Life,* chap. 26, no. 5.

31 Teresa, *Works, The Way of Perfection,* chap. 22, no. 6.

32 *Ibid.,* chap. 22, no. 6; chap. 21, nos. 2-3.

33 *Ibid.,* chap. 22, no. 2.

34 *Ibid.,* "Introduction," p. 25; see also chap. 25.

35 Teresa, *CW, Life,* chap. 28, no. 18.

36 *Ibid.,* chap. 27, no. 6; see also nos. 2-3 for Teresa's description of an intellectual vision.

37 Teresa, *CW, Life,* chap. 27, no. 14. Using the "categories of interiority" of Bernard Lonergan and his concept of intersubjective union, James Robertson Price III of Georgia State University has done a helpful study called *Lonergan and the Foundations of a Contemporary Mystical Theology.* One would think the study was done using Teresa, herself, as a subject for the research. See Lonergan's *Method in Theology* (New York: Herder & Herder, 1972), pp. 3-25.

38 See Elizabeth Johnson, "Incomprehensibility of God and the Image of God Male and Female," *Theological Studies* (1984): 462-63; see also Susan Cady et al., *Sophia* (San Francisco: Harper & Row, 1986). While Teresa's development, supported by John of the Cross' experience and teaching, may throw light from the mystical tradition on Wisdom studies, feminist research may open up new horizons in the interpretation of John and Teresa, too.

39 Teresa, *CW, Life,* chap. 27, no. 11; chap. 28, no. 1.

40 Ntozake Shange, *for colored girls who have considered suicide/when the rainbow is enuf* (New York: Macmillan, 1977), p. 63.

41 John, *CW, The Ascent,* Book II, chap. 15, no. 4; *The Dark Night,* Book II, chap. 24, no. 3; see also *The Spiritual Canticle,* st. 37, no. 2.

42 Teresa, *CW, Life,* chap. 28, no.1; Teresa tells us that she was always afraid of each *new* experience of Jesus Christ.

43 Elizabeth Koenig writes about this in her doctoral dissertation, *The Book of Showings of Julian of Norwich: A Test Case for Paul Ricoeur's Theories of Metaphor and Imagination.* Koenig draws on D. W. Winnicott's "Mirror-role of Mother and Family in Child Development," in *Playing and Reality* (New York: Basic Books, Inc., Publishers, 1971).

44 See John, *CW, The Ascent,* Book II, chap. 17. This is a key passage in understanding the developmental aspect of John's teaching. Moreover, it reveals his epistemology.

45 Teresa, *CW, Life,* chap. 28, nos. 5, 11, 13; see also *The Interior Castle,* VI, chap. 1, no. 4.

46 For this whole section, see Teresa, *CW, Life,* chap. 29, nos. 2-7.

47 *Ibid.,* chap. 29, nos. 13, 10; see *The Interior Castle,* VI, chap. 2, no. 4.

48 Teresa writes at length about seeing the devil. This is one of the ways she describes the Dark Night. See, for example, chap. 31, nos. 2,9. Darkness weaves its way in and out of Teresa's experience over a lifetime, as we see in her writings. Because I have written elsewhere about earlier phases of the Dark Night, I have chosen to concentrate later in this essay on Teresa's most profound experience of abandonment, just before the "spiritual marriage." See note no. 66.

49 In an article on Thérèse of Lisieux, I have written at more length

about the symbol of heart. See Constance FitzGerald, "Contemplative Life and Charismatic Presence," *Spiritual Life*, Spring 1983, pp. 18-30.

[50] John, *CW, The Living Flame*, st. 2, nos. 10-12.

[51] In the *Life*, chap. 37, no. 4, Teresa writes: "The vision of Christ left upon me an impression of his most extraordinary beauty, and the impression remains to this day."

[52] *Ibid.*, chap. 33, no. 11.

[53] *Ibid.*, chap. 33, nos. 14, 16; chap. 36, no. 24; chap. 34, no. 2.

[54] *Ibid.*, chap. 36, no. 17; chap. 33, no. 12.

[55] *Ibid.*, chap. 34, nos. 8, 3; see also *The Interior Castle*, VI, chap. 8, no. 4.

[56] *Ibid.*, chap. 34, no. 17; see also nos. 8-12.

[57] *Ibid.*; see vision in chap. 39, no. 1, and chaps. 38 and 39, to see how and why Teresa's prayers for others were answered.

[58] See Teresa, *CW, Spiritual Testimonies*, 2, no. 4.

[59] See Teresa, *CW, Life*, chap. 38, nos. 17, 18; chap. 40, nos. 1-4; *The Interior Castle*, VI, chap. 10, no. 7.

[60] Teresa, *CW, Life*, chap. 40, no. 5 with note no. 6; see also *The Interior Castle*, VI, chap. 10, no. 2; *The Way of Perfection*, chap. 28, nos. 9-12; *Spiritual Testimonies*, 20, nos. 13-14.

[61] St. 38, no. 1; see Cirlot, *Dictionary*, "mirror," pp. 211-12; *The Interior Castle*, VII, chap. 2, no. 8; *The Living Flame*, st. 1, nos. 9-13. To understand the kind of affirmation Teresa received, see *CW, Life*, chap. 39, no. 22; chap. 40, no. 12.

[62] Teresa, *CW, Life*, chap. 40, nos. 9-10.

[63] *Ibid.*, chap. 20, no. 9; see chap. 20, nos. 8-16; chap. 30, nos. 8-14. Teresa tells us this time of estrangement that occurred after everything else she writes of in her *Life*. However, she completed that work long before she died and before she reached the Spiritual Marriage.

[64] See John, *CW, The Living Flame*, st. 1, no. 20, and Teresa, *CW, Life*, chap. 40, no. 10.

[65] John, *CW, The Spiritual Canticle*, st. 36, nos. 7, 8, 13; see *Life*, chap. 20, no. 11.

[66] John, *CW, The Spiritual Canticle*, st. 1; see *Spiritual Testimonies*, 22, no. 2. In my article, "Impasse and Dark Night," in *Living with Apocalypse* (San Francisco: Harper & Row, 1984), pp. 94-116, I deal with Dark Night in the sense mentioned here. There I draw on Michael J. Buckley, "Atheism and Contemplation," *Theological Studies* 40 (1979).

[67] *The Dark Night*, Book II, chap. 3, no. 3; see also chap. 4, no. 1; chap. 16, no. 1.

[68] *Spiritual Testimonies*, 59, no. 14.

[69] See John, *CW, The Ascent*, Book II, chap. 2, no. 3; chap. 9, no. 5; *Life*, chap. 30, no. 8.

[70] To understand this interpretation, see John, *CW, The Dark Night*, Book II, chap. 4-12; *The Living Flame*, st. 1, nos. 20-22; Teresa, *CW, Life*, chap. 32, nos. 1-4.

[71] Teresa, *CW, Spiritual Testimonies*, 54, no. 14; *Life*, chap. 30, no. 13.

[72] *The Ascent*, Book II, chap. 6, no. 6; see all of chap. 6 for John's doctrine on the theological virtues; also see *The Dark Night*, Book II, chap. 21, no. 11; chap. 13, no. 11.

73 Karl Rahner, *Theological Investigations* X (New York: Seabury, 1977), pp. 245-47.

74 See *The Ascent*, Book II, chap. 3, for John's teaching on faith; see also chap. 4, 1-3; chap. 8, pp. 125 ff.; chap. 9, p. 129; *The Dark Night*, Book II, chap. 16, no. 8, par. 2; Teresa, *CW, Life*, chap. 30, no. 12.

75 Juan Luis Segundo calls this the passage from anthropological faith to authentic faith in *Faith and Ideologies* (Maryknoll, N.Y.: Orbis Books, 1984), p. 166. Karl Kahner has helped me to bring into dialogue contemporary experience and John of the Cross' teaching. See "The Experience of the Spirit," *Theological Investigations* XVIII (New York: Crossroad, 1983), pp. 196-97.

76 John, *CW, The Dark Night* poem, st. 4.

77 *The Dark Night*, Book II, chap. 21, no. 11; *The Ascent*, Book III, chap. 15, no. 1; chap. 7, no. 2; chap. 11, nos. 1–2; see Karl Rahner, "On the Theology of Hope," *Theological Investigations* X, pp. 242-59; "Theology of Death," *Theological Investigations* XIII (New York: Crossroad, 1983), pp. 176-84.

78 Marie Celeste Fadden, O.C.D., of Reno Carmel, has captured the reality of this solidarity in a painting of incredible power and feeling that she executed for Edith Stein's beatification. It shows Edith at the gate of Auschwitz, identified and one with the Jewish men, women and children being herded to their death.

79 For John of the Cross, purification and transformation are two sides of a single coin. The same fire that burns the log black causes the blackened wood to burst into brilliant flame. This realization pervades *The Living Flame*. See, for example, st. 1, nos. 1-25, especially no. 1.

80 John, *CW, The Spiritual Canticle*, st. 39, no. 4.

81 *Ibid.*, st. 38, no. 1; st. 42; *The Interior Castle*, VII, chap. 1, nos. 6, 7.

82 John, *CW, Spiritual Testimonies*, 31.

83 John, *CW, The Spiritual Canticle*, st. 38, nos. 3, 4. See also *The Living Flame*, st. 3, nos. 78-79, for equality.

84 Teofanes Egido, O.C.D., "The Historical Setting of St. Teresa's Life," trans. Michael Dodd and Steven Payne, *Carmelite Studies* 1 (Washington, D.C.: ICS Publications, 1980), p. 152.

85 John, *CW, The Spiritual Canticle*, st. 36.

86 *Ibid.*, st. 36, nos. 6, 7, 8; *The Living Flame*, st. 1, no. 31.

87 John, *CW, The Living Flame*, st. 1, no. 32; st. 2, no. 34; st. 1, no. 22; st. 4, nos. 5, 6, 7; *The Spiritual Canticle*, st. 37, no. 3; st. 39, no. 11.

88 Teresa, *CW, The Way of Perfection*, chap. 27, no. 6.

89 See Egido, "The Historical Setting of St. Teresa's Life," p. 130.

90 St. 1, no. 19.

91 Chap. 40, no. 8.

A Discipleship of Equals: Towards a Spirituality for Men

John Carmody

Early in the morning of the day I was to begin writing this essay, I had a beautiful dream. Usually I do not pay much attention to my dreams. Years ago I read Freud and Jung, and the unflattering dream about the Church that Jung mentions in his autobiography has long amused me, but normally I do not consider my dreams a theological source. This dream, however, was so strong and winning that I had to take it seriously. I had planned to discover what I wanted to say in this essay by working on my first draft. I had hoped in that way to resolve my ambivalence about the topic assigned me: did I think there was a spirituality distinctively for men? After the dream I realized I thought my essay should be about love, with more explicit attention to my male voice than usually I pay it.

Here is the dream: I was standing with my friend and teacher, Robert McAfee Brown, on the crest of a steep hill, in the middle of woods that seemed in early winter. There were rich, brown leaves on the ground and patches of snow. We were looking down upon a sizable church, the main features of which were natural logs and natural stones. Somehow I knew Bob Brown had built the church himself. The aesthetic effect was very pleasing: an amateur work in the best sense. The church evoked in me a powerful desire to enter what I knew would be a vaulted space in which I would want only to kneel, bow, and pray. I would feel small yet safe, and the space would release a great pent-up desire to be with my wholly good God in simple, wordless, complete love. I would experience with tears a love of God similar to what Ignatius Loyola suggests in the "Contemplatio ad Amorem" that consummates *The Spiritual Exercises*.

In the second scene of my dream, I found myself in the church for a wedding. Who were being married and who were attending were not clear at the outset, but by the end I was the groom. The mood was joyous, confident, earthy. The eros for God summoned in the first scene had become an eros for my bride, who filled my cup to overflowing by her responding desire for complete sexual union. At this point I awoke, moved by the beauty of the dream and laughing at its naked effect. "Where did that come from?," I asked myself. Then, I realized it might have been a message about the challenges of the day I was anticipating, as dreams of the morning supposedly tend to be.

I have taken the message to be a charge to write about love. On reflection, I find it has seemed a reminder of better thoughts I used to mine but have for some time laid aside. For, in two books I have worked with the thesis that the center of Christian life is the love stipulated for us by Christ's twofold command-ment.[1] And, I now realize, it was the absence of a clear focus on such love that was bedeviling my preparation for this essay. Neither what I had read as background preparation nor what I had sketched as preliminary outlines had shown me what I really wanted to say. Neither had moved me from the conceptual level, where one can simply shuffle the familiar notions once again, to the reasons of the heart that more writers than Pascal have realized are the crux of spiritual theology. I propose, then, to meditate on the twofold commandment, moving my thoughts about the trinitarian God, my self, and my neighbors toward the topic of this volume in which I am participating: the discipleship of Christian equals. The equality I shall stress is that between men and women, that which honors the "male and female he created them" of Genesis 1:27b. After completing these intro-ductory reflections, I shall treat successively of the one God, Christ, the Father, and the Spirit. My second section will treat of my self as embodied and my self as spiritual. In a third section I shall deal with women, men, and the Church. In each section, love will be the inquiry, the goal. How may men best love their God, themselves, their neighbors who are female lovers, friends, children, collaborators, enemies, their neighbors who are male friends, children, collaborators, enemies, and their neighbors who explicitly share with them Christian faith? I assume that most of what I say will wholly apply to women trying to love God, themselves, and their neighbors. However, it seems clear that in this volume I am being asked to deal explicitly with masculine overtones, so I shall try to let male hormones and social conditioning speak freely, that both what God would teach us through them, and the healing that experience shows they need, may be available for discussion.

Let me complete this introduction by returning to my initial ambivalance about my assignment. It stems from my dislike of disjunctive treatments of sexuality. I think men and women have differences, but that these differences should weigh less than what they hold in common. I think that each of us goes to God as a unique individual, shaped by genes, sex, family upbringing, social conditioning, education, and the gifts of a Holy Spirit who is not a generic Paraclete but a Comforter treating us as distinctive individuals she could no more abandon than her nursing children. And, I find the best community, the richest experience of romance, work, friendship, and communal prayer, to flourish when we attend to the concrete, individual whole that any person standing beside us is and chasten our tendency to perceive or react through stereotypes.

Consequently, I find myself slow to pick up books about male bonding, columns especially for men, invitations to join men's groups. These things embarrass me and, after I have admitted that some such embarrassment might be a good thing, a way of learning more about myself and other men, I find part of my resistance salutary. I do not want advice and preoccupation that set men over-against women, that do not from the outset distinguish only to unite. Equally, I am put off by women's writing that is separatist. I read quite a lot of feminist literature and theology, partly because I share an interest of my wife Denise and partly because I find much of it highly instructive. One of the things I have most admired about Doris Lessing, Margaret Atwood, Mary Gordon, Rosemary Ruether, Monika Hellwig, and many other women writers is their realism. They accept a two-sexed world. The graces they celebrate and the sins they deplore cut across stereotypes. With Dorothy Dinnerstein, they agree that the sexual malaise we suffer is a product of both sexes' collaboration. Sometimes they are hard on men, but almost always with good reason. I myself tend to be harder on men, thinking that real men take no pleasure in hurting women.

I have also been ambivalent about the topic of a spirituality for men, and its correlative, a spirituality for women, because it has seemed inevitably to raise the question of homosexuality. I do not want to have always to qualify what I am describing and make the distinctions gay men and women rightly can ask for, so let me say once and for all that I think some people have an unchangeably homosexual orientation, that this is part of their endowment from God, and that both they and any community they inhabit are healthier when this is as overt a part of their profile as their ethnic origins, their job skills, or their sense of humor. I think homosexuals are held to the same general morality as heterosexuals, that this morality boils down to honesty and love, and that genuinely homosexual relationships should neither bear any special restrictions nor claim any special exemptions.

From 1963 to 1966, I watched a young counselee/friend struggle to find himself and God. He succeeded only when he owned up to what he knew he was and took a wry pride in it. Three years ago he died of AIDS. I cannot bring him back to accept my apologies for the inadequacies of my counsel and friendship, nor to help him criticize his interpretation of his homosexuality. But, I can come out of the closet about what I think Christian faith says about homosexuality. In Saint Teresa's words, it says let nothing disturb you. In Saint Augustine's words, it says love and do what you will. I believe this advice, and all the other essentials of the Christian life, apply equally to men and women, to heterosexuals and homosexuals, to blacks and whites, to rich and poor. It leaves many further questions unanswered, of course, but it offers all people the evangelical bottom line: God is greater than our hearts, God is love. This is the line I now want to extend toward a spirituality for men.

Part One: The Love of God

Loving the One God

My division of this part owes a debt to the scholastic distinction of the tracts, *De Deo Uno* and *De Deo Trino*. It reflects, as well, some study of Judaism, Islam, and the theology of nature. From time immemorial, people have enjoyed moments when the world showed itself but the material face of an intriguing, almost crushingly beautiful mystery. Like many an Eskimo, the naturalist Barry Lopez has recently responded to the beauty of the Arctic with praise verging on religious poetry:

> I remember the press of light against my face, the explosive skitter of calves among grazing caribou. And the warm intensity of the eggs beneath these resolute birds. Until then, perhaps because the sun was still shining in the very middle of the night, so out of tune with my own customary perception, I had never known how benign sunlight could be. How forgiving. How run through with compassion in a land that bore so eloquently the evidence of centuries of winter.[2]

My spirituality for men would have a bigger place for love of the one God manifested in such beauty than the spirituality I was taught had. For personal as well as ecological reasons, I want to recapture the intimacy with the Lord of the Worlds, The Great Goddess of Life, that Muslims and Hindus, in their very different ways, have experienced. By virtue of the Christian understanding of creation and grace, men might experience the fields they tramp, the oceans they sail, as charged with the grandeur of God. They might nod with approval when preachers remind them that the biblical God is never captured by nature, always remains transcendent, yet reserve their heartier accord for those who claim that any fall of a cherry blossom might trigger enlightenment. One has only to dabble in present-day science—the physics of a Stephen Hawking or the neurology of an Oliver Sacks—to be staggered by the profusion of nature, the sweep and intricacy of the world. Job had his Behemoth and Leviathan. Men of today should read the natural signs of our times as Job's world to the nth power. For faith, our world should seem a constant series of theophanies. One has only to think about what is there, to admire what happens, to magnify the power of the one God, to minimize all human hubris, and to wonder, most profoundly, what is man, that God should care for us?

For present purposes, I am not much interested in the theodicy that a fully adequate treatment probably would enter at this point. Nature, like human culture, does present suffering, waste, destruction that make questions about the existence and goodness of God legitimate, even necessary. Moreover, these questions can persist within faith, always speaking up for the rights of atheists, always cautioning us not to get glib or saccharine. Our science is different from the science of Boethius's day, so our declarations that providence always orchestrates things for the best has to be similarly different. Yet, ultimately we should be able to say that the wisdom of God justifies creation. And, frequently we should remind ourselves that the profusion of goodness is at least as mysterious as the profusion of evil. Our regular memo to ourselves should be that we come from nothing and have no rights God has not bestowed upon us. Our regular prayer should be thanksgiving that we, and almost all other human beings, have enjoyed lives that make it relatively easy to say amen to divine providence, relatively easy to agree that God was good to have given us the light of the eyes and the air we breathe.

Another way of proposing this attitude toward the one God, the maker of heaven and earth, that I would like men to develop is by waxing ontological. Matthew Fox and others interested in a spirituality that pays as much attention to creation as to redemption have revived the convictions of the medieval mystics about panentheism. God is in us and we are in God. The medieval mystics (and any who, like them, find existence wonderful) meant this physically. That we are is more primordial than what we are. That God exists is more certain than what God is. Our culture generally has lost the contemplative orientation that makes such assertions significant. We rush and bustle midst concrete and neon, losing our ties with the quiet of early morning, when being seems fresh like dew, with the quiet of late night, when unknowing clearly is the way to a good night's sleep. I realize, of course, that monks and some nuns keep the contemplative rhythms. Most of the men I meet, however, find talk of contemplation less intelligible than Sanskrit. Indeed, they find it suspect: inimical to the pragmatism regnant in their worlds of business and education and so, subversive.

Recently, I agreed to review a book for *Religious Studies Review,* and so was sent James V. Schall's *The Distinctiveness of Christianity.*[3] It struck me as a piece of nostalgia, built on theses of G. K. Chesterton, Christopher Dawson, and other names I had not much seen for at least a decade. John Paul II was another prime source. Schall spoke pejoratively of justice, as though liberation theologians had made it the enemy of charity. He lamented the demise of Catholic higher education, charging that most American Catholic schools had sold their birthright for a bowl of secularism. He had little space for women, minorities, and the statistic realities of poverty around our globe. In most ways his book was what one would expect from the Ignatius Press in San Francisco that published it: Catholic triumphalism.

And yet, I loved the book. For its good style, its author's humanity (he always stayed on the near side of shrillness and vitriol), its call for a return to epistemological realism, and its devotion to contemplating the trinitarian mysteries, I was ready to forgive it the many sins that made it hopeless as a contemporary theology. It made me realize how hungry I was for the thought that had nourished me in the seminary. I was disappointed that Schall had not followed Rahner and Voegelin, whom he quoted several times, and Lonergan, whom he ignored, into the sublation of classical Catholic realism, its supplement by the positive aspects of the modern turn to subjectivity and empirical data. Yet, I still was moved and pacified by his Augustinian premise that God is the great treasure of human existence, that we are made to contemplate God and will have no rest until we rest in God.

The Catholic Christian vision of God as the mystery evoked in every decent luring of the human spirit seems more eloquent to me today than it has ever been. I am happy enough to see men cluster in groups to discuss the alienations caused by the inhuman pace of much American work. I admit that relations with women have been greatly complicated by the women's movement, herpes, AIDS, the economic depression afflicting the middle of the country, and maybe even sunspots. If men find it helpful to discuss these things, with or without basketball or bowling, fine and dandy. But, I myself am looking for a few good men with whom to discuss my shabby prayer, my forgetfulness of God's gifts, the relations between love and contemplation, the problems of getting religious experience into academically acceptable prose, the religious implications of my first significant appreciations of aging and so mortality, my emotional distance from the Vatican shenanigans I read about in *The National Catholic Reporter*, and my feeling that I am a man without a country, at home neither in academics nor in my local Catholic diocese, which interests me as little as I interest it.

The one God, the God common to all human experience as its basal mystery, seems to have clouded my mind, to have rattled my compass, and I would like to learn from my betters, from those who are better lovers, what this strange semi-disablement means. To date it mainly has meant keeping my own counsel, wondering why I still seem quite cheerful, thinking about de Caussade and other consoling writers I enjoyed nearly thirty years ago, thinking about Nietzsche, Tibetan gurus, Hammarskjold and others turned upside down and inside out. If there is one God, everything changes with shifts in one's relationship to him or her or it. I think men's spirituality, and women's spirituality, ought to be dealing with this, although, of course, usually not through formal, structured speeches. If it were doing its job, it would be creating many informal occasions, would be knitting together many friendships, in which sharing one's tears and fears, one's hopes and doubts, would be natural, regular, almost unthinking.

Christ

For the further refinements of the love of God brought by Christian belief in God's triune character, I begin with Jesus the Christ. In Schillebeeckx's term from some years ago, he is the sacrament of our encounter with God. This is congenial to Rahnerian theology, too, for Rahner finds Jesus to be God's eschatological Word of salvation. These could be triumphalist notions, of course, but certainly neither of these theologians makes them such. Both Schillebeeckx and Rahner are sufficiently religious to leave their readers thinking that, far from providing simple answers to the mystery of existence, Jesus deepens its wonder. Life is not a puzzle we shall solve. God is not an equation we shall balance. Jesus is not a cipher breaking a code that non-Christians continue to find meaningless.

One of Avery Dulles' recent books on the Church promotes the image of discipleship.[4] Jesus continues to be the main priest, prophet, king, and other traditional metaphors. Dulles is not out to deny the Pantokrator or the head of the mystical body. But, he is searching for something nearer, dearer, more enticing. He is verging on Loyola's notion of comradeship with Jesus, although without the military overtones. How should men, in particular, relate today to the God-man Jesus? What might the studies of bonding, friendship, work relations, and the rest suggest? I realized recently, though not for the first time, that most of my interactions with other men are pleasant but either functional or superficial. I like a great many men, but only with a very few does the prospect of our being together gladden my heart. When that does occur, I realize that male friendship should be more like male-female enjoyment and play than I customarily assume. Perhaps an example will help.

I went to the doctor this winter to have a wart removed from my sole—not so exciting a prospect as going to the dentist, but in the ballpark. Because of personnel shifts in our HMO—a story about I-Thou and I-It relationships well worth discussing in some other context—I did not know the doctor who would treat me. He knocked on the door of the examining room, came in, and introduced himself. I judged him about 35, perhaps 5' 7," 135 pounds, very trim, with dark blond hair, a short beard, and clear blue eyes. In three minutes I was convinced he was the born healer we all wish our doctor would be. He did not call himself Dr. Shultz and me John, as the folksy, patronizing local tradition encourages. He did not wear a silly three-quarter length white coat and make me wonder where was the beef. He was soft-spoken, gentle, respectful. I was intrigued, so I asked him a few questions, to prolong and deepen the interaction. This led to my giving him some advice about cardio-vascular exercise on a Nordic Track—imagine, a doctor interested in exercise! When I left, after barely ten minutes, I wished we could be friends. I had loved the healing touch that had gone out from him, much as many disciples must have loved the touch and voice of Jesus.

I am sure that many good devotional books about Jesus promote this sort of love, although I seldom go near them. From time to time I have thought about the beloved disciple reclining on Jesus's breast and about Jesus's weeping over Lazarus. But, despite lengthy indoctrinations in the splendors of the devotion to the Sacred Heart, and good advice in books by people like my friend, Bill Barry, about speaking frankly and intimately with "the Lord," I do not often pray or think in these terms. Jesus has not been my friend and, ever since I heard a group of elderly Methodist men singing from their Protestant hymnal, "He walks with me and he talks with me and he tells me I am his own" (or "his friend"—I cannot remember which), I have squirmed at treating him that way. And yet, of course, Jesus has not called us servants but friends. He has disclosed to us, whom spiritual reading of the gospels makes his contemporaries, the things in his heart. Presumably, he is interested in the things in our hearts, all theologoumena about his already knowing them not withstanding.

Occasionally, I have thought that discipleship ought to mean fascination with Jesus, response to his beauty and goodness, perhaps even rollicking laughter at the wit that the New Testament (a less than fully Jewish book) chooses to ignore. I have thought that female disciples ought to respond to Jesus as a very attractive man and that male disciples ought to respond to Jesus as a very attractive man, with all the implications that this term ought to carry in the two different cases. I have enjoyed times with male friends, especially in the early years of the seminary, when we were free to be scared and pious together, that filled my soul with contentment. If they were less charged than similarly fulfilling times with women, that was part of their appeal. I have had increasing, deepening experience of the fact that my wife and I are best friends to one another, and from this fact I have derived some central theses about the theology of marriage. It remains for me to take these matters up with Jesus, however, and until I do, my spirituality for men probably will not be worth very much.

With my best friends, strength and vulnerability change sides. We are open to one another, now more, now less, in good times and bad, in sickness and in health. The classical phrase was that a friend is *dimidium animae meae:* half of my soul. Can men apply that to Jesus? Are men in fact applying that to Jesus all the time, with me simply out of touch, marginal because of my secularism and sin? I do not know the way to answer the second question, except to say that most of the men I meet in a typical month tell me nothing about their prayer, indeed rarely give signs of praying. But, surely the answer to the first question is yes, men can apply the classical sense of friendship to Jesus, the sense of sharing one another's souls, of having a likeness of mind that makes communicaton almost instantaneous, of always being able to rely on one another's concern and loyalty.

For another day, one might reflect on the love of the Logos, but it is clear that for this day getting some purchase on the love of Jesus will be accomplishment enough. To consider Jesus my friend in the non-syrupy but fully affectionate way for which I am groping, I might of course pay more attention to his vulnerability. Christ on the cross not only died for my sins, as the old manuals constantly repeated, he suffered shamefully, most exposedly, as a criminal, a figure of contempt. The gospels certainly show him retaining his dignity, and their theologies insist that he kept control. But, the humanity in him touches the humanity in me most deeply when I realize the risks he took, the power of the shame that must have gripped him. He had lost, been rejected, been accounted a fool.

If I get a migraine headache, I feel ashamed. To lose my speech, to be wounded and dysfunctional, to cause bystanders to give me the look they give the crippled or the retarded, cause me to blush and withdraw. I want to be alone to lick my wounds, which are more psychic than physical. I need help to laugh at this passing debility and be reminded that things soon will be normal again. What can I do for Jesus, in his shame? Putting aside all the distinctions and guidelines orthodox Christology might prompt, how can I go to him and be compassionate, really enter into what he was willing to do and be "for us men and our salvation," as the old translations of the creedal phrase put it?

Would Jesus countenance my taking him in my arms, my not prefacing every sentence with "Lord," my telling him how much I admire his courage, my confessing I could never have done it, my more relevantly confessing I do not do even the sliver of it I might do if I believed he wanted to give himself in me and my circumstances today? Would he want gratitude, sorrow, succor? Obviously he would, if our faith is correct in insisting upon his full humanity, like us in all things save sin. Probably the women who stayed faithful at the cross while the men fled understood this. And so, probably what keeps men like me from doing it is a debility women might help us reduce.

The Father

In the next section I shall deal with a love of the Holy Spirit that might bear sexual overtones and with the perichoresis, the mutual indwelling, of the three divine persons. Here I want to continue the focus, the structure, implied when we take Jesus as the bringer of eschatological salvation. As is well known, Jesus's use of "Abba" for God was distinctive. Scholars may debate precisely how distinctive, rummaging through the contemporary rabbinic literature, but even if they narrow the novelty of Jesus's usage, we do well to take it seriously. Of the many books on Jesus I have read, Lucas Grollenberg's modest work still seems to me to have come closest to the likely heart of the matter.[5] Grollenberg stresses the singular trust that Jesus reposed in his Father. From that trust, Jesus was able to move through life much more freely than the rest of us. He did not need the defenses that keep us from appreciating, understanding, enjoying, and helping out one another as we might. He did not fear the establishment of his time nor avert his face from the divine mystery. Thinking, experiencing that the Father was always with him, on his side, for him, Jesus showed us what human nature might be, were we to let love bring our potential to maturity. The world was his oyster, because all good things descended to him from his Father of lights.

Two brief scenarios may suggest my own stumbling efforts to enter into this filial relationship to God, and so may illumine some of the considerations germane to a better spirituality for men. The first is rather negative. I have observed in several settings a marriage of theological suspicion of human nature with academic critical-mindedness that I believe has thrown up huge obstacles to a love of God on the model of Jesus's filial trust. The theological suspicion, in fact, has come from Calvinist tenets, but one could easily write the same scenario from Catholic Jansenist sources. Quite explicitly, colleagues have shown that they have taken to heart the doctrine of human corruption tended them by their masters, and the result has been a practical, political program with the motto, "We'd better get those bastards before they get us." More subtly, but ultimately more corrosively, this theology has made the colleagues I have in mind constantly second-guess, if not indeed hate, themselves. There, the motto has been: "Because I too am a corrupt bastard, I'd better rein in my natural instincts and favor the opposite of what I'd like."

When one couples this theology with the negatively critical mind sharpened by higher education—the ability to poke holes and debunk, which most graduate programs foster much better than they foster the ability to create and complement—the result usually is outright debacle. No exchange is straightforward. Most prejudgments are unfavorable. The hermeneutic of suspicion moves from the role of adjutant, where it is quite helpful, to the role of king, where it rides roughshod over the fragile bonds one needs to build collaborative enterprises, works of art, friendships, and people who pray to a Father they believe delights in them.

The second scenario, quite positive, comes from Ash Wednesday of the past Lent, when Walter Burghardt was preaching in our chapel in Tulsa. With a nice ecumenical touch, the choirmaster had prepared a Mozart Kyrie and Credo, which our kids in robes and sneakers sang like cherubim. I was amazed how quickly the tears came to my eyes and how long it took to swallow down the lump in my throat. Beauty ever ancient, ever new— how long since I had heard such praise of God? I thought of European cathedrals we have visited and the sense of tradition, continuity, solace handed down for centuries that they conjure up. I thought of Karl Rahner's forgiving the Church all its heartlessness and abuse, because it still has been a place where one could hear the words of eternal life, where one could receive the sacraments of immortality. Loving the almighty father, the maker of heaven and earth, of all things visible and invisible, that the Mozart credo was praising, I felt my cynicism melt away. Suddenly, it was minimalist expectations and stoic endurance that were on the defensive. Suddenly, the largess of God was obvious, and the burden of proof was on our human pusillanimity. And, with this came a Pauline anamnesis: If God is for us and has given us his Son, how can he fail to give us all things with him? Nothing can separate us from the love of God in Christ Jesus our Lord.

One of the several emphases of Rahnerian christology that helped to usher in a new phase of reflection on the meaning of Jesus was the insistence that we take seriously the fact that only the Logos, the Son, took flesh. On one level, this is stuff from the Baltimore Catechism. On another level, our failure to appropriate it in popular theology has contributed to our preaching and praying as though the community of divine persons did not exist. Practically, few Western Christians are trinitarians, aware that their exchanges of knowing and loving flow into and out from the processions of the divine knowing and loving. Practically, few Western Christians have appropriated with conceptual clarity the consequences of their being incorporated into the incarnate Logos, and so oriented toward the Father and the Spirit as Jesus was. Begotten from unbegotten, light from light—these primordial symbols mean little to most men I know, even those who pray. My own prayer is more apophatic than defined, but I love the drift of such symbols into the divine immensity, the fathomless memory that Augustine associated with the Father. The Abba of Jesus is the generativity of all creation, the explosive force of the stars, the strong bonds of the atoms, the light of the Logos who shines in every human insight. Yet Jesus, like Elijah, seems regularly to have experienced him as a small, still voice—as one so powerful he could be utterly gentle.

Primordial symbols such as these intertwine with our deepest psychic formation, making our relations with our parents what one might call our natal theological endowment. My father has been dead more than fifteen years; yet, as soon as I start to ponder trinitarian love, he is with me as though I were back in high school. It amazes me that my memories of him grow more and more compassionate. Apart from a few tearings up at beauty like that of a Mozart kyrie, I seldom cry. The last time I wept full out was at my father's wake, when the definitive proof of his vulnerability lay before me. I do not want to trade on his

alcoholism, his struggles to run a small business, his wasting by
cancer, but I do want to understand the poignancy they still
carry. The more he has moved away from my childish expectations of fatherhood, where I naturally looked for strength and
stability, the more patripassianism has seemed to me orthodox.
I do not mean, of course, that I want to contend literally for the
position that God the Father suffered on the cross. I mean that
the risk of God, the vulnerability of God, the engagement of
God the source in all the pathos of his creatures, have slowly
started to dawn. How one squares this with the perfection of
God, in which I also believe, can remain a question for another
day. Here, I am interested in the love summoned when one joins
the complete trustworthiness of God that Jesus depended on
with the risks of parenthood that any of our human fathers or
mothers has experienced. What could be more ordinary than
sexual attraction, conception, and birth—and what more extraordinary in creatures who now and then realize what they are
getting into?

Our Father, who is in heaven, presumably knew exactly what
he was getting into. Though creation as a work *ad extra* tradi-
tionally has been attributed to God as one, I find it especially
fitting to make the Lord's Prayer thanks for the decision of the
unbegotten source to communicate the divine substance beyond
the perfect, defectless sharing he has always had with the Son
and the Spirit to us very defective creatures. When God not only
makes us and saves us but divinizes us, takes us into the bosom
of the trinitarian relations, our mortal flesh should move on to
keeping silence, which often is our purest praise. The fatherhood of God, like the messiahship of Christ and the down-
payment on our immortality vouchsafed in the Spirit, is not too
strange to be believed but too good. Few things would do more
to revitalize the spirituality of Christian men than for us to take
to heart the trinitarian symbols of what God has given us, of the
way God always wants to be for us an Abba more intimate than
we are to ourselves.

The Spirit

Just as our conception of the fatherhood of God is shaped by
Christ's usage, so is our conception of the Holy Spirit. Jesus
seems to have prayed to God the Father and experienced the
guidance of God the Spirit.[6] And, I have already referred to the
role of comforter assigned the Spirit by the Johannine Christ.
But, average Catholic spirituality probably has done less developing the riches of the symbolism of the Spirit than it has done
with the Father. For weal or woe, our love of the Father is bound

up with our experience of human paternity. What experiences ought to give our love of the Spirit focus and resonance?

Certainly, we can explore the analogies to teaching, guiding, and comforting that Scripture suggests. Certainly wisdom, prophetic inspiration, brooding, and nursing also come to mind. The Johannine Spirit is "another" paraclete, which suggests that Jesus was the first and that the Spirit is carrying on invisibly what Jesus labored at visibly. I think any of these notions, perhaps especially those associated with wisdom, holds out rich promise. Whenever I have pondered the new, interior covenant foreseen by Jeremiah, I have hoped that the Spirit might be filling many hearts with ingiven, connatural knowledge. Whenever I have savored the Sequence for Pentecost, with its images of watering what is arid, washing what is dirtied, I have felt greatly comforted.

As many of these images suggest, the Spirit can bear us a feminine persona. God alone knows the way we may best handle the complications thrust upon us by today's awareness of sexist overtones in our traditional language for worship and our traditional theological conceptions, but, perhaps letting this feminine persona of the Spirit emerge into explicit consciousness would help. The reasons the Church fathers shied away from sexual analogies for the trinitarian persons no doubt were valid in their day, when the Hellenistic mysteries often had orgiastic overtones or dealt with fertility more materially than Christian instinct desired. In our day, however, divine fatherhood without divine motherhood can seem to warp our theology, and so our entire religious life. We may still want to avoid androgyny on the model of, for example, Hindu theology, but we should take a lesson from Jewish Wisdom, Buddhist Wisdom (*Prajnaparamita*), and Chinese reflection on the Tao, all of which carry feminine overtones. If we men were to begin to let the Spirit mother us, parallel to the way we should let the first trinitarian person father us, we might open a door to psychosymbolic energies we have kept shut to our detriment. The same would apply to women, all the more so in a time when feminists have been probing the ambiguities of mother-daughter relations.

My own mother is still living, and I have more work to do on my relation with her before I shall feel comfortable in publicizing implications for the love of God parallel to those I noted in my relations with my father. I can say, though, that a motif of deepening compassion for what she has suffered in her imperfect life and growing admiration for her courage suggests more likeness to what I have thought about divine fatherhood than difference.

The major hat that I wear is that of a writer, so sometimes I have experienced the Holy Spirit as a muse, a creative lover. Writing is a strange occupation, though perhaps no stranger than teaching, counseling, and other occupations greatly shaped by bio-rhythms and grooves one cannot control. If my experience is representative, those who write regularly never know precisely what they are going to come out with. We have our notes, our outlines, our heuristic suspicions, but what actually eventuates is always a surprise. Thus it is commonplace for novelists to speak of having a character lead them into situations they had not anticipated. It is common to hear theologians speak of unexpected twists and turns in the data, but less common to hear them speak of shifts wrought through their exposition of the data. That may suggest that most theologians are more scholars than writers: people more focused on their data than on summoning the phantasms in which insights into their data might be multiplied.

At any rate, writers like me are married to their muse. The conversation with the self that gets externalized on the screen of the word-processor involves more than the self, and sometimes quite obviously so. Probably the typical writer thinks that this more is the unconscious, the murky depths from which the most important glimmers and hunches pop up. However, there is no reason for the Christian writer, or the Christian worker in any other field that regularly depends on a modest inspiration, not to conceive of this process as an intercourse with the Holy Spirit. Many of the suggestions that come from one's depths carry marks of gratuity. Not all of them prove workable, of course— writers, too, must discern the spirits—but many of them imply that what is going on in one's depths includes a fairly regular reminding by a greater Spirit. If you can smile and abide it, you can use the simile of your mother's call not to forget your lunch (where you get your nourishment), or her rougher taking you by the shoulders and spinning you ninety degrees, so that you finally see the monkeys you were missing.

Intercourse with the spirit conjures up other possibilities, of course, and I want to use the rest of my space in this section to ponder them. Others thinking about a spirituality for men may have explored erotic love of the Spirit, but I have not seen much in this line. Usually, the discussion of spiritual marriage takes God as the bridegroom and treats the soul as the bride. From the Song of Songs to John of the Cross and Teresa of Avila, this has been a very profitable venture. But, I want to pursue the possibility of men extending their eros for women into spiritual depths where we would be romancing our God. If it is legitimate for women or the feminized soul to be both child of God and spouse, it should be legitimate for the masculine portion of our psyches to be both child of the maternal Spirit and lover of the divine beauty, fertility, subtlety, wisdom—all of the faces of God that by cultural tradition shine with a feminine smile.

Even in my acedia and secularity, I find days when I am ravenous for God. Sometimes it is the beauty of the day, with the sun dancing off the river. Recently, it was a delightful afternoon at the zoo, when two polar bears entertained us for an hour with their antics in the pool: wrestling, cannonballing, trying a little backstroke, hauling themselves out like the nimble Mark Spitz who never doubted he would win in a breeze. The play of nature in the spring, the release of all that sap, must have figured in the Aristotelian understanding of the good: that which all things desire. In the spring all of nature desires fertility, increase, prospering that we humans associate with intimate love. In the spring, the longing for God the consummate beauty seems but a gracious gilding of what all one's fellow creatures are feeling.

But, there are summer, fall, and winter variations on such eros. There is the love associated with the death of the days at the winter solstice, with the death of one's creativity in blockages, with the disappointment inevitably experienced with both fallible human beings and one's perhaps more fallible self. From depression and disgust can rise the most ardent longing: Get me out of this, help me find comfort, solace, fulfillment in a transcendent embrace. Pouring oneself into the Spirit, being taken to her bosom, perhaps we experience something of the divine mutuality and suffusion. In the Spirit the Father and the Son have their unity, their merely relational distinction. The Spirit who is their breath of love is also, in patristic usage, the kiss uniting them. Without the perfection and purity of the divine perichoresis, but still most usefully, we might play with the lovely Spirit, giving and receiving, praising and admiring. And, such a spiritual experiment might do wonders for our peculiarly, though of course not uniquely Catholic, unease with sexuality. If a fully passionate intercourse with the Spirit became legitimate, many of our questions about the theology of marriage and the single state, and many of our ethical dilemmas about contraception, artificial insemination, and even abortion might arrange themselves in new, less fearful patterns.

Part Two: The Love of Self

The Self as Embodied

If I were more clearly involved in a romance with the Holy Spirit than has been the leitmotiv of my spiritual life to date, I might do a better job at overcoming the dualism that seems to afflict all human beings, but perhaps especially men. This dualism appears in the masculine struggle to keep sexual appetite and love together and maintain an integral image of women. It appears in the many contemporary cultural movements to repristinate good health and emotional satisfaction, giving brother ass his due. Certainly, the struggles required to achieve wholeness are a major sign of our aboriginal division. Certainly, the Catholic convictions about sacramentality and grace's building on nature should be sufficient protection against the neo-paganism wafting in many discussions of diet, exercise, and emotional satisfaction.

At age thirty, I found myself in sunny California, looking for exercise. I went to the gym at Stanford and discovered that on the West Coast standing 5' 10" high meant never touching the basketball. Every kid seemed at least 6' 4." So, I bought Kenneth Cooper's book on aerobics and left the world of competition for the world of fitness, sure I was responding to a saintly daimon. Of course, immediately I began competing with myself, trying to get my time for the mile under seven minutes. And, whenever I could, I roared past some plausible equal on the homestretch, to the cheers of the Olympic crowd. But it was fun; it did push away the tensions of graduate school, and it brought back thoughts about my body that had first hatched when I was a "midget" swimmer.

As a ten year old, I was a great backstroker—the best in the circuit of New England Boys' Clubs at the awesome distance of twenty-five yards. As a twelve year old, I was into what was then considered serious training: a mile a day. And I did it willingly, somehow realizing that it was good for all of me, mind as well as body. When Cooper later gave me the concept, I realized that twenty years previously I had experienced the "training effect" prized by knights of the grail of cardio-vascular health. At the time, I had known only that when my second wind came, I would feel I could go on forever. Seventy-two laps made a mile, but one hundred were not beyond me.

I now swim and push the staves of a Nordic Track, still seeking the grail and enjoying the training effect. The swimming is like a return to the sea from which all of our genes came, a somatic homecoming. The skiing is a salutary exercise in working and working and going nowhere, perhaps like Gandhi's spinning wheel. For Gandhi, the spinning wheel symbolized *karmayoga*, the work done for its own sake, without desire. For me, each session on the Nordic Track now says things about aging and moderation, things the midget swimmer did not have to deal with. I have good days, usually correlated with winter cold and high pressure skies, when the temptation is to do too much. I have more draggy days, when the Tulsa heat and humidity call for another sort of caution. Slowly, I am accepting the fact that my tendency is to do too much rather than too little. Slowly, I am acknowledging the stitch in the side or the flutter in the chest that once I would have paid no mind. The body is such a marvel. It both does and does not have predictable patterns. Almost always I begin in heaviness, finding the exercise difficult and discouraging. At about 10-15 minutes the sweat starts to come, and my body says, "I like it." Anything beyond a half hour calls for conferences between body and mind, tricks to keep the legs pumping, reasons not to keep upping the goal. All of this is predictable, and yet, now and then I am sure I should go for a full hour. As well, now and then I cannot make twenty minutes, or the fine feeling that came from a brisk thirty-five minutes falls apart into a migraine. The fragile vessels in which we carry the life of God are not ours to command like computers. They are more like obedient servants who occasionally let us know they are fed up.

I imagine one could write similar reflections about patterns of hunger and satiety, patterns of sleep, patterns of sexual love, menstrual patterns, ups and downs in one's practice of medicine, teaching, or other works. In all of them the message I would expect is that our action is also a passion, our cooperation with the Holy Spirit is really a junior partnership.

As some readers perhaps noted, most of my suggestions for men's love of God suggested a more active role than traditional spirituality tended to propose. Especially with the Holy Spirit, but also with the Father and Christ, I found myself thinking thoughts of erotic initiative or compassionate appreciation that come from what might stereotypically be called men's strength. It is not that I want to deny men's weakness, nor the blessedness of feeling small yet safe in the house of God. It is just that when I tried to think of the ways of loving God that might engage me more than what I had been taught and now tend to do, these more active, perhaps more mature possibilities emerged. But, for this present matter of loving one's embodied self, the message coming to me from exercise and people-watching calls for greater moderation, seconding, and responsiveness. It sends me images of rejecting the workaholism I find rampant, the excess in many men's range of commitments. I want to take more time for prayer, thought, reading, leisure, romantic conversation, making love. I want to see more of God's beautiful world and show more flexibility in responding to cries for help. Maybe this, too, is a reflection of my trying to come to grips with middle age. This past year seemed to me a threshold, so that now often I no longer should, can, or fully want to swim an extra half mile or jam in another writing commitment.

I associate our so frequent overwork with the problem of loving the self that is embodied because usually the toll being taken shows itself in the ache in my neck and the irritability in voice. By the time summer comes and we get to the beach, I have narrowed my range of perception, appreciation, and pleasure to perhaps half of what it will be after the waves have worked their therapy. I am still not sure what the optimal balance is between the drive that gets things done and brings one to that peculiar fatigue that is highly creative and the drive that clearly is abusive and detrimental. Women, of course, have their drives, and perhaps more importantly the myriad ways they are put upon, but the paradigm of type A behavior I have in mind seems indebted to testosterone. With no wild boars and tigers to slay, no Visigoths to beat back, we men regularly displace our aggression onto our work, competing with nature, other workers, and ourselves for both the joy of it and the hell. Not only do we die younger than women, but we take a longer time to gain subtlety, wholeness, and what the Taoists call *wu-wei:* creative inaction, not-doing that makes everything run better. Good government, Lao Tzu says, is like cooking fish: the less stirring the better. Intrusive testosterone does not learn this easily. Receptive estrogen has a lot to teach it during those long winter nights when the hormones get to bundling.

So, to love the self God has given us, we middle-aged men probably need to think thoughts of letting go, praying for better perspective, trusting God to show us new, even better possibilities in ceding responsibilities, accepting retirements, appreciating the chant of ecological science that most intrusion is more complicated, and more deleterious, than we initially suspect. We need to convince ourselves that overwork is a vice—an ugly sin. We need to ask God for help in acting upon this conviction, when that will take us against the drift of our fellow-workers. And we need, finally, to think well of our bodies for finally forcing us to these matters. If we were wise, we would long ago have budgeted more time for our wives, children, and friends. Better late than never, though. As Rabbi Hillel said, If not now, when?

The Self as Spirit

Rabbi Hillel, like all religious masters, was especially interested in having people move their minds and hearts to the love of God. No doubt he wanted us to be kind to our bodies, but he realized that we come from dust and unto dust we all return. It is the spark in our clod, as Lonergan once put it, that rightly is judged more imperative. Only when we love the One God with whole minds, hearts, souls, and strengths, will our bodies be fully sacramental.

Extending the theme of mercy rather than sacrifice that I found exercise urging when it came to loving the self as embodied, let us now think kindly thoughts about our spirits, especially about the way the spirits of men usually have been formed to think, love, and pray. A book such as the recent and insightful *Women's Ways of Knowing* reminds us that the academic establishment still thinks of men's knowing as detached, impersonal, objective.[7] When it combines this assumption with an imposition of such a model on all students, women as much as men, it doubles the damages. Religious men and women may be somewhat comforted to note that the models of knowing suggested by prayer and community life dispute the academic stereotype. Any writers on prayer worth their salt soon come to contemplation, just as any epistemologists worth their salt soon deal with a judgment much deeper and more holistic than understanding. For a Michael Polanyi, our knowledge is more tacit than express, and in any venture it is wholly personal. For an Eric Voegelin, the only epistemologist who can appreciate the noetic breakthrough achieved by Plato and Aristotle is one who can sense the way God is the mover of our desire to know. *The Cloud of Unknowing* is perhaps the most apposite classic on the ways that interpersonal knowledge of God greatly relativizes what one can achieve by ratiocination. The advice of Einstein that one should attend to what scientists do in their creative work, rather than to the paradigms of scientific method they pontifically enounce, suggests that the regnant academic models no more respond to first rate science than they do to creative work in the humanities or the knowledge God gives in prayer.

The knowledge God gives in prayer, I suspect, is a knowledge well called faith, and well described as born of religious love. It is good to understand what one can of the creeds and the mainstream theologians, but God becomes a rock and salvation exorcizing our worst fears only when God has touched us heart to heart. We have to commune with God to know God, and unless we know God, we do not know the most important things about ourselves, other people, or the natural world. We have to speak to God, listen to God, and endure God's silences. Sometimes we will feel like a motherless child, adrift in an uncaring world. Sometimes we will feel like idiots, people so singular they neither understand others nor can be understood. These are the times when it is hard to love our spiritual selves, to think well of God's handiwork.

But, perhaps the hardest times come when we have run from God, hiding like our first parents. If we are honest, we know we have no excuse, not the thinnest fig-leaf to cover us. Adapting Augustine, we instinctively think, "It was foul, and I loved it." Imitating Judas, we exit into a night of further betrayal and despair, thinking even God can do little for us. Then, the love of ourselves has to hope that the Spirit will remind us that nothing can separate us, that God is always greater than our hearts. Then, we have to realize, in all humiliation, that we were but rookies, spouting the right words about sinfulness but not appreciating their omni-relevance. Let nothing disturb us, not even our sin? I want to believe it could be so. I want to think that love of self rests on the love of God that shines on just and unjust alike. If we ask God for the bread that is forgiveness as well as immortality, will God give us a stone? Is it possible to overstate the goodness of God, or our own foolishness in thinking we can block out the sun? No doubt we must not sin to magnify God's power of forgiveness, but when we do sin, must we not let that sin itself induce God to be Father, Brother, Lover?

The man who has an addiction, a dirty secret, the remorse of having been cold to his children, or just the fatigue of feeling himself a religious mediocrity probably finds it harder to bear these burdens than he might because his culture has warped his sense of self as much as it has warped his sense of the way he knows. When I worked briefly at the Boston City Hospital, or when I listened to friends who worked with the poor, I came to admire those who let themselves become familiar enough with grime, failure, and even betrayal to see them with clear eyes, even to feel them with forgiving hearts. Recently, I took a walk to a convenience store nearby to get some air, some oatmeal, a newspaper. On the way home, I saw a trio of Indians on the steps of a sagging house, marked "Bailbondsman." The two men were in jackets and jeans, appropriate to the forty degree weather. The woman, sitting on the steps, wore only a thin, short-sleeved blouse, and she was crying. I wondered why she was crying, but so many possibilities came to mind that thinking about that seemed futile. So, I seized on the reason she had no jacket, and the reason one of the men didn't give her his. I was well past before I thought of giving her mine, and somehow aware that the men would take offense. But, the woman is still there in my mind, cold and crying.

Ah, Lord, what do we do with all the cold and crying of the world's five billions? What does that do to their bodies, their spirits, the spirits of us spectators? I feel guilty not only for my own sins but for my place in the system of sin summoned to mind by an abused Indian woman. Comfortable and metaphysical, I probe the compassion that might ease the fallenness of history, realizing as I do that I have virtually given up on economics and politics. Voegelin took as one of his touchstones what the most idealistic people make of the politics of their era. Weaned on Socrates and Plato, forced to run for his life from Nazi Austria, he was not optimistic. What does it do to the spirit of good men when their impulse to take charge and set things right comes back at them like a boomerang stamped "useless"? What does it do to the spirit of any of us when our Church wants no dissent and insists that the female half of us cannot represent Christ at the sacraments?

We need gentle spiritual succor, offered to those most burdened by such evils, and offered by ourselves to ourselves. We need the Spirit's help in spreading on the wounds a balm that might keep depression from becoming despair. Nothing can separate us from God, not even the Church of God, which of course we are. As long as God is God, any idealistic generation may marshal the critical mass and start an exodus out of slavery, back to the foundations of genuine patriotism and pride in the Church. The problem is not that the spiritual masters have left us no wisdom about right order. The problem is that we, the mass of us human beings, do not know this wisdom and will not use it. Money, honors, and pride—what spiritual tradition has not estimated their dangers like an architect imagining every possible stress and strain? If we cannot achieve the full therapy of moving our culture to re-embody right order, we can at least succor our spirits in meditative reading and prayer.

For my own spirit, I am moving toward a redefinition of my work, with hopes that when I reach fifty, I shall have fulfilled the obligations incurred through years of trying to earn a living and be able to labor at a new sort of theology, a reflection interested in the traces of right order that God has left everywhere. The content is not so important at this present juncture as the therapeutic goal. I want to work at what offers the best prospects for healing and strengthening people's spirits. I want to pay back to the Rahners and Lonergans, the Voegelins and Polanyis, the pittance that a grateful disciple can. And, I want to do this with explicitly contemporary Catholic faith, occupying the hardly demilitarized zone between Roman theology and the riches of all the religious treasuries God has inspired. It is a quixotic task, but I love to contemplate it. In contemplating it, I find I am loving my spiritual self, because I am finding grounds for hoping that soon I may be able more leisurely, more avowedly, to study the ways of God, especially those as far from our destructive own as the heavens are from the earth, and to help publicize the freedom they offer.

Part III: The Love of Neighbor

Women

The Christian golden rule, presumably very important to any Christian spirituality, is that we should love our neighbors as ourselves. In the present section, let us reflect on what this might mean for the love today's men show women. My first impulse is to say that a spirituality for men would be innovative and helpful if it merely brought us to show women considerably more warmth, understanding, and playfulness. One of the important strands in the malaise between the sexes is our legacy of mistrust. This legacy, in turn, owes much to the spiritual writers who depicted women as the main dangers to men's religious fidelity. Other factors certainly pitched in, but the contribution of Christian tradition to the souring of what ought to be mutual delight between men and women is a sorry chapter. Our fathers have eaten sour grapes, so all of us today have our teeth set on edge about sexuality. In the popular mind, sex is the Catholic neurosis, and the popular mind is quite right.

Over the years I have dealt with a number of women suffering through bad marriages. I have been amazed how much they have accepted from blocked, stupid, hurtful husbands. They have had their own failings, of course, but again and again their disorder and sickness have seemed a mirror of their husbands'. One of the most poignant things I have witnessed has been the loss of confidence even gifted, beautiful women have suffered. They have been so grateful for a little admiration and affection that I have learned to offer these quite carefully.

I do not think this means that men should reenforce their stereotypical image of strength, silence, and having no needs. I do think it means that listening, showing affection, and being playful are no mean virtues. With spouses, friends, little girls, men have an opportunity to make the primordial other in women's experience, the most basic stranger, seem trustworthy rather than threatening. Certainly, women are not automatically bonded to other women and certainly, one of the rightful goals of feminism is to help women overcome the cultural trends that would make them distrust other women. But, it remains that men are somatic strangers as fellow women are not, and this is only intensified when most men are physically stronger and culturally more prized. More times than not, women are dealing with men who possess more power—physical, financial, institutional—than they do. More times than not, men first honor the Christian golden rule by being aware of this and trying to undercut it. When men communicate that they think of women

as their intellectual equals, when they suggest that they value
women's experience as much as men's and have at least a
glimmer about women's problems, they contribute a reconciliation, an atonement, at least as foundational as that redressing
economic or racial grievances.

From this initial stress on showing appreciation and affection,
men then have to move to the other side of equality, which
implies receiving as well as giving. Receiving is at least as
complicated as giving. Sacramentally, for example, men have
been willing to minister to women, but to date our male-
dominated Church is not willing to sanction a full ministry of
women to men. Of course, all sorts of ministries go on both
formally and informally, but many more are aborted because
male power-holders cannot see themselves receiving the eucharistic Christ from women. Giving and receiving ideally balance,
so the spirituality for equals we are probing implies an even
flow. Part of the flow is the gifts the two genders have evolved
throughout history, and part is peculiar to the given exchange.
So women offer receptivity and fertility, while men offer initiative and protection. Yet, Mary A is quicker off the mark than her
husband John Z, so in their household she initiates the financial
planning, the moves to new jobs, the sex, while he provides the
second thoughts, the seconding affirmations, the late night
"What a good idea!"

Their love of women should make men think of the biblical
"flesh of my flesh and bone of my bone," without the
patriarchalism of Adam's rib. It should be the main delight in
most men's lives, extended when the women they love are
reflected in their children. I do not think fathers should spoil
their daughters, but I can understand the reason they do. Here
is a miniature of the bounce and vulnerability that first seized
their hearts; so, even when it is bratty, they may tend to indulge
it. And, as long as our cultures ask women to represent beauty
more than they ask men, fathers will have a special obligation to
help their daughters feel they are beautiful. To be sure, this
should go along with helping them feel they are bright and
capable. It should not encourage manipulation nor the
daughters' becoming clinging vines. But, it should let them think
that snuggling in a man's embrace is part of their blessed
birthright. It should give them a foundational confidence that
they can give their beauty, their fertility, their competence, their
love because it will be cherished and returned.

I have the feeling that what I have said thus far risks
sentimentality, but I do not want to qualify it any further. Often
my wife's observations have led me to think that many women
who are in pain actually ask very little—which, of course, only

doubles the poignancy of their situations. I am not thinking of the statistics that show how many more of the burdens of poverty fall on women, and the children for whom women have the primary care, than fall on men, though these statistics are a fine antidote to sentimentality. I am thinking of the nun who works as a campus minister for $9,000 a year and cannot even get her bishop to answer her letters. I am thinking of the divorced woman who cannot get her ex-husband to visit their sons. I am thinking of the woman whose husband rarely makes love to her, largely because he stays up so late each night working and drinking. And, I am thinking of the myriads of women, the great groaning chorus, who complain that their men will not talk to them, are unwilling to share.

Sometimes women do not understand the pressures on men, and sometimes they do not understand a healthy male taciturnity; but, on the whole I find women usually willing to go 60% of the way. It is possible that the Indian woman who was sitting on the porch of the bailbondsman was the main culprit in that scene of domestic tragedy, but the odds seem against it. Women certainly have to work on their sins of weakness, but I sympathize with the complexity such work must carry. If they are able to preserve the receptivity, the slowness to rush to judgment, and the instinct to nurture people on which so much of childrearing, education, and healing have depended, women are bound to risk overindulging male egos and not standing up for their own rights. How much better it would be if men could muster the subtlety to offer women a love that was protective and caring without being patronizing or disabling. How much better it would be if, as equals, men and women got into a flow of mutual caring and mutual challenging, so that both could be receptive and critical. We are not going to overcome in a generation the patterns developed throughout centuries, nor are we going to outrun our bodies and our hormones. But, right now we could speak more frankly to one another, in both admiration and criticism, and we could play together much better.

This is the last point I want to stress. I think the attraction natural to men and women regularly should make our interactions delightful. When we joke, satirize, even flirt, we of course run all sorts of risks and set in play all sorts of stereotypes and conditionings. But, we can do this knowingly, with awareness, and so provide mutual correction. And, when we do develop male-female friendships—twosomes, foursomes, groups—in which healthy laughter flows in many directions, we provide ourselves prime analogates for the Church. The Church is the community bonded in Christ's love. Christ's love makes human existence a comedy, in Dante's sense of the word. So, the laughter of men and women, our mutual delight in the sexual existence God has given us, is virtually the same as our hymns of praise and thanksgiving. As a male psalmist today might put it, "What a work is woman—You've made her little less than the angels, and much more fun to squeeze."

Men

If I am to love other men as I love myself, I shall have to show them many of the same things I want to show women. My analysis of love of the self, both embodied and spiritual, suggested that a tender care is often the prime desideratum. There is no reason this should not be true for men's love of one another. Just as one can rightly add that love of self also has to include discipline and challenge, one can rightly add that good male friends keep one another on their toes. But, at the core of the male friendships I most treasure, as at the core of the love I received from my father and think I experience from Christ, is an acceptance both gentle and unconditional. My father did not push me faster than I wanted to go, perhaps because he observed that I was already pushing myself. Christ has been patient in the extreme with my neglect and stupidity, never overbearing. My best friends do tell me the truth. They do speak up when they think I am wrong. But, the wider context always makes it clear that whether or not I accept what they have to say, they will continue to love me.

Spurred by the task of writing this essay, I have thought about the characterization of men as most crippled by an inability to name their feelings. Women frequently voice this characterization, and now and then so do men. I think men have been making some progress with this problem, no doubt in part due to the sorts of groups I disparaged earlier, but we have many miles to go. One index is the rarity of easy exchanges of personal information and feelings among male acquaintances. If my experience is representative, even men I know quite well speak much more about their work than their hopes and fears, much more about educational theory or theology than about what they long for with their students or what troubles them at prayer.

The healthy male taciturnity that I mentioned previously can explain some of this phenomenon, but by no means the whole. As much as most men, I turn silent when I feel others are trying to hype up my emotions or get me to describe my feelings because it would be interesting. I feel fortunate in having been trained to discern the spirits working in me, and to have received an education that highlighted interiority. I have enjoyed many benefits from having been formed by childhood experiences toward quiet and introspection. So, I judge that if a man who has had much less opportunity to come to know himself and own up to his own feelings finds personal discussion difficult, he deserves a lot of sympathy. Often he gets this sympathy from women, and as long as they do not baby or flatter him, they do him a great service.

Too many of my intimate talks with men have occurred when they had had too much to drink; and yet, even at those times, I have felt that getting their fears out was worth the liabilities. I remember stopping my grammar school shop teacher in his tracks by asking him whether he thought people were more or less truthful when drunk. Ten year old kids were not supposed to ask such questions, were not supposed to need to know.

I think one of the things boys most need from men is assurance that the men once found sex troubling or sometimes struck out in the clutch, just as the boys presently are experiencing. I think kids have the right to adults' respect—to being told the truth, apologized to when it is appropriate, taken seriously, and even being let know that adults need them, would feel half of life's lights had gone out were the kids not around.

I have often thought about what I owe my niece, who is now ten years old, and recently I have started thinking about what I owe my nephew, who is charging toward two. I noticed that when he first met me, he let me pick him up, because he was used to that from people my size, but that it took several days before he would turn his head toward me. "You've got my body," he was saying, "but you've got to show you're worthy of my trust." I do not fear the task of earning his trust, because I believe that all anyone rightly can ask of us is honesty and love, that these are what we want to give, more often than not, and that, when we do give them, things usually turn out well. After being in my arms in a swimming pool for half an hour or so, my nephew fell sound asleep. No doubt this was more simple fatigue than any grand act of trust, but it completed his stealing my heart.

With nephews and male friends, as with nieces and the women we love, the trick is having our hearts stolen. Love is a willing entanglement. Ideally, we know what we are letting happen, but we also feel drawn by a Spirit with purposes beyond our ken. I know my nephew could turn out a bounder, a rotter, all those other things the British public school system has eloquently named. I doubt that he will; but even if he did, his stealing my heart should only help him. The prejudice in his favor love gives him should not mean I would turn my eyes from evidence of bad character or bad habits. It should not mean I would in the least countenance his doing drugs or not working in school. But, it should keep any problems such as this, as well as any successes he has, in perspective: framed by the gift of new life he made plain to me, the sacred benefaction he bestowed by letting me into his trust.

Friendship and care between adult men, of course, are more complicated, but many of the verities about trust remain. In listening to friends out of work grope toward acknowledging how demoralized they feel, I have found myself praying to be faithful to their confessions. In reflecting on another vaguely unsatisfying lunch with a bright colleague, I have found myself wondering whether we will ever get beyond scholarly notations and the exchange of new ideas. I have also wondered whether I am not more to blame for our superficiality than he, since I groan at the prospect of taking on another of the sets of burdens that intimate knowledge brings.

Love brings burdens—I have not worked this theme very much. Set me as a seal upon your heart, and I cannot so easily dismiss you when you are inconvenient. The impersonality of busy men, and busy women, may bespeak a sort of honesty: I just cannot make the commitment that seeing you whole might entail. Most people who find themselves in the helping professions can recall many times when they knowingly discouraged intimacy. From time to time I think of overtures to which I deliberately did not respond, feeling guilty that few of them came from attractive people. At some point all of us can plead finitude and fatigue, but we probably reach that point much quicker than Jesus, who has put up with so much importunity and neglect from us.

With the men whom I sense providence has sent me, I try to be attentive and trustworthy. I instinctively cut back on the wisecracking and try to listen more from the center. Men's codes are probably as subtle as women's, because most men have less notion of what they are sending. Indeed, by the rules of our game you are supposed to be sending polysemously. John Wayne says what he thinks, and neither friend nor foe ever gets it wrong. But, many men talk more than they listen, often talk to find out what they think. And, many men keep a firm defense against thoughts that would lead them to tender places of conscience, or to the hurts that could make them cry. So, we do business with a brief locking of eyes, a small softening of voice. For the moment, these convey sympathy, solidarity, willingness to be available should more be needed. Then it is back to the upbeat, positive projection that salesmen and clergy have inflicted on the mass of us. Our business has to be going well, showing a profit, because otherwise we would be wimps. I would like to see more positive projection about the grace we are sure God is always giving, and more honest, humorous discussion of the problems we have to solve. I would like to see macho men decisive and reliable, rather than brutal and inconsistent. Just as real men can learn to eat quiche, although I doubt it can ever become their favorite food, so real men can learn that strength means doing what one promises, what one knows is right, what it takes to love other people with at least faint echoes of the way Christ loves them.

The Church

My final focus for love of neighbor is the Christian community. In developing this focus I do not mean to imply that we should treat those who are not Christians with any less care and sympathy. Indeed, one of my touchstones for a healthy ecclesiology is the extent to which the Christian community is not dusting its own navel but is trying to serve the whole world the means of fuller humanization. By this touchstone, a depressing fraction of Church discussions seem unhealthy. For example, the participants in the symposium on the state of American Catholicism, published in the March, 1987, issue of *New Oxford Review*, seem unconscionably insular. First, one notes that all eleven of them are men. Someone, presumably the organizer of the symposium for NOR, has an impossibly narrow view of American Church membership. In less benign interpretation, someone sensed that the most volatile issues in the American Church now swirl around the status of women and so deliberately tilted the game. Second, I noted that these eleven men egregiously ignored what I, following Karl Rahner, would call the cardinal mysteries of Christian faith. Compared to the time the authors spent on abortion, Roman authority, obedience, the pros and cons of dissent, the accommodation to paganism, and other supposed peculiarities of American Catholicism, the time spent on Trinity, Grace, and Incarnation was scandalously miniscule. After reading these fairly representative pundits, I seriously doubted they have much understanding of Catholic Christianity.

For Catholic Christianity, the life of God is far more absorbing than the bickerings of Church members. No doubt few commentators would disagree with this thesis, so baldly put, but in practice the majority ignore it. Moreover, the life of God pulses in all human beings, at least virtually, and most of the function of the Church, in a sacramental ecclesiology, is to signify what is going on always and everywhere. Conservatives are quick to denigrate such a starting point, arguing that it minimizes the importance of the Church and takes the heart out of missionary activity. There is some danger of such a minimizing, but the more blatant reality is that divinity itself has set the agenda in these terms. If Christians are less than 25%of God's people, the explicitly Christian assembly should not hog the theology of the gathering of God's people. In my opinion, what ecclesiology should most be seeking is demonstrations, both lived and theoretical, of the blessings that Christian faith can bring to any culture's search for the fuller humanity. As Lonergan noted, theology mediates between faith and culture. The most important invariant of Christian faith is the saving love of God manifested in Jesus Christ, while the most important invariant of culture is human beings' need for meaning and forgiveness. A theology that makes more of the papacy or sexual morality than of these invariants has its head in the bowl.

The Church we must love is both the city raised on a hill, showing all people of good will the graciousness of God, and the motley crew of sinners and roustabouts who make the graciousness of God hard to accredit. Ideally, we Christians would treat other people as our equals, giving and receiving from the stores of wisdom both of us had received. We would not speak of chosenness. Any special status we would claim would be fully earned, by our demonstrable wisdom and service. Actually, we continue to be embarrassingly chauvinistic, as just about any document from Rome illustrates. Check the footnotes in the document on the norms concerning artificial insemination and other facets of the new bio-sexual technologies. Can any authority quote only itself and expect the world to find it a humble servant, to believe it cares what others think? Do manly authors eschew self-criticism?

And, of course, this authority only compounds its problems when it forbids dissent on all matters where it has pronounced, fallible as well as infallible. Charles Curran's account of his experiences with Rome merely confirms what has long been obvious.[8] The authorities given to us by God think of us, the Church general, as children who should be seen (contributing money), but not heard. Worse, they think of us as little cheerleaders, who should happily shake our pompoms to whatever tunes they presently are piping.

And yet, I think we must reckon with the God-givenness of this authority, as we must reckon with the sinfulness the Church has always carried, not least in ourselves. I have most been helped to love the real, gnarled, often ugly Church by those who focused on the treasures the Spirit still polishes within it. The more I despise the hurt many Church officials produce, and their stupid flouting of their own decrees on religious liberty, the more I am amazed that the stream of saintly wisdom, the beauty of Mozart masses, the reality of self-sacrificing ministry continue to flow. Bathing in that stream, I am able to forget for a while the detritus thrown up by Christian sinfulness and abuse of authority. God is greater than we who compose the Church. The branches have significance only in the measure they serve the vine. Many people who think they are leaving the Church never leave the vine. All people who continue to love what the Church sometimes has been, and always keeps flickering, can take as their birthright from God the right to speak their minds and vote with their feet.

Despite its many unattractive features, the Church continues to mediate God's grace. One of my colleagues in Tulsa is a Jewish teacher of creative writing. She has gotten immersed in the movement for nuclear disarmament, and the community she has sought out makes Catholic priests and sisters her main friends. Another colleague is a cradle Catholic, highly sophisticated and critical, yet always going back to what he learned at the Catholic Worker or from the leaders of the Neothomist revival. Any people seriously interested in spirituality soon look into the world religions, and usually they have a period of fascination with Catholic mysticism. Any people interested in liberating the poor soon run into Latin American liberation theology. One can argue that the papal dress and pageantry are anachronistic, but one cannot gainsay the fascination it still exerts.

What both amuses and pains me in the recent strategies of Church authorities is their shocking amnesia. Obviously, the most beloved Christian leader in recent memory was Pope John XXIII, but few Church leaders seem to have grasped the reason that came to be. So, altogether too much like our recent American presidents, they present the persona of the tough-guy. I think John XXIII was the real man, so let me conclude by reflecting briefly on his love for the Church.

It was a love full of warmth. It was a love wanting to promote freedom. John's first instinct was not fear, as the first instinct of Paul VI seemed to be. It was not to impose authority, as the first instinct of John Paul II seems to be. It was to convey solidarity, common humanity, the sense that all human beings are in it together. The "it" was God's romance with the world, as John's Christian faith led him to interpret history. The first word from God was yes, and the first word from John was yes.

I realize that John was quite traditional in his piety and that he made no radical break with the traditional papal symbolisms. Far more importantly, however, he broke with the almost hundred year old assumption that all wisdom resided in Rome and opened the windows to the rest of the world. Today, one has to sympathize with the burden that he has placed on his successors. He was a very hard act to follow. If we commoners in the Church were to take him as seriously as Paul VI and John Paul II have, no doubt he would seem more threatening to us, too. Yet, I hope we would still find his first word to be yes, his first instinct to be trust, and the import of these first things the lesson we should place first. Our faith is that God loves us, that God cares for us, that God numbers each hair of any of our heads. Whatever our nationality, race, sex, faith, virtue, wealth, intelligence, God cares more for the divine child he sees within us. Mothering this child, God remains the crux of any viable spirituality, past or present, female or male. Long live God.

NOTES

[1] See John Carmody, *The Heart of the Christian Matter* (Nashville: Abingdon, 1983); *Holistic Spirituality* (New York: Paulist, 1983).

[2] Barry Lopez, *Arctic Dreams* (New York: Charles Scribner's Sons, 1986), p. xx.

[3] See James V. Schall, *The Distinctiveness of Christianity* (San Francisco: Ignatius, 1982).

[4] See Avery Dulles, *A Church to Believe In* (New York: Crossroad, 1983).

[5] See Lucas Grollenberg, *Jesus* (Philadelphia: Westminster, 1978).

[6] See James D.G. Dunn, *Jesus and the Spirit* (Philadelphia: Westminster, 1975).

[7] See Mary Field Belenky et al., *Women's Ways of Knowing* (New York: Basic Books, 1986).

[8] See Charles E. Curran, *Faithful Dissent* (Kansas City: Sheed and Ward, 1986).

"Springs of Water in a Dry Land": A Process Model of Feminist Spirituality

Mary Jo Weaver

In the moving passages that begin Second Isaiah, the prophet speaks the words that Handel would later set so magnificently to music in the *Messiah:* "Comfort my people, . . . speak tenderly to them, . . . I will make the wilderness a pool of water and the dry land springs of water." Although these heavily messianic texts were later used by Christians to interpret the life and work of Jesus, they had a different meaning for post-Exilic Jews. In order to comfort a thoroughly demoralized people, the author of Second Isaiah made a radical re-interpretation of the ancient wilderness traditions of the exodus story. I believe that many Christian feminists are in the process of trying to re-define the desert for themselves, as the author of Second Isaiah did for his constituency.

Images of Wilderness

Although the original exodus did not lead to Jerusalem, the author of Second Isaiah says that now the people will walk through the waters, parted by God's powerful hand, and march, joyfully, to Zion, singing all the way (Is 51:9–13). The original exodus experience contains stories about thirst and the need for water, but they are stories of rebellion as well as comfort (Ex 17; Num 20; Dt 32.48.52), whereas the water images in Second Isaiah are pure comfort and lavish tenderness on the part of the deity. The later biblical author, therefore, used the most ancient and sacred texts of his tradition to create something new. He was able to give meaning to his own situation by reviving the old story of conflict and abandonment into a song of nurturance and delight. In so doing, he re-created the wilderness and gave the desert a new, celebratory meaning.

The original exodus experience, on which Second Isaiah built a new interpretation, was a troubled time: people were dramatically rescued from oppression only to be plunged into an experience of community and expectation that they claimed to find more oppressive than the Egyptian slave drivers from whom they had just escaped. When they believed they were dying of thirst and cried out for water, their needs were heard as complaints and their thirst understood as a metaphor for insatiability. The original wilderness, as remembered in the book of Numbers, was a harsh place, and the original characters, contentious wanderers, were apparently faithless, rebellious, and occasionally the objects of divine wrath.

The Isaian wilderness, on the other hand, was a *new* desert. There, people were tendered by God, and reminded of the loving deeds of creation; they were brought back from the abysmal experience of the exile and promised a new life in a new Jerusalem. They were encouraged to "sing a new song" and to put on beautiful garments. A new revelation unfolds in the poetry of the author: we meet a God who suffers with people; who comforts and serves; who persuades and responds. The Isaian re-interpretation, coming as it does after the destruction of Jerusalem, encourages people to rekindle their dreams and renew their trust in divine faithfulness. It makes it possible to believe in the future, to outstare the emptiness of the exile with the determined belief that still to come is a time in which all things will be made new.

Whether contemporary Christian feminists consider themselves to be in exile from their homeland, or on an adventurous escape from the land of the Pharaohs, they may find it useful to remember that beneath their fears and blindness, the liberated slaves maintained a conviction that God *was,* somehow, guiding them to the promised land and that the promises of a new Jerusalem grounded the hopes of the Jewish exiles. Christian feminists may need to hold onto these stories because their own wilderness experiences are very real and frighteningly similar to those found in the Bible. No longer "at home" in the oppressive land of Egypt, we cannot return there, however much we may long for its savory dishes and its painful, but familiar, security. At the same time, in exile from our religious tradition, we cannot yet see the "new Jerusalem," and so cannot always go forward with much confidence. Many feel abandoned by a divine being who has brought us to a morbid place where there seems to be neither food nor water. And, if we find solace in the promise of something new, it may be an ambivalent kind of comfort. Like those of the Hebrews who felt that they had to choose between dying in a wasteland or returning to slavery and oppression, our choices may appear to be bleak: religious alternatives are either not yet clear, or, if clear, not altogether congenial, and our own tradition[1] is killing us.

The biblical characters were alienated, oppressed, enslaved, and finally forced to flee in order to preserve their lives. Many women in the Catholic Church, when they discover the misogynist heritage of their own tradition, suffer profound alienation. They experience the liturgy as oppressive in a deeply painful way since it appears to betray the God of their deepest desire. In realizing how dramatically the parish structure depends upon the good will of the pastor and, at the same time, living under the direction of an insensitive or hostile priest, women know something of enslavement. Finally, the double bind they find themselves in forces them to choose between survival on someone else's terms or survival on their own.[2] Many flee to what I am here calling the wilderness. Although their desert is not a life-giving place, it may well be a life-discovering place. Contemporary women, like the Hebrews before them, can remember the covenant and hope that they will find the promised land. Failing that, exiled women, like the Jews addressed by Second Isaiah, can gather in the desert to sing a new song and anticipate something radically new.

The Experience of Alienation

The texts, traditions, language, pastoral care, and structures of Catholicism alienate women. All contain explicit, implicit, and structural devaluations of women.[3] One need only recall that before the women's movement began to have an impact on Catholicism, almost everything we read about ourselves—about our natures, aspirations, and sources of fulfillment—was written by male celibates. Paradigmatically, women were either subservient, ennobling creatures like Mary, or independent, temptresses like Eve, and behind this schizophrenic view of women lay centuries of misogynist writing aimed at avoiding real women either by mystification or slander.

Beneath the rhetoric about Mary and motherhood, Catholic feminists discovered a deep well of prejudice against women. In the texts and laws of the Church, women are said to be naturally unclean, spiritually dubious, unfit for service on the altar, intellectually inferior to men, dangerously seductive in youth, and garrulous in old age. Virtually all of this insulting material has been presented as God's will and has been used to justify the religious form of sex role stereotyping known as complementarity.[4] Since God created women as inferior beings, complementary to men, so the reasoning goes, Church teaching is bound to uphold and perpetuate the natural order of things by replicating the divine design. The literature and assumptions of Catholicism about women, therefore, assume divinely-willed differences that relegate women to secondary positions. In other words, they alienate women.

Oppression and Enslavement

In the weekly experience of liturgy and the ongoing life of women in the parish, oppression is real and very painful. In the few studies that actually ask women to name their own experience in the parish, it is clear that women still working within the parish structure feel invisible, powerless, unwelcome, and trivialized.[5] They hear the sexist language of the liturgy as rejecting or hostile, and many believe that the Church's refusal to ordain women is a reminder of division and inequality. Those women who manage to maintain a hopeful attitude in this situation admit to being tired and not nourished anywhere near the proportions in which they feel drained by their work for the Church. They are, in other words, oppressed, even in situations where they are working in some kind of ministry.

Furthermore, as the Hebrews were subject to the will of the Pharaoh, women are in bondage to the whim of their pastors. Those who are happy in their present situation can hope only that their bishop will make no personnel changes, whereas those who are currently enslaved by a misogynist pastor can pray fervently only that a new priest will make their lives better. Whether parish styles emphasize organization, social action, teaching, service, ethnicity, hospitality, or sacramental activity, the main character is still the pastor.[6] The climate for women in the Church, therefore, is set by the attitudes and behavior of members of the clergy and rests upon an adage many Catholics no longer believe, that "Father knows best."

Studies show that many women have difficult interactions with their priests. Those women who have been interviewed about their relationships with their pastors have struggled to define the sources of their discontent. Some of them acknowledge that general cultural formation leads to insensitivity toward women, and others blame seminary training and enforced celibacy; but, most felt that priests are simply uninterested in and unprepared to deal with family violence, rape, divorce, unwanted pregnancy, single parenting, birth control, abortion, widowhood, and other so-called "women's issues."

Women in a Double Bind

These experiences of alienation, oppression, and enslavement combine to put Catholic women in a tragic double bind situation, forced to choose between oppression and exile. If they stay within the structure, they are defined as secondary beings and given only tasks appropriate to those at the bottom of the hierarchical ladder. They may have relatively more status in these days of vocational crisis, i.e., women might be serving as parish administrators in some cases; but, they still operate under male direction and have no real power within the institution. Those who embrace traditional roles and structures have to cast a blind eye to the social changes for women in the world around them: they are in bondage to an identity that has been decreed for them.[7]

Those who simply try to survive in spite of the hardships of the situation, who are not happy where they are but have no where else to go, have to use a significant portion of their liturgical energy ignoring sexist language, discriminatory practices, and the invisibility of women's talents, ideas, and power within the Church. Every Mother's Day "Father" will tell them what motherhood is all about, and they can bask in the glow of a tradition that elevates "womanhood" while it denies power to real women and stifles their possibilities. They will have to explain to their daughters that they might one day be a justice of the Supreme Court, but never a priest; and, in searching for an explanation of that ban, they will confront a tradition that perceives women as ritually unclean, spiritually unfit, and physically inappropriate for sacramental service.[8] Whether or not middle-aged women can accept traditional explanations for inferior status is not so important as whether their daughters will. Beneath resigned acceptance, therefore, is the real possibility that subsequent generations will not benefit from it. Such is the life of those who remain in the land of the Pharaohs. Here in this tragic place, full of pain and frustration, many Catholic women attempt to survive.

Those who stay within the parish as rebels, who attempt to subvert the system, to make a case for women from within the Church, often find very little support from other women. Perhaps it is unrealistic to expect much support. Moses's passionate act in support of his people, the killing of the Egyptian taskmaster, neither galvanized the Hebrews nor inspired them to work together for a better life. Those who profess contentment with the *status quo,* or who see no viable alternatives, may actively work against rebellious women, whereas those with a raised feminist consciousness may have already moved on.

Because rebels are perceived by the pastor as meddlesome or threatening, and because they often cannot find a community within the parish, such women, at first fueled by and later drained by their anger, sooner or later may find themselves simply running out of steam.

Reform-minded women who stay "in the Church" in order to change it may be in the ironic position of finding their most spiritually enriching support from two groups that are *officially* defined as "out of the Church." The first group has, by *its own definition,* "left the Church"; but, if "recovering Catholics" are alienated from patriarchal Catholicism, they have not necessarily abandoned their desire for religious community and prayer. Today, many of them are involved in alternative religions, including meditation groups, Native American ritual practices, attempts to recover what many call "the Old Religion," that is to say, Goddess worship and witchcraft. As such, they make ecumenical dialogue a radically different experience, and they constitute a potentially rich source of new religious energy.[9] Members of the second group have been defined by Rosemary Ruether as "a community in exodus from patriarchy,"[10] though they are perceived by ecclesiastical officials as renegades, heretics, or in some other way effectively "out of the Church." Many of this latter group are actively involved in a still undefinable movement known as "womenchurch." Their search for religious alternatives, while genuinely open to insights from nature religions and alternative traditions, is also informed by and indebted to some of the rich heritage of Roman Catholicism.[11] One highly valuable feature of the womenchurch movement is its refusal to relinquish its place in the Church, a refusal that makes a clear distinction between abandoning patriarchy and "leaving the Church."

Womenchurch and Traditional Catholicism

Those of us who perceive ourselves as "womenchurch" understand that we cannot separate our lives in Church from our lives in the world, however much we might want to do so. We cannot protect ourselves and our children from reality. Ironically, we also know that we cannot protect the Church either: we cannot pretend that it lives in a time and space of its own, unaccountable to the ledgers of social justice.[12] I believe, therefore, that our redefinition of ourselves as Church, while it may be a metaphorical flight to the wilderness, is *not* a rejection of the tradition. We are not leaving the Church, but are, instead, abandoning a model of Church life that we no longer find persuasive.

Most Catholics grew up in a Church that gave us a sense of security. We belonged to the true Church. The pre-Vatican II paradigm was classical and conservative: it stressed hierarchical order and control, conceptual permanence, monarchical direction, edict morality, and clear lines of ecclesiastical demarcation. When James Joseph Walsh wrote *The Thirteenth, Greatest of Centuries*,[13] he invoked the pride Catholics had in the old paradigm, though he thoroughly romanticized it and joined a number of turn of the century conservatives whose ideal was a grateful and obedient people ruled over by a wise and benevolent pontiff.

Post conciliar Catholics follow a paradigm that began to emerge in the eighteenth century, the historical, progressive model that shaped much of the work of the Council. It stresses community and communion, developmental symbols, collegial leadership, representative ethics, and ecumenical diversity. I believe we are living in a time when these two paradigms—which we might call hierarchical and equalitarian, or, to borrow terminology from the women's movement, patriarchal and feminist—are engaged in a battle for supremacy. From the patriarchal point of view, women constitute the last *line of defense:* if their position gains support, then the walls of the old system collapse. From the feminist perspective, women's issues are the *last frontier:* our questions open up new worlds of possibility for humanity.

The old paradigm supported and was supported by an old deity. The dominant image of God as found in the Bible and in the accumulated traditions of the Church presided over a hierarchical system in which "He" was the controlling force. Since this God was immutable, almighty, and omniscient, the community formed by "Him" had a great stake in unchanging doctrines, lordly authority, and unquestioning obedience on the part of the faithful. All of these attributes—heavenly and ecclesiastical—were predicated on a belief in absolute Truth. The nature of God and the nature of "man" were clear, and the human task was to live according to their laws. Theology consisted in interpreting and translating what we knew to be "true" into terms that were accessible to people in all times and all places.

The fundamental question being posed by those whose experience suggests that the divine being might be richer than the sum of "his" patriarchal attributes is simple: what if the nature of God and the nature of humanity are *not* a static given, but a progressively created reality? What if God is not "in charge" in the ways many of us have always imagined? What if the divine self-communication found in Second Isaiah, a divine being who suffers with creation, is not meant to describe Jesus, but meant, instead, to describe the God of Jesus? What if God is not all knowing in the ways we have been taught, but is willing and able to respond creatively to genuine novelty? The Indian poet, Rabindranath Tagore (1861–1941), said, in one of his mystical reflections, "His own mornings are new surprises to God."[14]

Christian feminist theologians, members of womenchurch, reform-minded women who continue to stay within the structures of the Church, trying to change its policies, along with feminists who have abandoned formal religion in search for viable, women-centered alternatives, are all wandering in the same wilderness. As we look for new sources of spiritual energy, some of us are drawn into the mystical tradition which was born and nurtured in the experience of desert dwellers, those called to pray silently in lonely places. Others are searching for the passionate, creation-centered goddess who, they believe, was rejected and abandoned in an ancient desert by a hostile patriarchal priesthood. All of us are trying to find new models of community life, new rituals of celebration, new sources of empowerment, new relationships to the divine and new rules of conduct.

Feminist Spirituality in General

Feminist spirituality, a term which often embraces community, ethics and ritual, is, at its core, a relationship with divinity. On a more personal level, feminist spirituality reflects the search of the feminist articulating it. My vision of feminist spirituality, therefore, is personal as well as scholarly and is meant to reflect one interpretation of the current situation. To stay within the framework of my metaphors, I understand myself to be in a wilderness, in exodus from patriarchy. If I find a sense of adventure here, I also know that the desert is a cold, lonely place with frightening characteristics. As someone drawn to the classics of the Catholic mystical tradition, I find that I am in a new place where I have periodic, powerful senses of *déjà vu*. In this wilderness, where we are called to trust ourselves as well as the re-creative energy of the deity, I see an old God who has promised new things, and, at the same time, find that some of my "new" discoveries have probably been hidden here all the time.

Some of those seeking a feminist spirituality spend their time in the wilderness, creating new rituals to encompass the full, rich range of human experience and interaction. Others make the connections between spirituality and politics visible and urgent. Still others read and write in an attempt to imagine the way

everything fits together. We wonder about the way new understandings of God relate to traditional models, the way developing rituals can embody new religious experiences, and the way
this time in the wilderness might be a locus of new revelation for
us all.

I am drawn to alternative theological models and informed by
the history of modern theology. Feminist theologians have
gained enormously from the work of theological giants like Karl
Rahner, whose theory of the supernatural existential makes it
possible to consider human experience as a fundamental datum
for theology.[15] For Rahner, as for many of those searching for
a new spirituality, the divine permeation of the human is so
intimate and so complete—the divine Being is so clearly consti-
tutive of our human existence—that almost everything we say
about divinity can be translated into facets of human existence.

The efforts of modern theologians to open the question of
revelation so that it is understood in dynamic terms and in
contemporary situations of oppression and liberation[16] give
feminists a way to claim that their own religious experience
might well be a locus for divine self-communication. Also, the
work of metaphorical theologians like Sallie McFague, who
presents an imaginative picture of God and the world in which
God is mother, lover and friend while the world is seen as God's
body, urges feminists, along with all theologians, to experiment
with those metaphors that are most able to interpret the Christian faith powerfully and persuasively for its own time.[17]

Mostly, however, I am drawn to process thought, to those
theologians and philosophers who see the divine being as
creative, responsive love whose power lies in beauty and whose
life is involved in the adventure of our own. When I try to
imagine an ideal feminist spirituality, certain concepts seem to
reappear with regularity. Feminist spirituality must be rooted in
and take note of our collective and individual experience.
Sensitive to the connections among all forms of life, it seeks
respectful and appreciative coexistence between ourselves and
the non-human world. Needless to say, it rejects the body/soul
dualisms of older forms in favor of more holistic models: the
body and its rhythms are as important to us as the hidden world
of the psyche. Many have found spiritual insights in the work of
contemporary scientists. The notion that all reality is a process of
becoming, then perishing and becoming anew has a deep
resonance with human experience. Many also believe that there
are real clues for spiritual life in the laws of relativity and in the
statements about randomness and chance in the work of sub-
atomic physicists.[18]

Because, many feminists believe, so much of our spiritual past has been destroyed or vitiated by patriarchal fear and hostility, part of any feminist search for spiritual roots requires difficult excavations in dangerous places. We sift through the history of witchcraft and goddess religion, heartbroken at the destruction and energized by our sense of discovery.[19] Since it is possible that great reservoirs of spiritual wisdom might be still hidden, we look for the signs of divine love in unexpected places. Some women feel quite at home in pagan traditions, for example, while others look to the arcane symbols of Tarot cards or to the music that seems to come from unconscious memories. Still others try to find space in themselves for other traditions. They may look to the contemplative practices of Eastern religions or to stories of native American folklore.

In all of these ways, feminists, attempting to practice and formulate a new spirituality, long for and uphold freedom, and so seek a divine Being who genuinely respects our freedom. Since we have no single way in which to imagine divine activity, we often blend old and new insights. We create new rituals, re-create old myths, and look critically at theological systems already in place to see what we can learn from them. I believe that one modern established system can offer us an avenue to the minor themes of the biblical tradition, themes that focus on divine immanence and involvement in human life. Process thought takes the scientific view of the world seriously, refuses to place human experience outside nature, and holds it essential that every variety of experience be taken into account. Finally, process thought asks us to give up absolutes, to realize that everything is relative, even the deity.

Feminist Spirituality and Process Thought

The God of the patriarchal tradition was explained in Aristotelian categories in opposition to all that is not God. The attributes which defined the divine made God the supreme exception to human experience: we grew and moved, whereas God was perfect and unchangeable; we anguished and changed, whereas God was sublime and complete. It was fairly easy to imagine God having no essential relationship with the world, incapable of being known through modes of human experience.

Process thought is a systematization of the scientific and philosophical work of Alfred North Whitehead (1861-1947), who hoped to explain God in terms of modern experience. Whitehead, an English mathematician turned philosopher, worked on the assumption that all existence, all reality, is continuous: the building blocks of the universe are energy and process, undergoing incessant modification. Process thought, for him, was not a religious construct, but a vision of reality that identified the energy discovered in physics (relativity, chance, randomness, constant movement) with the emotional intensity of human life. Predicated on a modern scientific viewpoint, process thought claims that the universe is not made up of things, but is made up of energy. The basic structure of all reality, therefore, is process.[20]

If this assumption seems sensible when applied to human beings or to the material world, it may seem inappropriate when applied to God or the spiritual world; yet, for Whitehead, God is the supreme example of all metaphysical and human categories, not an exemption from them. Since for Whitehead all existence is continuous, with no breaks, God is part of the process; indeed, is the ultimate explanation of process. As the metaphysical ground of all process, God is that being who is conditioned and affected by everything that happens everywhere. God is not safely ensconced in some heavenly realm unrelated to our world. On the contrary, God is deeply and necessarily involved in the life of the universe and relates to absolutely everything.

If all reality is process and process is defined in terms of relationships, then perfection resides in movement, in ongoing creativity, and relatedness. Since there is no such thing as an isolated process in this system, it makes no sense to speak of God in the abstract, *in se,* to use a scholastic term. God can be understood only in terms of relationships as the most perfectible, most related and, *therefore,* most perfect being. Another way to think about divinity is to say that God is full of possibilities, is the vision of what might be in the world, and in the divine self.

Defining the deity in process terms means beginning with an oxymoron: God is absolutely relative. On the one hand, God is absolute and abstract and has what Whitehead calls the divine primordial nature. On the other hand, the divine being is relative and concrete, having what Whitehead calls the divine consequent nature. The divine primordial nature is the ordered realm of abstract possibilities. Here, God is the vision of what might be, embracing all the patterns of all the possible meanings and values relevant to existence. The divine primordial nature, therefore, is God as **possible,** and this side of God's being does not change: it is eternal, present in one timeless vision, the ground of the process. The divine primordial nature cannot be acted upon; it is simply there, or, to put it in scholastic terms, God **IS.**

The divine primordial nature, however, is totally abstract and has no concrete reality. And, since all reality is made up of energy events in constant relationship, this abstract divine vision needs fulfillment in relationship in order to be real. The vision of all possibilities exists only as an abstraction, and, for the divine nature to be concrete, to participate in reality, God must experience and relate to all "real things," what Whitehead called "actual concrete occasions."[21] The actualized nature of God, which Whitehead called the divine consequent nature, is *given* by this process. God is actualized by experiencing and relating to all actual concrete occasions. The processes of becoming, which are the real world for us, determine the experience of this divine being. In this sense, God is supremely and absolutely relational and is affected by everything.

The divine consequent nature, therefore, is the divine participation with creatures in the society of being. Why does Whitehead define God in this way? Because, if all reality is process, involving a set of relationships, and if relationships are themselves processes relating to each other in terms of going someplace, then all reality is continually becoming something else, moving to something deeper. The perfection of being is in the movement of the process. It is *in* the becoming, *in* the movement, in the process as it goes, What is most actual, most real, is that which is most related; in other words, God.

So, God is absolute, not in the traditional sense of final, total, unlimited, and unchangeable, but in the sense of encompassing in influence, related to and suffering with all entities, and being the ultimate and highest destiny of each. The divine experiencing is composed of the totality of all experience and is, therefore, larger and richer than any single actual experience. As single experiences enlarge and increase, which they do as we respond to the divine vision of what might be, God enlarges and increases. The divine experience encompasses, urges, and directs all actual experiences by being at once their fuller context and their most compassionate witness. Since the primary category of existence in this system is experiencing in process, God is the ever more Becoming One, ever more related, ever more involved.

Furthermore, since the process deity genuinely respects human freedom, God is not coercive. Divine power lies in the lure of beauty, in the tenderness of compassionate persuasion, not in force. In the old system God was the total, efficient cause of all things, able to produce anything, to create out of nothing. But in this system, the process contains its own inner dynamic. God has the vision of all possibilities and is the source of all value, but has no power of coercion toward the actualization of this value.

God has only the power of what Whitehead calls "suasion." The divine vision of the best possible interrelationships presents an aim to the process and functions as a lure to it, but cannot compel it. God shares the power of being with creatures and allows all of us freedom and spontaneity. The divine/human interaction, therefore, is a real history of intercommunication. We need God's primordial nature (the vision of all possibilities), and God's consequent nature needs our choices and experience in order to become actualized and real. Everything that happens, therefore, makes a difference to God because God has to respond to it, take it into the divine life, and adjust it within the harmony of the divine plan.

What remains fixed for God is the absolute integrity of the divine aim which looks toward the fulness of life for all creation. But, to move toward this fulfillment, God shares in the concreteness of events. Every achievement of good, or value, or meaning in the world increases the richness of God's being. God is not the world process, but God is IN the process, is the eternal structure and power which make the world possible and which participate in each moment of the world's becoming,. for the world is nothing without God.

As Daniel Day Williams says, "Process philosophy opens up for Christian theology a way of conceiving the being of God in historical-temporal terms. What it proposes is akin to the existentialist search for radical freedom for [hu]man[ity] and acceptance of the risks of being."[22] In the biblical sense, God works in time and history where people can refuse initiatives, overturn the most wonderful plans, and divert the most clearly articulated divine aims. Yet, the God of the Bible continually recreates good possibilities for those same people. God, as understood in process thought, is creative love that is persuasive, responsive and involved. The divine being in the biblical wilderness, who joins a wandering people with a sense of adventure, who works and acts within the limitations given by the actual situation, and who longs for things to go well, but is willing to present new possibilities when they do not, is very much a process God.

In terms of the feminist critique of Catholicism, whether we are in exodus from patriarchy or alienated and exiled from our religious tradition, we wander with a certain set of limitations and are lured on by visions of new possibilities. Like Yahweh, who promised a land of milk and honey, God, understood by many feminist interpreters in feminine terms, presents new visions to us and entices us toward their fulfillment. And, like the biblical deity, God is willing to adjust to our weakness or blindness or fatigue along the way, and stay with us on the journey.

Wandering in the wilderness is not lightly undertaken. It is a perilous journey on which we are searching for new language, new ways of understanding human interaction, new spiritual frameworks that contain political imperatives, and new ways of celebrating who we are in relation to the divine being and to the universe. The interactive aspects of the biblical God interpreted through process thought suggest that those in exile from patriarchy are accompanied in the wilderness by a divine being who has visions of our best possibilities, yet is willing to suffer with our defeats. Because God must work within human limitations, things might not always work out the way God envisions them. Because our lives in the wilderness determine the divine destiny along with our own, we are in radical partnership with a deity willing to take risks.

Religious experience has claimed that human beings relate to God in strength, love, vulnerability, and weakness. Process thought makes the same claims for the divine Being. God relates to us in strength because of the vision present in the divine primordial nature, in love because of a desire for more extensive and intensive relationship, in vulnerability because the divine destiny is tied to ours, and in weakness because God needs what we can give. Put another way, I would say that God holds on to nothing. Because of process, God lets go of everything all the time. Everything dies and becomes new at every moment with God. In the process God there is a sense of struggle which can support those whose religious lives are struggles.

Feminist Harmonies in Process Spirituality

The original desert of the exodus experience was a place of testing, as the desert of the Isaian re-interpretation was a location of nurturance. The wilderness many feminists find themselves in at the moment can be both: through suffering and solace we may be in a unique position to come to a deeper awareness of the kind of deity we long for when we reject the limited God of the patriarchy. In the present wilderness, feminists nurture and test one another as we search for and relate to a God of genuine mutuality. One might even say that the wilderness experience, the contemporary search for a feminist spirituality, is another way to understand covenant.

The Israelites experienced God through the covenant, a promise of relationship which carried a profound commitment to love and be present to one another forever. Yahweh's words, "I will be your God and you will be my people," are a promise to abide with and interact with that people. As Margaret Farley reminds us, we know from biblical history that the Jews fixed upon different aspects of divine abiding love at different moments in their lives. The covenant was identified with land and progeny with Abraham; with liberation and refuge in the Mosaic covenant; with peace and order in the kingdom of David; with wisdom and justice in the prophetic traditions; and after the exile, with the promise of a new kingdom of some sort.[23] Throughout these developments, however, we can find some constants. The divine promise is one of ongoing love; it depends, in part, on choices, as Yahweh's upholding of the covenant depended upon Israel's holding to its stipulations; it sustains life in the present moment; and it draws people toward a future realm of justice.

In the original exodus story, the biblical author focuses on Moses, the Red Sea miracle, the giving of the law at Sinai, and other important events. In an almost throwaway line, the author notes (Exodus 15.20) that Miriam, the prophetess, the sister of Moses and Aaron, took a timbrel in her hand, and all the women went out after her and danced. Let me focus on this story as a way to image "minor themes in biblical religion." Music is an integral part of new feminist spirituality. Songs accompany us on our journeys. Their sustaining rhythms and empowering chants have given us ways to achieve solidarity. Dance, too, is a special part of our spirituality, and, like the poets who saw the cosmic dance as encompassing and circular, feminists like to believe that we are "dancing Sarah's circle" rather than "climbing Jacob's ladder." All these musical moments can be brought to bear on process thought.

Marjorie Suchocki, in trying to describe the mysterious, intimate, joyful, related, triune reality of the process God, says that we *must* turn to metaphor and imagination to express such a reality.[24] Her analogy for the process God is that of a special, even fantastic, symphony. Imagine a symphony, she writes, in which each note is intensely alive. Each note feels the whole as well. The life that sustains the lives of the notes is the symphony as a whole. But, if we posit a deeper locus of awareness, suppose we say that the symphony as a whole is aware and alive, a living symphony sparkling with awareness of its own beauty, both from the perspective of the whole and from the multiplied perspectives of each part. The single beauty is intensified through the multiple awareness merged into the unified awareness of the whole. Now, imagine someone outside that symphony appreciatively attuned to its complex beauty. Imagine that every listener becomes a participant in the symphony, adding a new note, and that the symphony is ever deepening, ever intensifying, infinitely and inexhaustibly beautiful, and that it lasts forever.

If this metaphor gives some notion of the process God, then perhaps Miriam and the women were the only ones who really heard the deeper possibilities of that first exodus. Perhaps

Second Isaiah was profoundly insightful, telling the Jews to "sing a new song" and enter the new Jersualem dancing. Miriam and Second Isaiah saw, perhaps, what feminists attempt to see when searching for a genuinely feminist spirituality: that God wants our enjoyment of life's possibilities to be contagious, to increase the enjoyment of others, and to lead to a new understanding of the divine being in covenant with us.

Conclusion

In re-defining the wilderness, therefore, I am not concerned with being lost in the middle of a desert, but with what or who might be encountered in that place. The process God, a minor theme of the Christian tradition, has always been there. Some of the mystics have known it. Some of the poets have celebrated its sensuousness and ability to captivate the heart. Tagore sings eloquently of the pleasures of divine love in ways that feminist pilgrims might find attractive. "Deliverance is not for me in renunciation," he muses, talking to the divine Being, "I feel the embrace of freedom in a thousand bonds of delight. . . . I will never shut the door of my senses. The delights of sight and hearing and touch will bear thy delight."[25] His poetry is redolent with images of song and of ways to find interactive pleasure with a deity who longs for our joy as well as our company, who says, in effect, "You can sit mourning by the waters of Babylon forever, or you can compose a new song, a song with your own good parts of the past remembered in it."[26]

Whether feminists relate more directly to the original Hebrews or to the post-exilic Jews of the Isaian tradition, we can find some joy in our wilderness. Those who sense new life in the search for a feminist spirituality compose and sing new songs. Those who have left the land of the Pharaohs only to find themselves in an environment with new terrors and profound loneliness may not be inclined to take up their timbrels and dance. The only certainty at this point is that we cannot return to patriarchal religion. At the same time, many of us refuse to be read out of our heritage, and so seek the harmonies of its minor themes, and look for ways to relate to its life-giving aspects.

In this new territory, this wilderness of loneliness and desire, I believe we can find what has been there all along, waiting for discovery: a divine being infinitely richer than anything imagined by the patriarchs, containing a fullness of nature that makes sense of the divine image as male and female; a God passionately involved with our lives, eager for our enjoyment, supportive of our adventures, full of new possibilities and, therefore, hopeful, with us, for the future.

NOTES

[1] I am speaking from a Roman Catholic framework, but believe that the experiences I discuss can be generalized to include other mainline Christian traditions.

[2] For the literature on which these generalizations are based, see my *New Catholic Women: A Contemporary Challenge to Traditional Religious Authority* (San Francisco: Harper and Row, 1986), pp. 37-70, and notes.

[3] In her assessment of universal female subordination, feminist anthropologist, Sherry Ortner, offered three types of evidence to prove that a particular culture considers women to be inferior: explicit statements, implicit symbols, and social or structural arrangements. See "Is Female to Male as Nature is to Culture?," in Michelle Zimbalist Rosaldo and Louise Lamphere, eds., *Woman Culture & Society* (Stanford, California: Stanford University Press, 1974), pp. 67-89.

[4] Although modern ecclesiastical documents no longer suggest that women are "inferior," they hold to the claim that women have natures that complement those of men. Under the guise of divine will, or "natural law," women are portrayed as dependent, submissive, maternal, and naturally suited to secondary roles. See William B. Faherty, *The Destiny of Modern Woman in the Light of Papal Teaching* (Westminster, Md.: Newman Press, 1950). Conservative theologians usually invoke the same argument. See *Communio: International Catholic Review* 8 (Fall, 1981), devoted to relations between the sexes.

[5] Very few studies on women's issues have bothered to ask for women's opinions. As the British Laity Commission commented in its report to its bishops: despite the fact that "very little research ha[s] been undertaken to establish how Catholic women in this country regard themselves . . . there is no shortage of *authoritative* statements suggesting what women should or should not be doing." See *Why Can't a Woman Be More Like a Man?* (London: Catholic Information Services, n.d.). Now that the American bishops have decided to write a pastoral letter on women's issues, there have been lengthy and broad-based "listening sesssions," but the results of these sessions have not been collected and published. In the meantime, one of the most helpful sources for the voices of women in parish life can be found in *Task Force Report on the Role of Women in the Church of Southeast Wisconsin* (Milwaukee: *Catholic Herald,* supplement 9, December 1982), sponsored by Archbishop Rembert Weakland. The Weakland report is my main source for the generalizations made here.

[6] See Mary O'Connell, "Pastors: Parishes Still Follow the Leader," *U.S. Catholic* 47 (April 1982), pp. 17-24.

[7] This is not to say that one cannot find satisfied women in the parish. Indeed, some surveys have shown that women are quite content in secondary roles. See Florence R. Rosenberg and Edward M. Sullivan, *Women and Ministry: A Survey of the Experience of Roman Catholic Women in the United States* (Washington, D.C.: Center for Applied Research in the Apostolate, 1980). I argue, however, that the CARA Survey is flawed in design, and, even if it is not skewed, one has to ask about the ages of the contented women (most of them in the survey are over 40) and inquire whether this "contentment" is in its last generation? See *New Catholic*

Women, chapter two.

8 Any hopes that such arguments are "medieval" can be laid to rest by reading the Vatican declaration against the ordination of women and the commentaries following its publication. Best single source of all these documents is that edited by Arlene and Leonard Swidler, *Women Priests: A Catholic Commentary on the Vatican Declaration* (New York: Paulist Press, 1977).

9 Rosemary Ruether has noted that the willingness of different feminist religious groups to dialogue has led male critics to suspect "an excess of ecumenism" (see "For whom, with whom, do we speak our new stories?," *Christianity and Crisis* 45 (May 13, 1985), pp. 183-186). One of the distinctive features of feminist inter-religious dialogue (and ritual practice) has been its willingness to include contemporary paganism as a dialogue partner. Further, many of those working assiduously for new feminist visions that include a strong spiritual dimension are "former Catholics." See, for example, the introduction to the fine anthology by Charlene Spretnak, *The Politics of Women's Spirituality* (New York: Doubleday Anchor, 1982).

10 See Rosemary Ruether, *Womenchurch* (San Francisco: Harper and Row, 1987).

11 The Womenchurch movement aims at ecumenism, and it is becoming one united place for women of all religious backgrounds to gather for empowerment and celebration, but its roots are in a coalition of Roman Catholic women's groups. See my *New Catholic Women,* pp. 132-37. More information is available after the national meeting in October, 1987.

12 Even Vatican documents admit that ecclesiastical credibility depends upon the Church's accountability to the principles of social justice. See the major document from the 1971 Synod of Bishops, "Justice and Peace," in Joseph Gremillion, ed., *The Gospel of Peace and Justice: Catholic Social Teaching Since Pope John* (Maryknoll, NY: Orbis Books, 1976), pp. 513-29. It may be that this kind of accountability really had no consensus behind it and so does not really reflect "the mind of the Church." (So argues Gary MacEoin, "Forming a Catholic Conscience on Social Questions," *Cross Currents* 25 (Summer 1975), pp. 187-97.)

13 First published in New York by the Catholic Summer School Press in 1907, this book kept American Catholics mindful of the age of Aquinas, papalism, and other kinds of past glory. It has been reprinted continually since its publication.

14 From *Stray Birds* as found in Amiya Chakravarty, ed., *A Tagore Reader* (Boston: Beacon Press, 1961), p. 327.

15 The best introduction to Rahner's work is Leon O'Donovan, ed., *A World of Grace: An Introduction to the Themes and Foundations of Karl Rahner's Theology* (New York: Seabury Press, 1980).

16 I have in mind here especially the work of European political theologians like Jurgen Moltmann and Johannes Metz, and of Latin American liberation theologians like Gustavo Gutierrez and Leonardo Boff. See my *New Catholic Women,* pp. 147-54.

17 See her *Models of God: Theology for an Ecological, Nuclear Age*

(Philadelphia: Fortress Press, 1987).

18 See, for example, the work of Fritjof Capra, *The Tao of Physics* (New York: Bantam Books, 1976), and *The Turning Point* (New York: Bantam Books, 1982).

19 For some idea of the "sense of discovery" involved in the quest for "the Goddess," see Merlin Stone, *When God was a Woman* (New York: Dial Press, 1976). Although there has been serious and acrimonious controversy on the existence of a Goddess-centered religion, the existence of modern goddess celebrations do (as it said in a headline in *New Directions for Women,* November/December 1986) "lift women's spirits."

20 I am indebted to many general works about Whitehead's thought, among them Norman Pittinger, *Process Thought and Christian Faith* (New York: Pilgrim Press, 1979), and Daniel Day Williams, *The Spirit and the Forms of Love* (New York: Harper and Row, 1968). It may be best to read Whitehead himself, *Process and Reality: An Essay in Cosmology* (New York: Social Sciences Book Store, 1941), or his interpreter, Donald W. Sherburne, ed., *A Key to Whitehead's Process and Reality* (Chicago: University Press, 1966).

21 For a good introduction to the vocabulary and concepts on Whitehead's thought, see Marjorie Hewitt Suchocki, *God, Christ, Church: A Practical Guide to Process Theology* (New York: Crossroad Publishing, 1986).

22 *The Spirit and the Forms of Love* (cited, note 20), p. 107.

23 *Personal Commitments* (San Francisco: Harper and Row, 1986), p. 116.

24 Cited, note 21, pp. 214-15.

25 *A Tagore Reader* (cited, note 14), p. 305.

26 One of my students, Garbo Todd, in a review of E. M. Broner's *A Weave of Women* (New York: Bantam, 1978), summarized Broner's work with this fine sentence.

A Discipleship of Equals: Implications for Ministry

Maria Harris

My intention in this essay is to suggest some theory and practice for a ministry based on the mutuality and partnership of women and men. I will be arguing that such a ministry will necessarily include five major elements: receptivity, remembering, resistance, mourning, and reform. However, before examining each of these at some length, I will comment briefly on the context for ministry which exists in the Church today. In order to set the stage for the elements which follow, I want to make the preliminary observations that as a **term** (although not as an activity) ministry is new in usage in the United States Catholic Church; that any discussion of preparation and education for ministry is necessarily done with three publics in mind; and that education in the direction of the vocation to ministry is part of a paradigm shift in the larger framework of the religious education of Catholics.

THE CONTEXT

1. *The term "ministry."* It sometimes comes as a surprise to Church professionals that the use of the term ministry is very recent in the Catholic Church. In the index to the English translation of the documents of Vatican II, for example, the word is not listed at all. The closest we come in that index is the term "ministers," with the explanatory note, "see clergy; priests." Almost all of the Catholic writing which has been done about the meaning of ministry today has come subsequent to that time; for example, in such works as Bernard Cooke's *Ministry to Word and Sacraments* and in the two volumes of Edward Schillebeeckx, *Ministry* and *The Church With a Human Face.*[3] (Theological reflection in Protestantism has been going on for a somewhat longer time.) I raise this issue at the beginning to signal two factors. First, the term minister for most Catholics

still, in my judgment, refers to the Protestant clergyman (not woman, although their number continues to grow) down the block; still refers to persons who are ordained; and still remains, as a theological issue, in its beginning stages. In other words, we do not yet have a developed theology of ministry.

For our purposes in this volume, I believe that is very much to the good: we still have time, historically, to develop a ministry which is characterized by partnership, mutuality, and equality. Such partnership will not only be between women and men, but between the ordained and the non-ordained. It will also be a theology which does not assume two kinds of ministry: the "real" ministry which belongs to the officials of the Church, and a secondary (and unfortunately, second-class) ministry implicit in the use of the phrases, "Ministry" and "Lay Ministry" (a usage even more prevalent in Protestantism than in Catholicism). Being at the beginning can help us, if we are wise, to avoid such dichotomies.[4]

And secondly, because ministry is still being developed, not only by theologians, but by all of us working together in the Church, we need to specify what we are talking about when we use the term ministry, as a contribution in the ongoing conversation. Therefore, I need to say in this essay that the understanding of ministry with which I will be working here will be at least threefold: (a) I will use it to refer to what used to be called the "apostolate"; (b) I will use it to include what have always been known as the spiritual and corporal works of mercy, which many of us learned to memorize as children; and (c) I will use it as synonymous with the "work of the Church." In fact, I will specify it later on in this way: **Ministry is the priestly, prophetic and political work of the Church.** As such, it is a continuing of the work of Jesus the Christ embodied in the triple office of priest, prophet and king, a set of roles he received from his own Jewish people. Ministry is the Body of the Christ in the world today, continuing the priestly, prophetic and political work of Jesus of Nazareth.[5]

2. *The Three Publics.*[6] Preparation and education for Ministry at present focuses on three publics (although obviously these three do not exhaust all its publics): seminaries; graduate and undergraduate schools of theology and religious education (among which I would include such institutes as the Institute for Pastoral Life in Kansas City, Missouri); and local parishes. If we want to examine where actual lived understanding of ministy is being taught, developed and practiced—and the persons any of us would wish to reach in exploring meanings of ministry—these are the settings where the meanings are being hammered out.

One problem, however, is that the meanings being hammered out are not necessarily the same.

For example, we have at least three kinds of seminary education going on today. There are diocesan or regional seminaries where men are being prepared for ministry, and women are not permitted to enroll. The implicit understanding of ministry "taught" by such systems needs to be addressed. There are other seminaries, often run by religious orders (JST at Berkeley, Weston in Cambridge, MA) where women and men study together via an identical schooling, but where only some graduates are officially sanctioned by the official Church as ministers. And, there are many Protestant seminaries where Catholic women and men are preparing for vocations in ministry in ecumenical settings—indeed, at such places as Harvard and Yale Divinity Schools and the University of Chicago, Catholics often form the largest ecclesial group. These are also places (I have taught at several) where one meets many "former" Catholics— and as each new generation comes of age, the move to Protestantism may be even greater.

Ministry is also being taught and experienced in colleges and universities throughout the country. What began as programs in religious education have either shifted to being programs in education **and** ministry, or have begun to center largely on education for ministry alone. One needs only to study or to interview students in such large programs as the Boston College Institute of Religious Education **and Pastoral Ministry** (the name change over the past decade is significant) or Fordham University's Graduate School of Religion and Religious Education (which in the fall of 1987 began a new program of training for non-ordained leadership in parishes) to get some sense of the remarkable burgeoning of numbers of people who believe themselves called to ministry. In such programs, however, one also gets a sense of the number of women and men—in religious orders and increasingly from the laity; from the fifty United States as well as from around the world—who are remaking the meaning of ministry in ways which are only now **beginning** to be spelled out. One also gets a sense a few years later that some of these persons have discovered no place to call their own in ministry.

However, the most remarkable preparation and education for ministry going on today is at the local level—sparked in many instances by the people who have studied at those seminaries and colleges; sparked also by such phenomena as RENEW, RCIA, NCD and DREs—the ministerial alphabet soup. It is not unusual to find parishes in every diocese of this country and elsewhere (although "parish" often takes on a quite different meaning beyond the borders of the United States—witness the Latin American Church) which have regular "Ministry Days." These are occasions when all those substantially involved in the work of the Church come together for community, prayer, and further study. Many of these persons are even beginning to understand the daily work of their lives—as parents, insurance salespeople, taxi drivers, nurses and teachers—as expressions of a ministerial vocation begun in Baptism and Confirmation.[7]

3. *The Paradigm Shift.* These meanings being developed in study and practice coincide with a paradigm shift in the meaning of religious education as it goes on in the Church. Where such education could once have been described as "officials indoctrinating children to obey the official church,"[8] education is now far more accurately described as "the whole community educating the whole community to engage in ministry toward the whole world." In other words, every element in the description has changed: (a) the whole community—not only officials—have become the agents of religious education; (b) the work is no longer **indoctrinating,** but the fullness of **education,** which goes beyond schooling alone to include community, advocacy, liturgy and outreach (that is, not only *didache,* but *koinonia, kerygma, leiturgia,* and *diakonia*);[9] (c) the participants in religious education are not only children but the entire community—the entire Church: old and young, poor and rich, women and men and children are being educated together; and (d) the purpose, end, or intention of the education is no longer knowing the lore and the law in order to be obedient to the Church, so much as it is knowing the lore and the law in order to be obedient to the call of God to engage in ministry throughout the entire world and toward the entire world. Diagrammatically, the shift looks like this:

Agent:	officials	to	the whole community;
Activity:	indoctrinating	to	educating;
Participants:	children	to	the whole community;
Purpose:	obeying the Church	to	ministering to and in the world.

These are at least three of the conditions which contribute to the experience and understanding of ministry today. If it be granted, even for the sake of argument, that these conditions are present as context, then the implications for a ministry which would incorporate the gifts of all can begin to be suggested. And, although that future ministry cannot as yet be described, because it is still in the making, what can be done is this: as a community, we can describe the steps which are necessary to bring about a more responsive and responsible ministry which is the whole Church together, living its vocation to **be** the priestly, prophetic and political presence of the Christ in the world. We can describe the steps which are necessary to bring about a discipleship of equals.

I turn now to an examination of those steps, drawn from contemporary theology and practice of ministry, as well as from Church history. I do so, however, with one caveat: the word "step" is not used to indicate sequence, as steps on a staircase or as rungs on a ladder. Instead, the steps suggested as essential in the creation of a new ministry are akin to steps in a dance.[10] That means they will necessarily include bending, bowing, and backtracking; at some times moving forward, at some times sideways, at others stopping movement completely. That means also that there can be a gentle, organic rhythm to what is done. But perhaps most important, steps in a dance do not lead to a foregone set of conclusions. Only in the doing of the dance itself is genuine discovery made.

RECEPTIVITY, THE FIRST STEP

At its deepest, the human capacity for receptivity is the capacity to listen to Being in order to hear the address of Being. Receptivity is the disposition we bring to prayer, asking with the poet, "Lord, teach us to care and not to care; teach us to sit still." Receptivity is the disposition expressed in the comment, "Sometimes I sit and think, and sometimes I just sit." Receptivity means bringing our contemplative powers to bear on whatever reality lies before us and attempting to face that reality as a "Thou."

Among the most important forms of receptivity is hospitality—receiving others as they are:

> If we devote our attention to the act of hospitality, we will see at once that to receive is not to fill up a void with an alien presence but to make the other participate in a certain plenitude. Thus the ambiguous term, 'receptivity', has a wide range of meanings extending from suffering or undergoing to the gift of self; for hospitality is a gift of what is one's own, that is, of oneself.[11]

As an act, such receptivity applies not only to human beings with other human beings, but to the non-human companions with whom we share the planet: fire and water and air and earth, and all the other animals.

As a step in creating a ministry that assumes a discipleship of equals engaged in ministry, receptivity is incumbent on the leaders of the Church. Those in official positions are called not only to be speakers in the Church; they are called to be listeners to the Holy Spirit present in the lives of all people—and to the demands the Spirit makes on the shape of the Church of the future. Martin Buber refers to such listening as awareness of "a word demanding an answer happening to us."[12] (We also need to note here the responsibility of Church members to listen carefully and reverently to leaders—and then for both to be in dialogue). And although there are many Church leaders who do practice such receptivity/listening/hospitality, it needs to be said that the perception of many women and men in the Church today is that they are not listened to by those in leadership roles. The receptivity of leaders, however, is not my concern here. I would propose, in fact, that a far more important receptivity deserves attention if we would move to a discipleship of equals. And, that is a receptivity to ourselves.

Such receptivity has been described in a number of ways. Paulo Freire, for example, writes of the discovery of the onto-logical vocation to be a subject, rather than an object, of existence.[13] Receptivity implies this discovery, this sense of one's own subjectivity and the subsequent coming to understand the power within ourselves which accompanies it. Soren Kierke-gaard, in distinguishing direct and indirect communication, teaches that, whereas in a direct communication *information* is delivered to another, an indirect communication is address of another in such a way that that other *is delivered to herself*.[14] In the Church today, much indirect communication is going on—in conferences such as this—where together, persons are being delivered to themselves.

Poet Marge Piercy puts it more simply: she calls it "unlearning to not speak."[15] And, Margaret Atwood describes some of what is necessary in order to achieve it:

> This above all, to refuse to be a victim. Unless I can do that, I can do nothing. I have to recant, give up the old belief that I am powerless and because of it nothing I can do will ever hurt anyone. A lie which was always more disastrous than the truth would have been. The word games, the winning and losing games are finished; at the moment there are no others but they will have to be invented, withdrawing is no longer possible and the alternative is death.[16]

The receptivity I am calling for here is all of these: refusing to be a victim; unlearning to not speak; and knowing we have been delivered to ourselves: as free, responsible, intelligent human beings acting as subjects in the world. It is acting not only for ourselves, although that is critical; it is acting also for the sake of the Church, for the sake of the Christ, and for the sake of a world yet to be born.

When such a receptivity to ourselves as participating subjects in Church and world occurs, an eventual (although granted not immediate) result is the discovery of our equality within the Church: not only as women and men, or clergy and laity, or teachers and students, or pastors and parishioners, or DREs and catechists, but as faithful and hierarchy—equal before God, not in office, but in being. This is a gift those of us who are teachers and preachers, and ourselves in leadership roles, need to assist developing in our students and parish colleagues—at times we must admit to being among the leaders who may not listen! And, when this step of receptivity—**to** ourselves and **with** others—is taken with care, two further implications become apparent.

A first is a deepened understanding of the other, especially the one who appears to be adversary. For that other, no matter how seemingly intransigent, vicious, or duplicitous, is, like ourselves, only human. (Try drawing, sketching the face of your adversary while it is in repose, suggests one of my students—it can lead you to receptivity of that other, to understanding.) And, when that understanding becomes deepened—**received,** if you will, then a further implication may surface. This is an implication which tends not to be addressed when the positions are of inequality in the Church. But, it is an implication born out of a sense of mutuality, even if that mutuality is surrounded by conflict. Ironically, the implication is this: a genuine receptivity to ourselves as participating subjects who know ourselves to be equal allows us to take, where necessary, the paradoxical, ecclesial step of **non-receptivity.**

Writing of the tension between Church order and alternative practices, Schillebeeckx reminds us that, against the background of existing Church order, new and perhaps urgently necessary alternatives have usually been seen through the medium of what must provisionally be called "illegality." He reminds us, however, that this is not a new phenomenon in the Church and that the old, medieval scholasticism sometimes elevated this provisional illegality to the status of a theological principle, especially in its theory of the ***non-acceptatio legis,*** the rejection of the law-from-above by opposition from the grass roots.[17] He goes on to say that, from the history of the Church itself, it seems that there is a way in which Christians can develop a practice in the Church from below, from the grassroots,

> which for a time can compete with the official practice recognized by the church, but which in its Christian opposition and illegality can eventually nevertheless become the dominant practice of the official church, and finally be sanctioned by the official church. (whereupon the whole process can begin all over again, since time never stands still). That is how things have always been![18]

Eventually, practices which diverge from Church order can and have been actually received into the Church on principles which the western Church has developed—the extraordinary minister, the intention to do what the Church does while not knowing the form, and the one which applies here: the non-receptivity of a doctrine. The last is the ancient doctrine which says that a Church law, while being valid, can in the long run become irrelevant because it is in fact no longer accepted by the great majority of believers.

Where we have arrived at a discipleship of equals who question existing Church laws **by engaging in alternative practices,** non-receptivity of doctrine may be necessary and appropriate. The celebration of Eucharist without an ordained presbyter, the refusal by homosexual persons to be written out of the Church, the massive dismissal of the ruling on birth control are only some of the practices which may be indicative of this direction. In his tightly written *Concilium* essay on "Reception as an Ecclesiological Reality," Yves Congar noted a number of cases of non-reception, including *Humanae Vitae,* asking, "is this 'non-reception' or 'disobedience' or what?," and responding to his own question with the brief commentary, "The facts are there."[19] In similar circumstances, when we learn to receive ourselves and unlearn our not-speaking, it may be up to each of us to proclaim the non-receptivity of doctrine once more—as a symbol of our having first taken the opposite, but in an ironic way essential, step of Receptivity.

REMEMBERING, THE SECOND STEP

Among the central aspects of ministry in the Church from its beginning has been another step: Remembering. Indeed, the ancient term **anamnesis** situates remembering at the heart of the Church's prayer life—the re-membering, that is, the making present, of the Christ in the Eucharist. This memorial of the Paschal Mystery has never been taught as a simple reminding; rather, it has always existed as our fullest expression of the depth of the step of Re-membering: bringing into conscious awareness a presence which is always with us, the presence of God in the Christ.

In a related way, Catholic Christianity's emphasis on Tradition as a source of revelation, along with scripture, has also served to keep Remembering alive. Again, at its fullest, that which is handed on and handed over—traditioned—has never been words or dogmas or verbal formulas alone, but the life to which those words point. At its fullest, what is handed on continually in the Church is a life—and life is passed from generation to generation by living, breathing people. G.K.

Chesterton captured this understanding with wit and wisdom, reminding us of the nature of the Tradition which is remembered:

> Tradition may be defined as an extension of the franchise. Tradition means giving votes to the most obscure of all classes, our ancestors. It is the democracy of the dead. Tradition refuses to submit to the small and arrogant oligarchy of those who merely happen to be walking about.[20]

The *leiturgia* of *anamnesis* and the *koinonia* of tradition are complemented, in turn, by the remembering of the story which is the work of *didache* and *kerygma*. In these forms of remembering, what is repeated and retold is the story: we remember the night when he took bread and took wine and washed feet; we remember the people with whom he walked and the people he healed; we remember the stories of the people who made us **us** through the centuries, our forefathers and our foremothers. And all of these are good. But, once again, they are not enough. Further forms of remembering are necessary.

A contemporary theological emphasis on remembering has been made by John Baptist Metz. This is his notion of the form of memory called "dangerous memory," the kind of memory which makes a demand on us:

> There are memories in which earlier experiences break through to the centre-point of our lives and reveal new and dangerous insights for the present. They illuminate for a few moments and with a harsh steady light the questionable nature of things we have apparently come to terms with and show up the banality of our supposed 'realism'. They break through the canon of the prevailing structures of plausibility and have certain subversive features. Such memories are like dangerous and incalculable visitations from the past. They are memories that we have to take into account, memories, as it were, with a future content.[21]

Metz specifies these dangerous memories in conclusion by saying they circle around two great human experiences: they are memories of freedom and memories of suffering.

These memories, these dangerous memories of freedom and suffering, are the ones a ministry based on discipleship of equals must recapture. Among the memories of freedom which could assist us are the memories of change in the Church throughout the centuries, especially around the meaning of priesthood, with the accompanying remembering that the Church continues to possess this freedom.

In different periods of the Church's history, several different theologies and models of priesthood have come into prominence.[22] First is the **jurisdictional** model, which sees the priest holding a fullness of authority, where the meaning of "to teach" is to impose authoritative doctrine as a matter of obedience. In this model, admission to and denial of sacraments are quasi-juridical actions. Second is the **cultic** model, found in much patristic and medieval theology, in which the priest is regarded as the performer of sacred mysteries. In this model, the priest offers sacrifice in the place of the community. Third is the **pastoral** model, evident in much of the New Testament but recovered in Vatican II, in which the priest is viewed primarily as pastor or community leader. A fourth model is the **prophetic** model. Here a person is seen predominantly as proclaimer of the word of God, the role being based on the conceptions of prophet and apostle found in the Hebrew and Christian scriptures. This is a model especially evident in Protestant theology, in which the term priest is shunned as too heavily weighted with cultic overtones. Fifth and finally is the **monastic** model, in which the priest is viewed primarily as a holy, sacred person, a guru or a spiritual director. In this model, monastic spirituality is in great part imposed on diocesan seminaries and diocesan priests, and practices like meditation, recitation of the office, community life, and celibacy are extended to all. The priest, in this model, is expected to be withdrawn from the world and its "vanities."

This typology, drawn from the work of Walter Burghardt, is critical for dangerous memory. Its value lies in illuminating the historical reality that, in the course of Church history, not one but many models of priesthood have existed and, in several cases, overlapped. And although his focus is on priesthood, it is not difficult to make the shift to ministry. This suggests to me that, although models of priesthood and ministry develop, even with the guidance of the Holy Spirit, no one meaning can be canonized or considered forever normative. We can be strengthened as we remember that different historical and social reality has **always** called forth different and more appropriate models and meanings. New Guinea missionary William Burrows, for example, points out that all five of these understandings arose in the Second Church, that is, the Church of western Europe and North America.[23] Had ministry developed from the lives of the people of the Third Church (the churches south of the equator, who will comprise 72 percent of the world's Catholics by the year 2000), we would undoubtedly have come to different understandings of priesthood, and by extension, ministry. Similarly, these models rose almost exclusively out of **male** experience. If women had continued to exercise ministerial and priestly roles, as we did in the early Church, we would understand priesthood differently today.[24]

And we shall. For, the second exercise of dangerous memory and remembering going on today is the reclaiming of these first century women as well as their successors. I wrote above of Tradition as a remembering of forefathers and foremothers. It must be acknowledged that much of the Tradition remembered into our own century has been of forefathers alone, or only those foremothers who were virgins and martyrs. But in our own times, we are finally learning the names and the stories of the until-now-unremembered women who were responsible for making us who we are. Schüssler Fiorenza is right in saying we must do the work which is "In Memory of Her." And, that is the remembering demanded here, for a discipleship of equals: the *anamnesis* which names and celebrates Hagar and Lilith and Elizabeth and Dorcas and Hildegarde and Mechtilde and Juliana and Mary Dyer and Elizabeth Fry and Mary Slusser and Sojourner Truth and Angelina and Sarah Grimke. They are our inheritance—and the dangerous memory of their freedom can nourish us and make us whole.

But, so too can the memory of suffering women. For a last element in remembering is the recovering of the stories of tragedy and travesty: the burning of more than a million European women as witches, a story largely untold in the history of the Church; the genital mutilation of millions of African women with the quiet compliance of too many missionaries; the death by burning of Hindu suttee of millions of Indian women and the destruction of the feet of millions of our Chinese foremothers, crippling them for life; the still continuing practice of womb and breast mutilation in so-called "advanced" nations such as our own where unnecessary mastectomies and hysterectomies have never been protested[25]—all of these of far more destructive power over women than the pronouncements concerning contraception and homosexuality which so dominate present official statements. We need to surface and face these dangerous memories and keep them alive. And why? So that nothing like them can ever, ever, happen again. In such a step of Remembering lies the way to a fuller ministry, a holier discipleship, a Church of human beings equal in the presence of God and one another.

RESISTING, THE THIRD STEP

A third step necessary for ministry in this emerging discipleship is one which is specifically intellectual—a work of the mind. The kind of resistance I want to address is the opposite of conformity to the *status quo*, especially in the working of human intelligence. It is a resistance which is especially the work of people in an adult Church who minister through teaching, worship, and preaching—who use **words** as our major vehicle, as we at this conference are doing. It is the work which has to do with **thought.**

The heart of the step of Resistance is raising questions: asking why, asking says who, asking (as Jesus did) and what do you think, asking could this be changed, asking how. Resistance is basically an attitude, a decision to take a questioning path. Resistance is the step where we attempt to ferret out the causes of ignorance, injustice, and inequality, and where we attempt to make our receptivity and our remembering an educated receptivity and remembering. Its basic operating principle is, "Accept no dogma without investigation: it may be wrong; reject no dogma without investigation: it may be right." In other words, resistance is a refusal to set closure, to say all the data are in—even, perhaps especially, to the revelation of God. Resistance is the sister of a hermeneutic of suspicion.

The capacity for resisting begins in the youngest human beings, as a child of two or three learns to say "No." That child is saying the **no** over against adults in large part because the child is trying to understand what it is to be a human self. But, that first no is made legitimate or illegitimate, generally, by the kind of authority and adult power they face. If the adult power is genuine and humane, it will not be coercive authority, not an authority put on and off like a cloak—assumed. Instead, it will be a demonstration of truth and sincerity offered in response to the young person's resistance. All great teachers, whether in schools or otherwise, listen to the "no" of resistance and explore the reasons it is said.

Throughout our lives, we are continually offered the choice of exercising this power to resist. Often we assign it to the realm of those striving to overcome governmental power which they deem unjust, people with names like "partisan" or "guerrilla" or "freedom fighter"—as in the Resistance Forces of World War II. But, when our own political vocations in the polity of the Church are recognized and the re-forming of the Church and the world is entertained as a vocational issue, what does resistance mean? To what in the situation of the Church's life must "No" be said? Universal answers are hard to come by, but allow me to make three suggestions.

1. Resistance needs to be exercised toward privatizing, ghettoizing, and domesticating ministry. To "domesticate" an animal is to tame it and thus render it harmless. Used metaphorically, domestication is the process whereby groups in power seek to channel or neutralize the potentially resistant forces which are let loose when people realize their own capacities and

abilities are either not being used appropriately or are being exploited or manipulated. It is even possible to domesticate the Word of God, which has often been imaged as an avenging fire or as a double-edged sword, yet is too often reimagined in order to make it soft and palatable. In this context, I am warmed and encouraged along the path of resistance by two suggestions— both having to do with liturgy. The first comes from Annie Dillard who says, "Ushers should issue life preservers and signal flares; they should lash us to our pews. For the sleeping god may wake some day and take offense; or the waking God may draw us out to where we can never return."[26] The other is a reminder to work consciously sometimes at shaking ourselves out of complacency by using instead of a serene benediction, such as "May the Lord bless and keep you; may the Lord's face shine upon you and be gracious to you," this one: "May the Lord plague you and torment you; may the Lord set an impossible task before you and dare you to meet it; may the Lord give you strength to do your best and not to falter. Then and only then may the Lord grant you peace."

2. Resistance needs to be exercised to the practice of leaving persons out of shaping the institutions in which and through which they live—in this case the institutions of Church and ministry. Here, those of us in the Church moving toward a discipleship of equals need to resist a double tendency: on the one hand, to be too independent, not sharing power, not engaging in mutuality, which is often not done out of malice but because it is easier to do things ourselves; and on the other hand, to be too dependent, in a dependency unworthy of adults, where we refuse to take responsibility for the shaping of our worlds.

Thirty years ago, in the United States, we had a dramatic instance of the exercise of resistance from a Church people, a resistance which has literally changed the face of our country. At that time, on December 5, 1955, the newly appointed head of the Montgomery Alabama Improvement Association stood in a church pulpit and issued a cry for resistance, claiming the future as the power energizing his cry and the tradition of the past as its source:

> If we protest courageously, and yet with dignity and Christian love, when the history books are written in the future, somebody will have to say, 'There lived a race of people, of black people, of people who had the moral courage to stand up for their rights. And thereby they injected a new meaning into the veins of history and civilization.'[27]

It may be that, in the Church today, taking the step of resistance in whatever form is demanded of us will be the injection of a new meaning into the veins of the Church, the Body of the Christ, and of its ministry.

3. Resistance needs to be exercised to the tendency to understand God too quickly. As we read the stories of the tradition and as we tell and retell them; as we seek to illuminate the meaning of Scripture in our lives in order to be obedient to God, let us take counsel from two Jews. The first is Martin Buber who, in reflecting on his life and the study of the scriptures, says he was always stopped short by reading the Book of Samuel. In that book, the prophet Samuel tells Saul he may no longer be king because he did not slay the kindly, aged king of the Amelekites in battle. Buber remarks that even as a boy it had been dreadful to read this as the message of God—this injunction to kill—and that he had finally concluded, quite simply, "I believe that Samuel has misunderstood God."[28] Resistance in our own time need not take the form of anger toward those with whom we disagree. Instead, imitating Buber, it may quite simply be the truth that one of us has got God wrong.

A similar story is told in the essays of another Jew, Woody Allen. Here, in his brilliantly humorous way, Allen invents a dialogue between Abraham and Sara—with Abraham sure that God has commanded him to kill his only son and Sara resistant to the end. "How do you know it was the Lord, and not thy friend who loveth practical jokes," Sara asks her husband. "Because," Abraham answers, "it was a deep resonant voice, well modulated." In the end, the Lord intervenes and stops Abraham's hand, with an obvious suggestion that Abraham should have resisted. And when Abraham says, "But does this not prove that I love Thee," the Lord's cryptic response is that it proves only one thing: that some people will accept any counsel, as long as it comes from a deep, resonant, well-modulated voice.[29] And the point: it is a very, very difficult thing to know the mind of God, and any resistance to too-quick assurance that we do may be a holy and grace-filled activity.

MOURNING, THE FOURTH STEP

Receptivity, Remembering and Resistance all bring us to the brink, to the border of new activity, to a step which may be spoken of as Reform. Yet often, in the past, careful, thoughtful action has been taken in the Church and has not borne fruit. I want to suggest a reason here. In my judgment, one of the great necessities in a move toward new forms—toward forms which will enable us to live out a discipleship of equals—is the need to let the old forms die: consciously, and attentively, and with ritual. Otherwise, unfinished business will always remain.

Therefore, before moving to the fifth step in the necessary elements I am naming, I want to suggest a fourth step as essential passageway. A step which is not a going out, but a going down. A step which is not a giving birth to the new, but a burial of the old. A step named Mourning.

Mourning is the step where we give time to the recognition that if ministry is to **attend** (to listen) and to **tend** (to care for) and to **extend** (to all in the Church as right and responsibility); if ministry is to be a discipleship of equals; if, more pertinently, it is to be shaped and designed and formed from a base which incorporates and takes seriously the experience of those who have till now not been included, much of our present limited concentration and practice will have to be abandoned. In its place will be a sea change, a different course, where ministry is understood as the work and the interplay of the visions and vocations of all.

The call for such change is voiced especially to those who have the power to make such change. And the best metaphor I know for this time-of-passage and at-tending to the present context is mourning, grieving, discarding what is no longer viable, able to carry life, no longer appropriate—and turning toward purging, enlarging, re-forming, and re-creating it. For that to happen, something must die.

In 1942, after the Cocoanut Grove night club fire in Boston in which 492 people perished, Erich Lindemann interviewed survivors and bereaved and gave us one of the first technical descriptions of what is involved in mourning. Six characteristics were especially evident: somatic distress; intense preoccupation with the image of who or what was lost; guilt; a disconcerting lack of warmth; disorganized patterns of conduct; a sense you no longer fit.[30] In naming these, I find a remarkable congruence with what is happening in the Church today, reminding us that the journey toward a full ministry of and discipleship of equals is not always filled with pleasure; indeed, it is often necessarily uncomfortable, painful, sorrow-filled. For, we **are** talking about a genuine death.

Elisabeth Kübler-Ross continued this research and elaborated five stages which anyone to whom ministry has been denied recognizes: denial, anger, bargaining, depression, acceptance.[31] I think of my own denial, of my initial disclaimer that I had been a victim of inequality. I had been to school; I had held a Diocesan position; I was on a seminary faculty. I think of my own anger as well and that of many of my women students, and instead of turning from it, learning to celebrate it. I am made strong by thinking of Beverly Harrison's counsel of the power of anger in the work of love[32] and of Augustine's dictum that hope has two lovely daughters, anger and courage—anger so that what must not be will not be and courage so that what should be will be. I am supported even by Chrysostom whom Aquinas quotes: "Whoever is without anger when there is cause for anger sins."[33] In other words, I and others recognize mourning in a deeply personal sense.

But, at the same time we know that mourning is not just personal; it is systemic too. Therefore, I am proposing that taking the steps which lead to a discipleship of equals will include moving with entire communities—classes and parishes and schools and dioceses and religious orders—**through** mourning, in the knowledge that grief is caused by systemic loss as well as by personal loss; and that we are undergoing systemic loss today. When old ways, old forms are being let go (as is our very way of **being** Church today), we need time to acknowledge their passing, whether those old ways are comfortable but unequal ways of relating, patterns of belonging, attitudes toward and exercise of authority, reinterpretation of sacrament, design of institutions, or living responsible, adult lives.

Further, the mourning of dying systems and dying structures, the mourning for procedures and patterns and forms, echoes in the planet itself, waiting to see what the humans will do. The rest of creation joins us, groans and travails, as with the great mystical and religious figures we descend into hell, make the passage down into grief and darkness on our way to light. The Christian Creed says of Jesus, "Descendit ad inferos (he descended into hell, into the depths)." So must we all.

REFORMING, THE FIFTH STEP

And once we have done that, like Jesus of Nazareth, we can be born again. We can get up and take the fifth step in this dance, the step of Reforming. Reforming is a recapitulating step, including, as we shall notice, the former steps of remembering, resistance, receptivity, and mourning. Reforming is also artistic work, for it has to do, at root, with the creation of form. In the Church today, reforming means stretching our hearts and minds and intelligence into the experience of being an ecclesial people and giving **form** to that experience. The great, archetypal forms of ministry have not changed since the time of Jesus—they are still the Priestly, the Prophetic, and the Political. But, the **meanings** given to these forms have continued to change through the centuries, as we have seen, and in our time this is no different. We continue to be the *ecclesia semper reformanda,* the Church always in need of being re-formed. For us, at this time in history and even more specifically in the context of concluding this volume, what might this mean?

As with all the other steps, any response to such a question must be addressed and created together, in community. But, as we reflect on the great work of Reforming: reforming Church, reforming ministry, and reforming ourselves, allow me to make three suggestions.

1. We need to reform priesthood. As we have seen from the Burghardt essay quoted above, priesthood has been modeled many ways in Christian history. We may have forgotten, however, the universal teaching throughout that history: that actually there is only one priest. The rest of us are partakers in that priesthood—and this has been taught to us from the time of Peter, who reminded us of it in his first epistle, to and through Vatican II, which taught in *Lumen Gentium* that all of us participate in the priestly role of Jesus.

Priesthood, as I understand it, means living fully in the present out of the past. The key roles in priesthood are **remembering** that past through liturgy and teaching; **mediating** the presence of God through sacramental activity; and **hallowing** the presence of divinity everywhere through blessing. What needs addressing in our own time, however, is the dis-covering and claiming of these roles of remembering, mediating, and hallowing by all of us. For, the simple truth is, it seems to me, that in each of our lives these are central activities. We are a people of memory; we are, in our being and relations with others, the mediators of grace. We are also sacraments to one another—or can be—and, unless we offer blessing and grace to one another, hallowing does not happen.

In other words, each of us exercises priestly ministry every day of our lives. What we need to do is claim that as our identity, thus contributing to a reformation of the meaning of priesthood. (I taught a woman this past year who belongs to a small congregation in the southern United States. During the previous year, her sisters had petitioned each of the bishops in the five dioceses where they work for the sisters to hear confessions. Her recording of that story before a room full of other students was a source of imagination and hope. And her story is one of many similar ones.)

Thus, instead of responding to the question, "Do you want to be ordained?," with a yes or no answer, I would advocate a different question, which in turn would call forth a different response from those who are not formally ordained. The different question is, "In what is your priesthood manifested and how can you re-form it in order to make it more manifest?" If we begin responding to that question, we might find ourselves publicly identifying ourselves this way: "I am a Roman Catholic priest of the Archdiocese of New York, or Philadelphia, or St.

Louis; I am a partial embodiment and incarnation of the one priesthood found in Jesus the Christ."

2. We need to reclaim prophecy. Ministry and priesthood are so closely associated that the entire meaning of ministry might be relegated to that one form—and sometimes is. But, the ministry of Jesus is not only priestly; it is prophetic. And prophecy is living in the present out of the future—a future where we demand that justice be done.

As much as anywhere, we receive our understanding of prophecy, just as Jesus did, from the great Hebrew prophets. They were people who spoke of justice, not because they had learned the six stages of normal development, but because they had encountered the God of justice, and they had also encountered the little ones who suffered injustice. They were the ones, and in our own day are the ones, who, instead of taking us to the mansions of the soul, make sure we see the slums.[34] They were the ones, and in our own day are the ones, who embody the pathos of God—God's grief over the human condition. They are the ones who will not keep silent, who continue to shout an agonizing "No" in the face of the evil surrounding us. They are the people, often, of non-receptivity to dogma, of resistance, and of dangerous memory.

Many places demand our prophetic voice, but I shall name only two. The first is in those realms of our own life where injustice lives and survives, the places where we have been hurt by the absence of justice and are in need of healing. It is not unhealthy narcissism to name ourselves as recipients of injustice, especially if we are women in the Church; to deny this is to keep an infection untreated. Therefore, we must confront injustice and evil as it directly affects us and say, "Not any more; not any more," a step which may prove amazingly difficult—and, for some of us, may even now still be shrouded by denial.

But, at the same time we must say the prophetic "No" in the face of the evil in our world. For this work we can find few models more eloquent than the women of our day: from the mothers standing in a living circle, with their children, at Greenham Common; to the grandmothers of the Plaza de la Mayo in Buenos Aires, continuing to search for the *desaparacedos* —the disappeared ones; to the women running shelters for battered women and victims of incest and rape; to Molly Rush, mother and grandmother from Pittsburgh, who finally acted "illegally" in non-receptivity to the United States government's policy on nuclear arms buildup. It is Molly Rush who supplies us with a theme for prophetic ministry in the question she tells us finally moved her to action. It is the simple question which could transform our world into a world of peace: "What about the children?"

3. We must address political ministry as essential in the Church. In that way we can be helped to move away from the extreme and dangerous **privatizing** tendency which always lurks in religious understandings. Even when we accept the priestly and the prophetic as aspects of ministry, we shy away from the political. Either we sanitize the word with such related terms as "royal" or "kingly" (queenly?) or "administrative," or we do not admit this as an aspect at all (although this is changing: a recent Network seminar, drawing on the feminist principle, "the personal is political," noted in its advertising, "the **pastoral** is political"). But, if and when we avoid political ministry, it helps to recall that the third title of Jesus, as king, is a manifestation of Christos as Kyrios and of the Divinity's address to power—and judgment on power—as it is exercised in the world at large and in the world of the Church. To suggest the Church is not a political body is, to my mind, not only naïve, but manifestly untrue.

If anything is the issue at the heart of a conference such as this, it is the political nature of a discipleship of equals. For, what we are searching for is some way to reshape, redesign, recreate and **reform** the polity, the structure, and the organization of the Church, so that, **as a Body Politic,** it is the Body of us all. It is precisely such re-forming which will then make it more, not less, the Body of the Christ. The political aspect of ministry means attending to such realities.

We need to do this on a global level where we recognize we are not solely a white, middle-class, North American Church, but far more extensively a Church of the young, the poor, the non-white, the African, the Asian, the Americas south of ourselves. We need to do this on a local level where we recognize the desperate reforming needed in our parishes, so that, instead of conglomerations of three or four or five thousand units who are supposed to be "communities," they are small units of 20 or 50 or 75, bonded with one another in larger communities of communities. We need to take seriously suggestions regarding re-forming such as that proposed by Enda Lyons of Dublin. His thesis is simply this: We assume the task of the laity is to assist the bishops and priests in their mission and ministry. But, this proposition needs to be stood on its head. For, bishops and priests exist so that the mission and ministries of the laity—men, women and children—may flourish and grow.[35]

And finally, we need to continue doing exactly what we are doing here: exploring the meaning of the Church which is already with us while it is yet to be: a Church of men and women and children before God who are leaning into and living into becoming a discipleship of equals. For, it is not only by talking about and urging receptivity, remembering, resisting, mourning, and reform that a new ministry will be born. It is also by the being and the doing of these in suffering and in freedom, and as communities of equals, that we shall bring it about. And, if we do continue taking steps such as these, in fidelity and in hope, we may find we have lived ourselves into being a people manifesting the presence of God in the world. We may find we are creating anew the priestly, prophetic, and political work of the Christ which is the vocation to Ministry.

NOTES

1 *The Documents of Vatican II,* edited by Walter M. Abbott, S.J. (New York: Guild Press, 1966), p. 775.

2 Bernard Cooke, *Ministry to Word and Sacraments* (Philadelphia: Fortress, 1976).

3 Edward Schillebeeckx, *Ministry: Leadership in the Community of Jesus Christ* (New York: Crossroad, 1981); *The Church With a Human Face* (New York: Crossroad, 1985).

4 See Maria Harris, "Questioning Lay Ministry," in Regina Coll, editor, *Women and Religion* (New York/Ramsey: Paulist, 1982), pp. 87–110.

5 I would also note here the influence on our understandings of ministry derived from Henri Nouwen's *Creative Ministry* (New York: Doubleday, 1971), p. 116: "Ministry means the ongoing attempt to put one's own search for God, with all the moments of pain and joy, despair and hope, at the disposal of those who want to join this search but do not know how."

6 The notion of "publics" is developed in David Tracy, *The Analogical Imagination* (New York: Crossroad, 1981), especially chapter one.

7 See George Peck and John S. Hoffman, editors, *The Laity in Ministry* (Valley Forge: Judson Press, 1984).

8 See Gabriel Moran, *Religious Body* (New York: Seabury, 1974), chapter five, for the seeds of this idea.

9 See Maria Harris, *Portrait of Youth Ministry* (New York/Ramsey: Paulist Press, 1981), for extended development of *didache, koinonia, kerygma, leiturgia, and diakonia* as classical forms of ministry.

10 I am indebted to Judith Dorney for this insight on the nature of steps.

11 Gabriel Marcel, *Creative Fidelity* (New York: Farrar, Straus and Company, 1964), p. 28.

12 Martin Buber, "Observing, Looking On, Becoming Aware," in *Between Man and Man* (London: Kegan Paul, 1947), pp. 9–11.

13 See Paulo Freire, *Pedagogy of the Oppressed* (New York: Herder and Herder, 1970).

14 See Soren Kierkegaard, *Concluding Unscientific Postscript,* translated from the Danish by David Swenson (Princeton: Princeton University Press, 1968).

[15] Marge Piercy, "Unlearning to Not Speak," in *To Be of Use* (New York: Doubleday, 1973), p. 38.

[16] Margaret Atwood, *Surfacing* (New York: Simon and Schuster, 1972), pp. 222–23.

[17] Schillebeeckx, *Ministry*, pp. 76–77.

[18] *Ibid*, p. 77.

[19] Yves Congar, "Reception as an Ecclesiological Reality," in *Election and Consensus in the Church, Concilium* 77, edited by Giuseppe Alberigo and Anton Weiler (New York: Herder and Herder, 1972), pp. 43–68.

[20] Gilbert Keith Chesterton, *Orthodoxy* (New York: Dodd, Mead and Company, 1943), p. 85.

[21] Johann Baptist Metz, *Faith in History and Society* (New York: The Seabury Press, 1980), pp. 109–10.

[22] The following section is drawn from the work of Walter Burghardt, "What Is a Priest?," in Michael Taylor, editor, *The Sacraments* (New York: Alba House, 1981), pp. 157–70.

[23] William Burrows, *New Ministries: The Global Context* (Maryknoll: Orbis, 1980), p. 118.

[24] See Maria Harris, "Education for Priesthood," in *Education for Social Justice,* edited by Padraic O'Hare (San Francisco: Harper and Row, 1983), pp. 14–25.

[25] For development of these dangerous memories of women's suffering, see Mary Daly, *Gyn/Ecology: The Metaethics of Radical Feminism* (Boston: Beacon, 1978), who quotes David and Vera Mace on Hindu **suttee,** p. 124, in an especially powerful way. See also Andrea Dworkin, *Woman Hating: A Radical Look at Sexuality* (New York: E.P. Dutton, 1976); Phyllis Trible, *Texts of Terror* (Philadelphia: Fortress, 1984).

[26] Annie Dillard, *Teaching a Stone To Talk* (San Francisco: Harper and Row, 1982), p. 40.

[27] John C. Raines, "Righteous Resistance and Martin Luther King," *Christian Century* (January 1, 1984), p. 53.

[28] Martin Buber, "Autobiographical Fragments," in *The Philosophy of Martin Buber,* edited by Paul Arthur Schlipp and Maurice Friedman (La Salle, Ill.: Open Court, 1967), pp. 31–32.

[29] Woody Allen, *Without Feathers* (New York: Warner, 1976), pp. 26–27.

[30] Erich Lindemann, "Symptomatology and Management of Acute Grief," in Robert Fulton, editor, *Death and Identity* (New York: John Wiley and Sons, Inc., 1965), pp. 186–201. Reprinted from *American Journal of Psychiatry* 101 (1944): 141–48.

[31] Elisabeth Kübler-Ross, *On Death and Dying* (New York: Macmillan, 1969).

[32] See Beverly Harrison's inaugural lecture at Union Theological Seminary, New York, "The Power of Anger in the Work of Love: Christian Ethics for Women and Other Strangers," *Union Theological Seminary Review* (Supplementary, 1981), pp. 41–57.

[33] See Daniel Maguire, "Abortion: A Question of Catholic Honesty," *The Christian Century* (September 14–21, 1983), p. 807.

[34] See Abraham Heschel, *The Prophets* (New York: Harper and Row, 1962), p. 3.

[35] Enda Lyons, *Partnership in Parish* (Dublin: Columba Press, 1987), quoted in Peter Hebblethwaite, "Irish Laity's No-Blarney Call for Say in Church," *National Catholic Reporter,* 10 April, 1987, p. 14.

Index of Persons